Praise for *Impact Hiring* by Frederick W. Ball and Barbara B. Ball

"This book offers compelling insights into the psychology of negotiations as well as providing the depth of commitment necessary for successful interview results."

— *David I. Fisher, Chairman, Capital Guardian Trust Company*

"Provides a step by step process for ensuring that a busy executive team takes all the factors involved in the hiring decision into account."

— *Dag F. Wittusen, President & CEO, Aker RGI Seafoods*

"We interview others—and sell ourselves—in every aspect of our business lives. The authors thoughtfully provide the guidance and skills most of us need—but seldom develop."

— *Kenneth M. deRegt, Managing Director—Head of Worldwide Fixed Income Division, Morgan Stanley Dean Witter*

"Competition for top talent has never been more intense given the wide array of choices for the best candidates. This book's ideas and pragmatic advice provide a competitive advantage in the hiring process."

— *Clifford S. Cramer, Managing Director—Global Healthcare Investment Banking, Merrill Lynch*

"A book that connects with every reader who has ever felt uncomfortable or unprepared as an interviewer. It will help you to avoid costly hiring mistakes."

— *Gregory J. Zorthian, COO, Forbes.com and Vice President Business Development, Forbes Inc.*

"A great guide for interviewing. It will serve you well no matter the job function, level, profession or industry."

— *John P. Bankson, Jr., Telecommunications Legal and Policy Specialist and Past President of the Federal Communications Bar Association, Drinker Biddle and Reath LLP*

"The authors' buy/sell model of interviewing is unique and powerful."

—*T. Timothy Ryan, Jr., Managing Director-Global Head of Government Institutions, Central Banks and Real Estate, J. P. Morgan & Co. Inc.*

"Practical, insightful wisdom for executives who understand the critical importance and challenge of hiring top talent."

—*C. Douglas Mercer II, Managing Director, Pendleton James Associates, Inc.*

"A terrific guide for developing strong interviewing skills, a necessary skill set for every executive."

—*Katherine J. Trager, Vice President and Deputy General Counsel, Random House, Inc.*

"Unforgettable vignettes that should be shared with senior management who are seeking top talent."

—*Susan F. Goodrich, Managing Director, Madison Investment Partners, Inc.*

"This is not only a 'how to' book; it's a 'why to' book."

—*Wayne E. Hellmann, Vice President-Human Resources, Lehigh Portland Cement Company (Subsidiary of Heidelberger Zement AG)*

Impact Hiring

Impact Hiring

THE SECRETS OF HIRING A SUPERSTAR

FREDERICK W. BALL • BARBARA B. BALL

Prentice
Hall Press

Library of Congress Cataloging-in-Publication Data

Ball, Barbara B.
    Impact hiring : the secrets of hiring a superstar / Barbara B. Ball,
Frederick W. Ball.
            p.   cm.
    Includes index.
    ISBN 0-7352-0228-1
    1. Employee selection.   I. Ball, Frederick W.   II. Title.

HF5549.5.S38 B357 2001
658.3'112—dc21
                                                            00-045662

© 2000 by Frederick W. Ball and Barbara B. Ball

HF
5549.5
.S38
B358
2000

Printed in the United States of America

10 9 8 7 6 5 4 3 2 1

ISBN 0-7352-0228-1

ATTENTION: CORPORATIONS AND SCHOOLS

Prentice Hall books are available at quantity discounts with
bulk purchase for educational, business, or sales promotional
use. For information, please write to: Prentice Hall Special
Sales, 240 Frisch Court, Paramus, New Jersey 07652. Please supply: title of book, ISBN, quantity, how the book will be used,
date needed

 Prentice Hall Press Paramus, NJ 07652

http://www.phdirect.com

>

To Jay and Katherine
who demonstrate
an exceptional ability
to form partnerships

Contents

PART 1
THE BATTLE FOR TOP TALENT

PART 2
PREPARING FOR THE INTERVIEW

PART 3
BUILDING A PARTNERSHIP

Foreword

The business world is a complicated place. On the one hand, working in corporate America can be like an epic adventure—exploring uncharted territories, full of exciting opportunities, rewards, and surprises. I consider myself fortunate to be a part of this fascinating world.

However, the business world is also marked by competition—fierce competition. Competition for innovation, market share, revenue, and profits. As the saying goes, it's a jungle out there! No wonder so many analogies have been drawn between business and warfare.

The most critical battle being waged in business today is the war for talent—highly skilled employees to handle a wide variety of jobs and responsibilities. Talent drives innovation, market share, revenue, and ultimately, profits. Make no mistake, talent has always been important, but the competition for talent has never been greater as the balance between supply and demand has shifted. Those companies who today recognize the significance of that shift and the importance of hiring and retaining top talent will thrive for years to come—and those that don't will not.

At Roche, we are privileged to have some of the world's leading talent on our side. Undoubtedly, these gifted individuals have made Roche one of the world's leading pharmaceutical firms.

Our company was founded on talent with vision. In 1896 in Basel, Switzerland, Fritz Hoffmann started the company when he was just twenty-eight years old. His goal was to develop and manufacture new drugs of uniform strength and quality, and to market them internationally. In the 1930s, Roche became the first company to commercially synthesize vitamins. Our work today includes groundbreaking research in the treatment of AIDS, the management of obesity, and the prevention of organ rejection.

What started as one person's dream is today Roche Holdings, Inc. parent company of Hoffmann-La Roche, an organization employing approximately 70,000 people worldwide with operations in more than a hundred countries.

We are proud of our many distinctions and accomplishments, none of which would be possible without our distinguished cast of "A" players. What's more, Roche recognizes that a corporation must plant seeds and invest in its most important asset, people. Recently, our firm and six other pharmaceutical companies joined forces with Rutgers Graduate School of Management to offer a new Master of Business Administration in Pharmaceutical Management.

But these days no firm can afford to rest on its laurels. Today's top candidates expect more, and the old standard approaches to interviewing and hiring simply don't work. Companies large and small must operate within this new reality to reach out to prospective employees. Understanding this concept is essential—and doing something about it is even more so. Fortunately, Fred and Barbara Ball have developed an interviewing and hiring model that is both sensible and effective. Simply stated, *Impact Hiring* is a practical, no-nonsense guide to hiring the best candidates time and time again.

Arm yourself with the wisdom found in this book and you will win the ongoing war for talent. Win the war for talent and your company will soar!

PATRICK J. ZENNER
President and CEO, Hoffmann-La Roche, Inc.

Preface

Most CEOs agree that hiring the best people, those who have the vision and the ability to drive the business forward, is one of the two or three most important goals. Hiring a star involves great risk and great reward for any hiring executive or hiring team. Hire someone great and your stock in the company rises; hire someone mediocre or poor and your stock falls.

To understand the importance of making an impact hire, it is helpful to understand how we have arrived at today's hiring practices. From shortly after World War II until the early 1970s, the American dream flourished. During that time, certain conditions prevailed:

- U.S. companies were dominant in the world.
- We could afford to be arrogant because we held such high market share.
- There was a limited pool of employees to service our expanding businesses.
- We were so successful we could tolerate low achievement while enjoying tremendous economic prosperity.
- Our prosperity spawned a culture of entitlement.
- The expectation was that in exchange for complete loyalty, obedience, and modest competence, employees had a contract for life.
- Organizations were rigid, with clear lines of authority and well-enunciated policies and procedures.
- Control came from the top, where it was presumed the outstanding decision makers would guide the company.
- Generation after generation could assume they would achieve the dream by moving up the economic ladder.

In the early 1970s, however, changes in economic conditions and the state of world competition began to change the landscape. Business became much more competitive and turning a profit became less predictable. The current conditions are:

- World competition is fierce; The U.S. is no longer assured of dominance or constant growth.
- The U.S. is still strong, but is no longer leading all industry sectors.
- Capital is readily available.
- Companies enjoy technological advantages for only short periods of time.
- The shift to a global economy means "your customers" are everyone's customers.
- Companies have to earn your business continuously by offering outstanding new products and performance.
- Organizations can no longer guarantee job security; hundreds of thousands of workers have been fired to maintain profitability.
- The concept of lifetime employment has vanished.
- The new employment contract demands that companies offer challenging work, performance-based rewards, and opportunities for development in exchange for employees who are entrepreneurial, willing to develop skills the company needs and client-centered.
- Organizations are flatter and more flexible and have less red tape.
- Small teams are customer-centered. They are empowered to make quick decisions and have the authority to commit resources.

During the 1990s, there has been yet another technological phenomenon. The waves of start-ups in technology and Internet commerce industries have been spawned by ready access to information and capital. New trends are emerging:

- Revived entrepreneurial spirit;
- The chance to invent new economic models;
- A "figure it out yourself" culture;
- Huge potential and risk, but uncertain rewards;
- A meritocracy in which your success depends upon your productivity;
- Minimal company hierarchy and internal politics;
- Cross-functional teams in which everyone is fully engaged.

All of us have observed the fallout caused by such radical shifts occurring in such a short period of time. One of the most important problems to surface is the psychological effect on the American executive. While senior management has often been able to see and adjust to the changing landscape, those at the middle and lower levels haven't always gotten the message. Even if they have intellectually understood how the employment contract has changed, they haven't been prepared for the psychological and emotional impact that would have on them. Perhaps the saddest cases have involved middle-level executives who were originally hired under the "womb to tomb" or "cradle to grave" unwritten employment contract and then, in the middle of their careers, were told that the contract had changed (without their input). As these executives watched the American dream crumble beneath them, the toll has sometimes been terrible on them, their spouses, and their families. Their children, often at especially impressionable ages, have observed and internalized the vulnerability of their parents' lifestyles. Those children are now the adults you may be recruiting.

It has been easy to predict that this generation of job seekers would have different characteristics from their parents. They are less trusting, more skeptical, less loyal, and more in it for themselves. In addition, they have skills that are easily transported and they are willing to take their intellectual capital elsewhere. In fact, they will tell you as they are leaving for a better position that it is corporate America, and not they, that brought on the changes.

The role of the hiring manager and the interviewing team has become more complex, not only because of the difficulties in attracting talent but also because there is no reason to believe that we will see a lessening in global competition. If anything, competition will be more fierce. The CEO, knowing that human talent is the key to increased revenue and profit, values those executives on the team who can recruit, retain, and develop "A" players. We see a number of additional trends on the horizon:

- The organization's drive to maintain profitability through cost cutting can only be successful to a limited degree.
- The ongoing need is for the infusion of "A" players who have the ability to provide the next generation of products and services that produce revenue and profits.
- Global competition is making it more and more difficult to hire "A" players.
- There is a greater need to have the right executive managing the recruiting process.
- Interview systems are being monitored and upgraded constantly.
- Interview training has become an essential part of every line manager's skill development.
- The hiring manager's credibility is on the line every time he or she hires new talent.
- A senior executive has the responsibility to "keep score" regarding the hiring manager's success in hiring, developing, and retaining new staff.
- Some companies are linking a percentage of compensation to success in hiring high-potential staff.
- The hiring record is a major area to examine and discuss when considering a candidate for internal promotion.

THE THESIS

Having briefly examined the business landscape since the 1950s, let's look at the impact of those changes on the interview process. We have seen how we were forced into major changes in the way business is done. These changes are necessary if the U.S. is to remain a vital world leader. It's clear that interviewing processes need to keep pace as well. When a rigid, top-management dominated structure mandated loyalty and obedience from staff, an interviewer-dominated approach to the interview may have been appropriate. Under this structure, the hiring manager fired salvos of his (it was most often a male interviewer) favorite questions at the candidate and the candidate reacted to each one in an attempt to show how nimble and quick she could be. At the end of the interview, the candidate went home and hoped for the best, usually having little or no idea how well she had done or even whether she was still on the interviewer's radar screen. There was little attempt on the part of the company to remain in touch with the candidate, because it was obvious that "the candidate will be lucky if we make her an offer and she has a chance to work with our company." When the company did reach out with an offer, there was an expectation that the candidate would immediately jump at it.

It's clear this type of interviewer-dominated system is not going to make it with the new breed of "A" player. The new system needs to be client-centered. This requires a major change of focus for some interviewing team members, because if even one person "doesn't get it," he or she can torpedo the efforts of the entire team. The key is to reach agreement on the basic principles of conducting the recruiting process while allowing individual interviewers to maintain their unique personal styles. Showing the candidate respect in every phase of the interviewing process will be critical. If you don't do it, the candidate will decline your offer. As the interview begins, you need to form a partnership from the first moment, to learn about one another and then to examine the business needs and goals of your organization and how the candidate can help you to achieve the goals. The idea is to help the candidate to present at the top of her game, to look her best. The focus, then, which is positive and inclusive, is completely different from that of the old structure.

Although it is not an easy task, if you help each candidate to do his or her best, then you level the playing field and put yourself in the terrific position of being able to select the best of the best. (*Note:* Under the negative system, many great candidates do not present as well as their glib counterparts, because they are not as extroverted or don't market themselves with the same flair as others, and they are eliminated.)

The interview with the "A" player is not the "buy" interview that we saw in the management-dominated approach. Rather, the conversation integrates the "buy" and the "sell." This candidate, after all, has the complete skill set to make your company a winner and will likely have a number of offers from which to choose. Yours is only one of a number of outstanding opportunities. The formation of the partnership with the candidate is critical to your success during the "sell." If you and each of the members of your interview team form a bond with the candidate, then you'll be in the game and have a chance to win.

The sell process continues after the interview is complete, because it often takes a series of interviews and from a few days to a number of months to land the top candidate. This is a time when the great recruiting individual or team stands apart from the rest. The critical ingredient will be maintaining a close dialogue between the candidate and the member(s) of the interview team with whom he or she bonded most closely. Your interviewers must be highly professional and be able to anticipate and resolve candidate needs during the decision-making process.

An important phase of the sell is answering the candidate's questions about the reasons she should choose your company. The interview team must spend time dealing with these questions. The best answers should be prepared well in advance of the candidate's question, if there is to be any consistency in the answers. Outstanding candidates are typically looking for the following:

- A dynamic organization with a strong reputation and company culture.

- A boss and division that respects them and really wants them.
- A highly respected management team.
- A chance to become part of a winning team.
- Exciting work with the potential to learn new skills.
- Goals that are clear, measurable, and attainable.
- A defined career path.
- Competitive compensation and benefits.
- Immediate responsibility and visibility.
- Smart and likeable colleagues.
- The opportunity to attend training programs.
- The answers to questions about your company's perceived weaknesses.

THE FORMAT OF THE BOOK

Hiring the best is not a fad. Knowing the profile of the candidate you need to hire and knowing how to conduct an outstanding interview are critical competencies in your individual skill set. When building entrepreneurial teams with the authority to produce (and fail), it is critical to include team members in the hiring process. Having the candidate meet more people affords the opportunity to get input from those who are on the firing line and will be the colleagues of the new hire. This provides a sense of involvement for the team members as well as an increased likelihood that the correct candidate will be chosen. Consequently, outstanding interviewing skills are no longer for the senior executive alone, but for anyone in the organization who might be part of an interviewing team.

Hiring theory suggests that you develop a recruiting process that is consistent with the culture and size of your organization. Although the basic principles of the hiring process are the same in a small, mid-size, or large company, the procedural aspects differ for an organization with 5 to 50 employees as opposed to one with 5,000 to 50,000.

Showing respect for the candidate is so simple a concept to discuss, yet so difficult for many people to implement, that we start with the concept in Part I and continue to deal with it in other parts of the book. Professional interview systems and outstanding preparation are often the ingredients that determine a win or loss when dealing with the outstanding candidate, and they are the subject of Part II. The discussion includes the ownership and accountability of the process and how to define the ideal success profile.

Part III deals with building a partnership with the candidate. This involves understanding both the candidate's and the interviewer's agendas. Building a partnership requires bonding, which will increase your chances of a successful sell. The partnership will also enable both you and the candidate to complete your business agendas during the meeting. This section concludes with strategic and tactical considerations, including your questioning approach to gather the information you need.

Part IV is concerned with the sell. The best candidates have more than one offer, which means that you will be selling them on why they should join your company. We discuss the research-based due diligence that the best candidates employ to pare their list of companies, and the emotional basis on which the final decision is often made. Chapters on negotiating a win/win solution and on sealing the deal conclude the book.

Interviewing to hire the best is highly competitive. It takes preparation, outstanding strategy, a great interviewing style, and hard work to win the outstanding talent. If you're interested in learning the secrets of hiring a superstar as your hiring team becomes involved in *Impact Hiring,* we invite you to read on.

Acknowledgments

Our mission is to communicate the importance of forming an effective partnership with the outstanding candidate. We are grateful for the partnerships we have established with friends and colleagues who have given freely of their time and talents to help us examine the interview from broad based perspectives that cross industry, function and company size. We thank them for their perceptive comments and for their specific assistance in various parts of the book.

For the development and production of the book we feel a deep sense of gratitude to:

- Louis Wolfe for his continuing effort to mentor and guide us in the ways of publishing.
- Bill McCord for the study that job applicants undertake when deciding whether the company is right for them and his thoughts on reference checks.
- Jim Borland for his knowledge of the process, refining the content and suggestions regarding style.
- Tom Shea and Dan Patrick for their keen insights into the recruiting process in the large organization.
- Andy Sherwood for his entrepreneurial spirit and continuing advice and encouragement.
- Kathy and Alan Trager for the constant opportunity to share ideas.
- Lou Paglia for his assistance on the preface of the book and his overall critique.
- Pamela and Richard Scurry for their vision and faith in the power of partnerships.

- Jim Sullivan for examining the partnership between line executives and human resources professionals.
- Rick Kendall for his thoughts on the role of the hiring manager in the process and the case studies.
- Julie Connelly for her insight on presenting information effectively and for her gift of the book's subtitle.
- Bill Brittain for the psychologist's perspective on understanding the interviewer's agenda.
- Ken Shulack for his expertise in case interviewing.
- Diane Glynn for her advice in communicating the message.
- Betsy Ross and Greg Slattery at Forbes for their professional competence and project leadership.
- Paul McCarthy for his expertise in graphic design.
- Colleagues, and former colleagues, at the New York office of Goodrich & Sherwood Associates, Inc. for their thoughts and reactions to our ideas
  - Tom Miller
  - Chuck Wright
  - Louise Maxwell
  - Dave Peaseback
  - Diane Sherwood
  - Chris Lowden
  - Whitney Williams
  - Gregory Gabel
- Hans Wittusen, Patrick Rea, Jake Perlman, and Sara Dawes for their knowledge about the interview process from the new hire's perspective.
- And finally, to our families for their ongoing love and support.

PART

1

THE BATTLE FOR TOP TALENT

Part 1 focuses attention on the changing nature of the job market. Presently and for the forseeable future, outstanding candidates will have considerable leverage because there will be great demand for their services. Consequently, they will look for organizations that are dynamic and growing, that have strong values, and that treat people with respect.

The War for
Talent Escalates

The image remains long after the remote has been clicked off: Tiger Woods' fist pumping the air emphatically after demolishing the competition. The gesture conveys a personal satisfaction and a hunger for victory far more powerfully than any commentator's words. Yet the offhand remarks of two sportscasters who are trying to fill air time after the match are more compelling than they may realize. One muses aloud that it's interesting Tiger doesn't hug his caddie after the final hole, nor does he approach the fans. The second commentator responds with an observation that it looks like Tiger is satisfied to please himself and is most motivated by the competition from within. If that is the case, it isn't keeping the fans away. The mission of any sport is to draw in the fans and Woods is doing it better than anyone else in sports today.

Tiger Woods is not merely a golf phenomenon; in fact, he is far more than the newest sports icon. Respected writers who are not given to hyperbole have called Woods the embodiment of the millennium. In an age of start-up companies with twenty somethings at the helm and an established generation overwhelmed by hordes of young, smart, supremely confident talents who know exactly what they want and won't settle for anything less, Woods may be the apt personification. He is young, well-educated, racially diverse, absolutely certain of his talents and abilities and is making money faster than maybe even he envisioned. In addition, he just keeps getting better.

Some observers are stunned by Woods' lack of loyalty; he has fired almost everyone who has been part of the "Tiger Team," citing not quite the right fit for his goals. His single-mindedness is clear. He has a tough mentality and is bent on constantly taking on new challenges and improving himself. He is physically and emotionally fit with a competitive drive fueled by his game plan to win every time he enters a match.

It only takes a slight shift from Tiger Woods' outlook to understand today's top talents in the workforce and, equally important, how to recruit them and then retain them. Naya Collins is a perfect example. She is a 27-year-old graduate of a well-known school in the East who had nine job offers before taking a position as an E-commerce manager in the arts and entertainment industry fourteen months ago. When asked what her goal is for five years from now, she answers that it is of utmost importance to her that she continues to enjoy what she's doing and have personal satisfaction. "If I'm not learning and growing every single day, then I'm out of here." It is interesting that the goal doesn't include "making partner in five years," or "hoping to make my first million by my thirty-second birthday." The take-away message is that Naya embodies the attitude of the sought after candidates across industries and companies.

> *I am motivated by new and challenging things to do; I need to keep growing to be satisfied.*

*   *   *

Georgia Bittner agrees with Naya's motivation, but takes it a step further. "I love my job even though it can be frenetic and twelve-hour days are the norm." She has changed jobs twice in the last three years and is now an editor at a new and fast-growing magazine. What Georgia most enjoys is the independence and the autonomy to make decisions with her staff without continually checking with her boss. "I value the breathing room; I know I'm competent and I have the skills and talents to do a job well," she stated. "What drives me crazy is when someone is constantly looking over my shoulder. I'm being paid extremely well to do the job. Trust me and let me do the work. If I screw up, fire me." Her confidence and independence are benchmarks of the top talents in today's marketplace.

I am motivated by independence; I need some autonomy for my own sense of self-worth.

*   *   *

A common thread among highly recruited candidates, regardless of industry, is that they're looking to achieve professional success without sacrificing personal happiness. Recruiters can learn from Naveen Shah's priorities. At 30, Naveen is re-entering the workforce with an MBA from a prestigious business school where he maintained a perfect grade point average. He has made the rounds of the best-known investment banks and most respected consulting firms, garnering impressive offers from all of them. To the surprise of some, he is taking the offer from one of the smaller consulting firms. "I'm going to make plenty of money and I know I'm going to work some ungodly hours," Naveen allowed. "But that's a given at all the places where I've interviewed. What made my decision easy was the diverse and creative ways this firm shows their employees that they're valued. Yoga classes and massage therapy are offered on-site. Even the newest employees are involved in aspects of the firm's decision making. Everyone gets close to the clients and there is a lot of flexibility in work schedules. The partners regularly entertain employees and they do it in their own homes, rather than keeping employees at arm's length."

I am motivated by personal satisfaction and happiness; I need more from work than an impressive paycheck.

*   *   *

Recruiters in the talent chase should be heartened by the vignettes from Naya's, Georgia's, and Naveen's job hunts. They represent the motivations of the best and the brightest. They are interested in working hard and in making significant contributions, but the work has to be "real" and it has to be challenging to keep them from moving on. They know they're good and they want an environment that allows them to show their worth. If they're not learning, they're not growing; and if they're not growing, they're becoming stagnant, and that is a fate worse than death.

Facing surging competition from dot-coms in an intensively competitive job market, companies are becoming more aware of the need to recruit actively and well. For some, the pitfall has been to rely on gimmicks or bells and whistles which the top recruits will accept only if coupled with genuine interest in them as individuals. "Sure, I'll accept an invitation to dinner at a restaurant where reservations are impossible to get, but if the recruiting team isn't staying in regular touch with me and getting to know me as a person, the dollars spent on me won't matter at all," says one savvy recruit. Top-of-the-line recruiting isn't an option but a critical necessity.

Despite increased globalization and the prospect of continued expansion, sustaining growth at the corporate level will be more of a challenge than ever. There is increasing evidence that growing top-line, bottom-line, and shareholder value for even a few years is difficult. To sustain that kind of growth over many years is a huge challenge.

A key factor for the most successful companies is their constant ability to generate new ideas that benefit their customers. This requires a corporate culture that encourages innovation and a senior management that believes in hiring outstanding management talent who can nurture and grow big ideas into action.

HOW AVAILABLE IS TOP TALENT?

The demand for top talent is moving in the opposite direction from supply. Studies have shown that there will be a 15 percent decline in 35- to 44-year-olds, the traditional executive talent pool, over the next fifteen years. There will also be a decline in the 44- to 54-year-olds. These shifting demographics suggest an acute shortage of management talent that is only going to worsen.

In addition, there are at least four other trends adding to the difficulty of hiring top talent:

1. There is an increase in competition caused by the Internet and the growth of e-commerce. The recent exodus to these small, high-risk, high-reward companies, has happened because high potential individuals decided to "take a risk" for a huge pay day and they left their old economy companies.

2. There is weaker bench strength in many companies following a period of repeated downsizings. Many of these companies have a skeleton executive crew and no longer maintain developmental positions from which people were traditionally promoted.

3. Companies today expect their executives to demonstrate more sophisticated leadership and management skills than ever before. An example of this change is the CFO position which requires vision and proactive leadership while less than ten years ago it was a reactive position in many companies.

4. There are changing values among the up and coming talent of today. Many of the top candidates don't aspire to climb the corporate ladder; rather, they opt for a great job that doesn't demand all of their time and take away from their lifestyle.

WHAT CHANGES RESULT FROM THESE TRENDS?

We have begun to see changes in the marketplace that would have been unheard of a few years ago. We have evidence from the top MBA programs that over 10 percent of the graduating class is starting their own companies or joining a classmate in starting a new venture. Most of these are Internet-based in an effort to cash in on the new economy. With competition coming from the old economy, new economy and global competition, recruiting teams are under pressures that has rarely, if ever, been seen before. New recruiting strategies and tactics are needed.

The rules are to keep it simple, be flexible, and move quickly. If the recruiting effort isn't netting top talent, your team better adapt fast or you'll be out of the game.

From a strategic point of view, senior management in the best companies realize that hiring the finest talent and keeping it is their most important job in this economy. Consequently, many more resources are needed for this effort than in the past. No longer is recruiting left in the hands of the company recruiter and the hiring manager alone. Increasingly, we are seeing members of the candidate's potential team join the effort, especially those who can create a close bond with the candidate. It is also common to see senior management involved in the recruiting of the top candidates. This includes regular involvement by the COO, CFO, and CEO.

To remain competitive, the head of recruiting must receive market information constantly. She should be a member of the executive committee and have the authority and resources to change direction on a moment's notice since it is often necessary to reinvent tactics in the middle of a recruiting season.

Turning to tactics, the initial focus is usually on compensation programs. In an effort to stop the exodus of talented employees, law firms, financial service firms, and consulting firms are taking some painful, but necessary steps. Recently, a prestigious New York law firm announced that it was raising the starting salaries of first year associates from $100,000 to $150,000, a move that could cost partners up to 20 percent of their compensation. This followed the financial initiative by West Coast law firms to stem the resignations that had moved from a few percentage points to beyond 20 percent. The argument made to first year associates was simple—you can stay here for a lot of money or try the high-risk company that may not be there in a year.

In the last year, some well-known investment banks and consulting firms have offered summer interns bonuses of up to $5,000. This was unheard of a year or two ago and was in response to on-campus recruiting seminars where the high-tech and Internet seminars were drawing most of the students. The rationale is that, in the short term, money talks or at least gets your attention.

The education industry is experiencing the same dilemma. Creative proposals offer new teachers increased pay, sign-on bonuses, and even the unprecedented step of not having to pay state income tax. Everyone knows the difficulty of recruiting and hiring great science and math teachers; now the demand is for teachers in all disciplines.

WHAT ADJUSTMENTS ARE BEING MADE?

Efforts to recruit top candidates today must go far beyond compensation and the standard benefits issues alone. Some of the tactics are designed to provide more or better benefits than the competition and some demonstrate that the recruiting team and potential colleagues really want the candidate to join them. Several examples of each follow:

Benefits

- Casual dress certain days or every day.
- Unique benefit programs such as a menu of holistic services with a preset spending limit.
- Low-cost day care facilities.
- Cafeteria outfitted with high chairs for parent/children lunches.
- Free access to corporate gym.
- Golf driving range and putting green.
- Car service if working late.
- Loans for various purposes.
- Dinners prepared by the firm's food services for employees to take home.

Commitment to the Candidate

- Proposing flexible work schedules.
- Sending care packages to former interns during exam time.
- Offering to fly the candidate back to the company campus for additional conversations and data gathering.

- Taking the candidate to dinner, a show, professional sports event, or other entertainment.
- Communicating directly with senior management.
- Assisting the candidate with individual issues that will enable him to accept the job.
- Offering resources to a spouse who may be job hunting as well.

It is important to remember that these are only examples that change rapidly in this fast-paced, creative recruiting environment.

WHAT DOES THE TOP CANDIDATE WANT IN A JOB?

We are in a seller's market and the top candidate is in a great position to evaluate carefully before making a career choice. The decision rests on a number of factors that we will examine briefly now and in more detail throughout the book.

1. A Dynamic, Highly Successful and Demanding Organization with a Strong Corporate Culture

The Internet has brought with it access to information that was unheard of a short time ago. The top candidate today is willing to study, network, and gather information regarding the best companies in the most desirable industries. This information may be subjective and rapidly changing; however, it may put a company in an excellent position to recruit or, if the information is nonexistent or damaging, to make recruiting particularly difficult. The information that the candidate gathers from company insiders and chat rooms will also influence decision making.

In addition to gathering generic information about the company, recruiters must remember that each candidate comes with his own set of dreams and desires. A top candidate will want to work for a company that provides something more than a place to go to work. He wants a challenging job in a great company that also enables him to give something back to mankind.

Sometimes, companies have powerful reminders of their commitment to others. In Merck & Co.'s corporate headquarters, for example, there is a life-size statue of a small boy leading a blind man. The statue is so realistic and compelling that everyone is immediately drawn to it. The inscription states that Merck developed an inoculation to prevent river blindness disease. When it became apparent that many of the developing nations in Africa had neither the finances nor the communication mechanisms to eradicate river blindness, Merck donated the vaccine and has contributed manpower and dollars to lessen the impact of the disease.

Everyone knows that Merck & Co. is one of the top pharmaceutical companies in the world. Everyone may not know about their philanthropic outreaches. When a top candidate who is interested in a job that also offers the opportunity to give something back to mankind walks into Merck, the statue and its inscription is sure to make a powerful statement.

2. Competitive Compensation, Benefits, and Equity

Previously, we have discussed why there is little loyalty left toward the company. Given these attitudes, there is a much greater likelihood that the top candidate's objective will be to seek and accept an exciting job where he can learn new skills while making as much money as possible. The thought process is that he will do his own long-term investing since the "company will not be taking care of him." If the top candidate comes with compensation as the number one criteria, then he will look for a dynamic company in the industry that pays the most.

Since the 1980s, investment banks, large law firms and consulting firms have been riding high on the ability to pay. Myths, for example, have been created on some of the exorbitantly expensive recruiting tactics that these firms have enacted to upstage their competition in an effort to win the top talent. That tactic, however, is only successful while you have the greatest ability to pay. When the new economy companies surfaced, the balance changed in their favor. It has actually taken less than two years to see the dramatic shift in interest to high technology and Internet companies. How long this will last is the content of heated debate. Some say that when there is a dip in high technology and Internet stocks for a period of time, there will be a mass exodus back to the old economy. That remains to be seen.

Fortunately, the top candidate has more than one criteria on his "most desired list." It is these other elements that lessen the "money only" approach and make the process much more competitive.

3. Challenging and Exciting Work with Continuous Learning

Imagine the rush you would feel if you were one of the contributors to a recent NASA space mission. Your work would be of great interest to others. You would be on the cutting edge of technology with a challenging job that places you in the forefront of learning new and marketable skills. In addition, your work would be designed to bring greater good to humankind.

Those who have actually worked at NASA agree with the components we just mentioned. They also add that working on a highly sophisticated project with committed, smart, high-energy people was a great deal of fun as well. In addition, there was energy generated from having a big goal driven by a "we can do anything" mentality. Work was as much a happening as it was a job.

Today, the top job candidate would like that same experience of great excitement, challenging work, continuous learning, and a chance to build a company. This can happen in many different ways. It can be a small, growing advertising agency that is built vertically so that the team works on assignments together, giving everyone a chance to grow. It can be in an Internet startup with all of the energy inherent in working on a new idea with a group of smart people. It can also happen within a large division of an established company or on a small project team where a committed group of people take on a challenging assignment and have the resources to make it happen.

4. A Team That Respects Me as an Individual and Wants Me as a Partner

Respect will be a topic throughout the book because it is a major topic on the minds of job seekers in the sellers' market. Think about it. We have a marketplace where top candidates are clearly in demand. The candidate is being shown and told that he is sought after in every way possible. Respect is assessed in a very practical, comparative manner: How am I being treated by this company as compared to the other companies that want me? It isn't defined by the way that job seekers were treated ten or fifteen years ago. The concept: When I was interviewed, I was told that I should consider myself lucky if I got a job at this company, is completely foreign to today's top candidate and if the interviewer conveys that attitude, her company is immediately eliminated from the candidate's short list.

It is extremely important to understand who you are dealing with in this strong seller's market. The candidate, as we have discussed, is less trusting of the corporation than previously, doesn't think about longevity and may not care about "moving up the corporate ladder." Hence, the candidate views the interview as an opportunity for the company to show him what kind of exciting job and great compensation package it can provide for him today. It is expected that every person will show him respect, meaning that no stone will be left unturned in the team's effort to recruit him. Any missteps will be regarded as uncaring acts.

Can you imagine the disbelief inside those companies who have been automatic winners in the talent race as recently as two or three years ago? Previously, small or even large mistakes in the recruiting process were never even factored since the top candidates were going to accept the company's offer anyway. Now, the old economy established company is in an incredibly competitive struggle with the new economy company. Any recruiting error will be noticed and quickly exposed. In fact, repairing leaks in the old recruiting system will not work; a new and more responsive system is needed. Every person in the company is a recruiter and new and innovative tactics are required immediately. One of the easiest ways for the top candidate to evaluate the team's respect and commitment is to evaluate the quality and the quantity of the contacts and communication from the company between the job interview(s), the offer and then the acceptance of the offer. This is one of the most precarious times if you are attempting to recruit a top candidate because if your competitor is doing a better job than you are, you lose.

5. Outstanding Boss, Mentor, and Coach

The leadership literature over the last quarter century has been making the case for a change from a militaristic leadership model based on power (e.g., Senior management has made a decision and you therefore will do X) to a more participative model based on authority (e.g., Ted will direct today's discussion because he has more knowledge and experience than the rest of us. *Note:* Ted may not be the boss). The record on better leadership practice in the real world is spotty at best. Progress has been based more on individual initiative than on organizational commitment. Over the years, companies have increased training efforts to encourage a more participative leadership style, but the bottom line still depends on the leader deciding to make a personal commitment. Think of your own company and the huge variance from supervisor to supervisor.

More recently, some companies have begun to make more serious commitments to changing executive behavior. Most people today simply will not work for a boss who doesn't involve them and give them meaningful assignments. This is not so difficult in concept, although it is extremely difficult to stick to the plan for any length of time. The change works only when it becomes part of the company's business goals, is made part of the annual performance review and is tied to compensation, typically bonus dollars, which are determined by the degree of success. Typically, the supervisor and the subordinate examine the success the person has had in hiring the highest ranked candidates, the retention rate of those people, the record of promotions of the best and the brightest, the rate of internal transfer out of the group and the results of exit interviews when the high potential person leaves the company. Once this is accomplished, those companies are setting improvement plans for each supervisor to help them to improve upon her record in the years ahead.

Now there is another and stronger impetus for change. It is coming from outside the company. Enter the seller's market and now the top candidate has increased negotiating leverage. The top candidate may look you in the eye and say, "I am really excited about coming to work for your company. If I can work in X area of your division and have Y as my boss, I'll be happy to accept your offer." Do you think that the top candidates talk to former graduates who are working at the company concerning the great boss and the poor boss? Can the top candidates learn which bosses really value new people and give them meaningful assignments? Is it possible for a potential star to ascertain who will value him, mentor him, and coach him? You can count on it. This impetus will force changes in management behavior and it will happen much faster than it did during the buyers' market when change was not forced upon organizations.

6. High Profile Tasks with Authority and the Ability to Make an Impact

As we saw in the case study of Tiger Woods and others, the new hire doesn't always enter the new company with the "keep your mouth closed and your ears open and learn how to be a team player" philosophy that proved to be good advice in the past. Rather, the focus is often on "how fast I can get a high profile job with a lot of visibility and with the chance to make an impact?"

This attitude is causing the hiring executive to rethink her strategy. Let's face it, every job inside a company or division isn't necessarily going to be a high-profile, high-impact job initially. There will only be a limited number of jobs where a new hire will have the authority and autonomy to impact the business from the first day in the position. Consequently, the hiring manager is going to have to make some decisions early in the process concerning her most important vacancy, second, third, and so on. In this way, she will have a clear picture of her needs and priorities. When she is interviewing and offering jobs, she knows she will offer her top candidate her most important vacancy.

This is not to say that there is only one high-impact job. There are many and it is the hiring executive's job to help each candidate recognize the potential in the job that is offered. In today's marketplace, it is the hiring executive's job to fill each vacancy and the candidate's role to accomplish the job successfully while understanding the possibilities of expanding the job scope to provide the greatest possible challenge.

7. Flexibility and Autonomy to Control the Work

In addition to the other elements of the ideal job, the top candidate wants to have the job on his terms. This means, simply, as much autonomy as possible and the flexibility to work in a way that is congruent to his lifestyle.

The issue of lifestyle is an important one and the hiring executive must be aware of the candidate's concerns. The best candidates are the best prepared and have determined those items that are "must have" and those that are "would like to have." If a candidate has determined that a balanced life/work formula is what he seeks, then the wise recruiter will understand this need and address it to the maximum her company will allow. This negotiation may very well represent the most critical determinant in her success or failure to land the candidate.

Grace was the number one student in her class at a prestigious graduate school and was being heavily recruited by a number of companies. She was an only child and she and her parents were extremely close. As the decision-making process wound down, Grace received a distressing call that her father had a heart attack and was unable to manage the family business. The decision was a non-event, Grace went home. The interview process simply stopped.

After a few weeks, Grace received a telephone call at home from Sharon, her potential boss, at one of her two favorite companies. Grace started to apologize for not getting back to her until she realized that Sharon was calling to tell her she was sorry about her father. During the short conversation, Sharon showed a level of caring that Grace couldn't believe. Sharon told her that everyone who met her thought she was great and that the interview process would be placed on hold. Whenever Grace decided that she was ready, the process would restart. Sharon went on to say that if Grace found that the family business didn't take all of her time she would be interested in hiring her on a consulting basis for whatever amount of time Grace could afford. Finally, Sharon was able to provide Grace with some wonderful leads for service providers that Grace needed to hire quickly to maintain the level of the family business. It was no surprise to anyone that Grace eventually joined Sharon's company.

A PRACTICAL COMPARISON

As we will stress throughout the book, people want to feel valued and respected in every aspect of their lives; the premise of our thoughts is that it is the critical component necessary to every step of the recruiting and interviewing process—no exceptions. It's interesting to see the effect of that belief when inserted into everyday life.

We are not frequent guests at San Francisco's Ritz Carlton Hotel; however, we do stay there every time we're in the city. It's tough to ignore the hotel's excellent location or the building's beautiful facade, but the initial impression comes from the hotel's staff. The valets smile and look the guests in the eye when they greet them and then bring the correct luggage (not always a given in some hotels) immediately into the lobby. When the desk receptionist asks for our name and checks the reservation, she promptly says, "Welcome back, Mr. and Mrs. Ball," since the hotel's impeccable records indicate that we have been guests there before. She continues by saying, "I know you enjoyed staying in room 424 overlooking the courtyard on your last visit; I'm sorry that the room is not available for you this time, but we have reserved a room for you on the sixth floor which overlooks the courtyard as well. Will that be acceptable?"

The room is well-appointed and every detail has been checked. The Ritz Carlton refurbishes all guest rooms every three months without fail, cleaning carpets and draperies, checking all electrical outlets, replacing tiles or wallpaper if necessary, guaranteeing that every accommodation will be comfortable and pristine. In our room when we arrive is a handwritten note from the concierge, welcoming us by name and offering whatever assistance we may need. The note is accompanied by a large bottle of sparkling water and a plate of cheese and fruit. Neither is an expensive offering, but it's an effective gesture which we appreciate after flying for almost six hours.

That evening we decide to have dinner in the hotel's dining room. During the first course, the maitre d' comes to our table to thank us for joining them for dinner when there are so many wonderful restaurants in the city. The Ritz Carlton's dining room gets top recommendations in every guide book so it is an easy choice, but the point is that the maitre d' acknowledges us as guests of the hotel and tells us that they appreciate our decision to join them. The next afternoon there is a brief note for us at the desk. One of the reception clerks has noticed that we left the hotel that morning with a camera; he wants us to know that the Ansel Adams exhibit downtown might be something we would enjoy if we have the time. We are home less than five days when we receive a handwritten note from the manager of the hotel, thanking us for staying with them and asking if there is anything they can do better for us the next time we visit.

The Ritz Carlton's mission of being the best in the business and making every client feel like a welcomed and valued guest is pervasive and evident in everything they do. We never consider staying anywhere else and recommend the Ritz Carlton to everyone because of their careful attention to details and their quick response time to any need. Every staff member projects the same attitude of being genuinely glad that we have chosen to stay with them.

It's possible to make a fluid transition from the Ritz Carlton's point of view to the necessary outlook for today's recruiting and interviewing teams. Creating an outstanding interview team in the current market requires senior management who are passionate about the vision to hire top talent and are able to communicate the vision clearly to everyone connected with the mission. The team must understand the need to build a partnership with the candidate and the critical attention paid to showing the candidate utmost respect. No detail can be overlooked and impeccable records must be kept on the process for every candidate. It is imperative to acknowledge that it takes far more than excellent interviewing skills to hire the superstar. It takes sincerity, honesty, a willingness to go the extra mile, and a commitment to do the right thing for the candidate as well as for your organization.

The Balance of Power

We are conditioned to think that the balancing scales in the hiring process are totally skewed in favor of the interviewer. The balance shifts dramatically with the best candidates, those who have the potential to make a dramatic impact on an organization's bottom line. With these candidates the scales are almost equally balanced, with the interviewer holding an exciting job and the candidates a marketability that numerous outstanding companies want. David is one of those outstanding candidates.

Career Profile _____

David's Choice

David sat back and thoroughly enjoyed the moment. As confident as he had been throughout his interviews, he was still a little surprised at receiving offers from his top three choices. This was a defining moment for him and he was justifiably proud. The seriousness and sense of purpose he had shown through high school, college, and graduate school suddenly seemed worth the effort. He knew that graduating summa cum laude from college and in the top tier of his graduate school class made him a valuable candidate.

The first 24 hours were euphoric. Then reality began to set in and David realized that he had to make the choice as to which of the offers he would accept. How would he make the choice? Which criteria were the critical ones? After pondering his enviable dilemma, he decided that he needed to go back to the criteria he had set at the beginning of his job search. He had hoped to:

- Work for a recognized and well-run organization.
- Be involved in challenging, stimulating work.
- Interact with smart, interesting people who had values similar to his own.

After establishing some lists and reviewing his criteria, David came face to face with the difficulty of his task. Although he had business experience, the task of determining which of the three companies had the best reputation was not easy. They all had excellent reputations. Besides, he knew that the job with the greatest potential for rapid career growth might be in the number 2 or 3 company and not in the number 1 organization. After struggling with his lists for a few days and making little progress, he called his graduate school mentor, Professor Carvallo, who was a well-known consultant to the business community in addition to being an outstanding teacher and coach.

Fortunately, David was able to get on Professor Carvallo's calendar. At lunch they caught up on personal issues and then got to the business at hand. David updated Professor Carvallo on his interviewing process, the three offers, and his dilemma in making a wise choice. Dr. Carvallo's questions were penetrating and right on target. At one point the professor asked, "Do you remember how, when we were examining case studies in class, we would try to assess the culture and values of the organization by studying the behaviors of the people?" David nodded. The professor continued:

> The behaviors that you experience in your personal interactions during the interviewing process give clues to the way you will be treated if you are hired. It's interesting to note that Bob Harrington (the men's basketball coach) and I have had this conversation. He says that a player's behavior in practice is an accurate reflection of the way he will behave in the final two minutes of a really competitive game. Under pressure, the player will revert to those good or bad habits that have been developed in practice. The same is true in interviewing a company. The interview is a pressure situation for both interviewer and candidate, and under pressure there is a strong tendency to revert to normal behavior or to give clues to everyday behavior. Perhaps the most interesting aspect is that it is not the overall behavior in the interview; rather it is the subtle comment, the glance, the add-on, the interruption, or the silence that

give you the biggest clues to the true underlying behavior. And as Coach Harrington says, you can't hide the truth on game day, no matter how hard you try. The trick then becomes comparing your beliefs about the way people should interact with the data you have collected about the way people actually interact with one another. This comparison will be a critical determinant every time you make a career decision. When there is an excellent match, there is a much greater chance you will have an excellent business marriage.

David was silent for several seconds. What the professor said made sense. Finally, he said, "You know, it helps to hear that again." Dr. Carvallo smiled. "Most people go through their entire business careers and never learn this lesson." David asked if the professor could give him an example of the subtleties. "Sure," said his mentor, "let me give you both a business and an educational example." The educational example came first, as the professor told David this story.

Career Profile

Concern for the Individual

My daughter is a senior in high school and is looking at colleges. She is an excellent student and soccer player and her goals are to attend a great academic institution where she will also play soccer. The process of getting these goals aligned is complicated by the fact that some coaches are very good salespeople in the interviewing process. It is up to you to determine whether their remarks are truth or fiction. Recently, we asked a coach about one of his players whom our daughter knows personally. The coach knew all about the young woman, including where she grew up, background about her family including her twin sister, and how she was progressing academically including her major, grades, and academic standing. This was one excellent sign that he cared about his players beyond their performance on the soccer field.

"You were able to evaluate the coach's integrity based on this one incident?" David asked.

"No, not entirely; but it was one important piece of evidence that the coach volunteered in the course of normal conversation," Professor

Carvallo said. "It was clearly an honest reaction to a question and not a canned or calculated response. My daughter felt it was honest and caring. He didn't have to refer to any file on the player or refer to any notes. My daughter wants to play for a coach who cares about her as a person."

"That's interesting," said David. "But when do you make the jump from one isolated comment that sounds like the right stuff to the decision that this person is a high-integrity individual who will care about your daughter?"

"That's the key question," said Professor Carvallo. "It is certainly not based on one comment; rather, it is the series of actions, comments, and nonverbal signals we discussed earlier that ultimately form your final conclusion and help you decide which option is best for you." The subtle comments and signals generated during David's interviews were beginning to flash through his mind. He caught himself from wandering too far into the interactions he had during his interviews and asked the professor for the business example. Professor Carvallo told David this story.

Career Profile

The Bosses Overrule

Kim's initial conversations and her search of the promotional literature suggested that outstanding client service, a supportive internal environment, and a cohesive team environment were critical values of the company where she was interviewing. In her third round of interviews, she was scheduled to meet Yvette and then her prospective boss, Ralph. When Yvette appeared, Ralph appeared with her. He told Kim that he had an unscheduled meeting later in the morning and asked if she would mind if he sat in at this meeting. Kim said it was fine with her.

Yvette began the interview and conducted some normal rapport building chitchat. After about ten minutes, Yvette directed the conversation toward business. The style of the meeting was informal, with a lot of give and take. When an opportunity surfaced, Kim asked about the goals of the division and Yvette volunteered three goals.

Ralph, who had been quiet through most of the interview, suddenly came to life. He corrected two of the three goals Yvette had mentioned. From that point on, Ralph adjusted what Yvette said at least four more times.

The worst instance occurred when Yvette said, "To be successful, you'll need strong organizational skills, flexibility, and the ability to implement solutions quickly." The words were no sooner out of her mouth than Ralph countered with, "No, no. Strategic vision is what we are looking for. That is the critical ingredient. Then flexibility and the ability to implement solutions quickly and efficiently in a pressure environment." Yvette, who had been taking Ralph's interruptions in stride, glared at him. Kim saw the look, but Ralph was oblivious to it.

"Sounds like something I experienced," David said with a surprised expression. Dr. Carvallo laughed and said, "David, when you have been consulting inside companies for as long as I have, you've seen it all. Interviews like this do sometimes occur. Since you had an experience somewhat like Kim's, tell me how you felt about that interview."

DAVID: My potential boss was Courtney and her boss was Richard. The interview wasn't as extreme as the one you just described, but Richard seemed very overbearing. He frequently talked over Courtney and regularly inserted his own spin on Courtney's comments.

DR. CARVALLO: How did it make you feel about the company?

DAVID: You know, I hadn't given it much thought until now. I clearly didn't like Richard's behavior. But my decision is a very difficult one because the company has a great reputation and a lot to offer. Everyone else seemed very pleasant.

DR. CARVALLO: Would you have much contact with Richard?

DAVID: Well, Courtney would be my boss and I liked her a great deal. But I would also have interaction with Richard. I guess the question I raised before becomes important again. How do I know how much weight to give something like this as I do my evaluation?

DR. CARVALLO: There is no exact answer to your question. It is as if you were a detective collecting evidence in a case. You gather facts, you experience subtle interactions, you form hunches, and you keep testing them as you meet additional people. The more interactions with different people, the better. Eventually, you reach a conclusion you have based on fact and intuition. Remember, you can never know 100 percent about any situation; some gut reaction goes into any decision.

DAVID: Just to review, you suggested that I go back to my original goals which were to work for a recognized company, doing challenging work, and interacting with smart people who have similar values to my own.

DR. CARVALLO: That's right. Evaluate the companies on that basis. What I'm suggesting is that since you are looking at three outstanding organizations, your decision may very well come down to the last part of your statement: Who has similar values to my own? Gathering evidence on values is evaluating sound bites that happen in interviews at times when interviewers let down their guard and you see who they really are. The more interviewers you see, the better the chance that you will get a true reading of the culture of the organization.

DAVID: When you were talking about sound bites, specific interactions in various interviews jumped into my head.

DR. CARVALLO: Were they good interactions or bad ones?

DAVID: The bad seemed to jump out.

DR. CARVALLO: That's right. For some reason they always seem to surface first.

DAVID: Then you would recommend that I go though an evaluation, put the pieces of the puzzle together, reach my conclusion based on both the facts and my gut reaction, and accept the position that seems to offer the best fit.

DR. CARVALLO: That's it, plus one more thing. There is neither bondage nor a "cradle to grave" philosophy any more. You are a highly desirable candidate and you're doing your best to make the best decision. If that decision isn't right, you will always be able to move on.

David thanked Professor Carvallo and left to think about the encounter and complete his evaluation. The companies were all outstanding and David did not find his evaluation easy; but as he thought about the interviews in light of Dr. Carvallo's comments, the issues became much clearer and he was able to discriminate between them. Dr. Carvallo's comment that the decision would probably hinge on values turned out to be correct. David found that listing some of his criteria in written form helped with his task. Here is his scorecard, based on a 5, high, 1, low ranking:

Criteria	Company 1	Company 2	Company 3
1. Show mutual respect	1	5	5
2. Energy, enthusiasm	3	4	5
3. Know company direction	2	3	4
4. Sense of team	2	5	5
5. Integrity	3	5	5
6. Accomplish aggressive targets	5	4	5
7. Produce profit	3	3	4
8. Self-confidence	3	4	5
9. Enjoy working for company	3	4	4
10. Smart and adaptable	4	4	5
11. Pride in company	3	4	5
Total	32	45	52

It was intriguing to David that the professor had given an example of a business issue that he had experienced. As he reviewed the other interviews he had with that company, he reached the conclusion that mutual respect and sense of team were not as highly regarded in that firm as in the other firms. He wasn't quite sure to what degree the negative interview colored his recollection of the other interviews with that firm, but David recalled another interview at the firm when an interviewer made a remark about a colleague that David felt was unkind. He recalled the professor's suggestion that, although there are thousands of words in an interview, it is the negative comments and impressions that stick with you. That's clearly what happened to David, and company 1 was eliminated.

The choice between company 2 and company 3 was more difficult, but the decision came down to the same type of subtleties. David felt that the company 2 interviewers were not sufficiently clear on divisional goals. One said, "The development of Area X" while another interviewer said, "The development of Area Y." David also felt that in terms of commercialism or the drive to succeed financially, there was a little less confidence in company 2. One interviewer said, "We'll never be a _____ (he mentioned another company), but we're still profitable." Another interviewer made a similar comment: "We're not rated too highly in that business." Due to these bits of information, David's rating of company 2 was a little lower than company 3 in the areas of self-confidence and intelligence. Consequently, David eliminated company 1 and company 2 and chose company 3.

SUMMARY

Attracting the very best talent demands a high level of commitment and focus from everyone on the interview team. Great candidates have great antennae. You will be evaluated to the same degree that you are assessing the candidate. At the top of the candidate's list will be issues like respectful treatment, sense of team, and bright colleagues who are interested in learning and having fun, as well as the more traditional issues like working for a highly regarded and profitable company, doing challenging and visible work, and earning a highly competitive compensation package.

Why Critical Hires
Are Lost

We have seen that the interview scales are balanced and the playing field is almost level for the very best candidates. Any interviewer can hire a "B" or "C" player but it is a different proposition when the "A" or "A+" player walks in. Now the stakes for winning and losing are higher, the visibility is greater, the participants are smarter, the conversation level rises, and both interviewer and candidate are on the line.

It is fascinating to watch executives at all levels who do not focus on that equalization of power and who lose outstanding talent before the lesson hits home. There are numerous reasons for the losses, none of them acceptable. A few of the most prevalent ones are worth mentioning. There remains an arrogance among some executives who feel that, "I work for a company with a great reputation and you will be fortunate to work with us if we offer you a position." What they forget is that the great candidate may opt to sign with an Internet company that may go public in 18 months, with the hope of amassing impressive wealth. Some executives who have not kept pace with the times don't realize the difficulty of attracting top talent and the need to offer a candidate challenging and exciting work, the ability to make an impact quickly, an exciting career path, and outstanding compensation. By the time they get the message, the candidate has gone elsewhere to receive those benefits. Many hiring managers do not understand the degree of respect that top candidates expect to be shown.

Let's be honest. The best candidates are intelligent and savvy and have demonstrated that they can make a major impact on the bottom line of a company that is clearly ahead of its competition. They assimilate ideas and they often reach conclusions quickly, and sometimes unfairly, about companies and people. It will help you to become a stronger interviewer if you understand some of the reasons why outstanding candidates reject companies.

MOTIVATION

The relationship between an individual's motivation and drive and that person's fit with the culture of a company is one of the critical variables in determining the probability of making an outstanding business marriage.

Career Profile _____

Drive to Succeed

Bob and his brother Ned grew up in turmoil. Their father bounced from one job to the next, never able to hold a position for long. Money was always tight. At very early ages, both brothers were expected to have jobs after school and to contribute to family finances. There was also very strong competition between them, perhaps because only 14 months separated them in age. When they became adults, both Bob and Ned were highly motivated to be successful and not to repeat their father's financial instability.

Ned eventually put himself through college by working two jobs and attending school at night. Upon completion, he secured a commission sales job selling computer hardware. His individualism, drive, and determination made him an almost instant success. His commission income was paid out quarterly and his checks were sizable. He became the envy of the family.

Bob was in his third year of college at the time. He was a better student than Ned and was working his way through a better college. Despite the positives, this was a very tough time for him. Ned was doing extremely well and he was Bob's yardstick of success.

Two years later, Bob graduated. He had done extremely well by anyone's standards, especially since he had completely funded his own college education. Bob, like his brother, had been forced into very independent, do-it-alone, bottom-line type activities. In addition, he had a strong desire to achieve financial success.

Soon Bob was interviewing with two computer software companies. One had a better reputation; the other one was in the process of establishing itself and seemed to be on the verge of making it. The company with the better reputation was considering Bob for two positions, one in its entrepreneurial sales division and the other in its corporate marketing and account management division. This company clearly had the inside track because of its reputation and the ability to sell its established product line. As the interview process played out, two strong managers, one in sales and one in marketing, each wanted Bob badly. When push came to shove, the marketing manager was a little more powerful than the sales manager and the decision was made to offer Bob a marketing position. As far as the organization was concerned, it was a simple decision—great company, great reputation, great career path. The only problem was that no one had probed for Bob's needs or wants, which had not surfaced in any of the interviews.

Bob was disappointed with the offer because he understood his own underlying values and drives. It was clearly important to him to do well financially as quickly as his brother. He didn't know, nor would he have cared, that it was internal politics that resulted in the marketing offer rather than the sales offer. Suddenly, the sales job at the second firm with heavy emphasis on commission income started to sound a lot better. Bob had a series of meetings with both salespeople and sales management. There were some minuses, such as the number of quality products, but he was assured that would change in the near future. Basically, the job was a sales position with a defined territory that would be his alone. The salary structure included a base salary and a very generous commission structure above a certain sales volume. Bob was certain that he could reach the targeted sales volume very quickly and move into the commission structure.

By the time the original company finally focused on the fact that it was losing Bob, it was too late. Bob had "fallen in love" with the other organization, its people, and the chance to realize his goals to equal or exceed his brother's income. Despite the fact that they had been in an extremely strong interviewing and negotiating position, the managers in the original company lost a potentially great sales associate to internal politics and failure to uncover the candidate's motivation.

RESPECTFUL TREATMENT

The expectation of respectful treatment is a given for all candidates, and most especially the outstanding candidate. Most interviewers are respectful when they are with a candidate. Any number of circumstances, however, such as time pressure, arrogance, lack of sophistication, or ego can make otherwise caring individuals behave in strange ways. When they do this, they lose the respect not only of outstanding candidates but of their own constituencies as well.

Career Profile _____

Hoop Dreams

A well-known college we'll call Jones State fired its basketball coach after five years and began a search for a new coach. The college had within the last few years entered a new conference that was high-profile and extremely competitive. Jones State was not consistently at the top of its previous conference, so it was a huge step to enter the more competitive conference and expect great results. Because the coach had not achieved the desired results, he was fired.

The university president knew that the men's basketball record had been a sore spot for years with alumni who clamored for a winning program. With great fanfare and media coverage, the president announced that he would personally oversee the hiring of the new coach. Furthermore, he indicated that his preference was for a high-profile, successful coach from an established program.

Certain longtime sports writers questioned the strategy as well as the splash. Here was a Division I program (the highest and most competitive level) that had been at the bottom of the heap for most of its existence because neither the school nor any of its previous coaches had ever been able to recruit top talent. Here was a program that had recently joined one of the most competitive conferences in the country and the possibility of winning for a number of years was in serious doubt, no matter who was selected as coach. Here was a university president saying that he would personally recruit a big-reputation, high-profile coach to lead the program out of the wilderness when the simplest of research proved that virtually every successful coach in this conference had come from a successful coaching tenure at a lower-profile college. The successful coaches were not high-profile. Rather, they were young and had boundless energy and enthusiasm and a work ethic that would not quit. That was the kind of passion it took to drag an unsuccessful program, inch by inch, into the winning category.

At the beginning of the search, three coaches were mentioned as the top candidates. Two were the high-profile coaches the university president sought and the third was Wayne, who had built an enviable record of five straight seasons with 20 wins at a school one step below Jones State's level on the basketball ladder. The athletic director spoke to Wayne early in the process and then moved on to other candidates. A number of additional candidates surfaced and the press was kept informed every step of the way. When the athletic director spoke with the first of the high-profile coaches, the media had a field day, speculating that he would be the next coach. Every day for a week, the newspapers wrote of the possibilities and who the new coach might choose as his assistants and what system he might install. Then, as suddenly as he had appeared, he disappeared. A week later the press reported that he had never interviewed at Jones State; rather, he had decided to remain where he was and his university had offered a $100,000 per year increase in salary.

At this point the president turned to candidate number two, another wily veteran. The same process played out as a day-by-day serial in the newspapers. This time the university did get to interview the coach and Jones State made him an impressive offer, in the $500,000 per year salary range. The president wanted to make sure that the offer was highly competitive. When the candidate ultimately rejected the offer, he reiterated how flattered he was and how seriously he had considered the offer. Within a week it was announced that he had accepted a $125,000 per year increase in salary from the administration at his university. Later that week, one of the longtime sports writers systematically documented how that coach had used the new offer to leverage his current position for the third time during his career.

Although there were numerous other candidates, Jones State turned to Wayne next. His story played in the press for over a week and it had a very different ring. The articles stated that the university had looked at the high-profile coaches and been rejected, so now they were turning to Wayne. Surely he would accept without question. It wasn't even a consideration that he might reject an offer. The university was so sure that he would jump at the chance that the salary terms were stated in the newspaper. The papers were told that it wouldn't cost nearly as much to get Wayne. The package would be in the $300,000 to $350,000 per year range. Finally, the athletic director caught up with Wayne two or three days later to discuss the position.

The next day Wayne pleasantly and professionally rejected the offer, saying how much he enjoyed and appreciated where he was, that he didn't have to be in the spotlight and he would wait for the right opportunity. The Jones State administration was devastated. Many observers felt that Wayne was the right candidate for Jones State from day one and that he had demonstrated every skill that would be necessary to resurrect the program. The president and athletic director, however, had been on an ego trip that had them talking to the high-profile coaches. The problem was that they had been taken for a ride by two experienced coaches. In addition, they did not show respect for Wayne as a coach or as a human being. In the process, they lost an outstanding candidate for the position.

Higher education, government, and other public institutions aren't the only places where this happens. The same thing happens in industry and is driven by the same kinds of issues. Although not usually as public as the case study, it is no less damaging. The critical mistake often comes down to the offhand remark that the candidate was not supposed to hear, such as, "Do you think that we'll be able to land the candidate we saw last week?" Actions often speak louder than words in the interview process. Letting an outstanding candidate sit in the waiting room for three-quarters of an hour after the appointed time or acting as if you are bored during the interview are examples of disrespectful behavior that will cause you to lose great candidates.

INTERVIEW TEAM CONSISTENCY

Defining the characteristics of the ideal candidate prior to beginning the interview process is a critical function of the interview team. It is then the function of each interviewer to play his or her part, however defined, in helping to identify the best candidate for the organization. This requires playing a team role that is sometimes in conflict with the manner in which interviewers conducted themselves when the process was more individualistic and ill-defined.

Career Profile ———————————————————————

Gotcha with That One!

Sara and Marlene had gotten along very well in their initial rapport-building conversation. Marlene felt that, as the interviewer, she had helped Sara, who was interviewing for a marketing position, to become comfortable in the new surroundings and had found some interesting topics to begin the rapport building part of the discussion. Sara felt the same way; she felt comfortable both in the surroundings and with Marlene.

What Sara did not know was that Marlene was the top salesperson in her firm and was regarded as the rainmaker. Although she had never had any formal interview training, Marlene fancied herself as a tough interviewer. She enjoyed the fact that her questions came from left field and right field and were often "gotcha" questions. The fact that her group had received interview training and now each person had a role didn't deter Marlene. She had been out of town during the training and she continued to do exactly what she pleased.

What Marlene did not know was that Sara was one of those truly outstanding candidates who had lots of choices. In fact, Sara had an offer in her pocket but had heard good things about Marlene's company and wanted to see whether it might provide her with an excellent home.

Marlene made the transition easily and smoothly from rapport building to the content of the interview by saying, "I've really enjoyed spending some time to get to know you on a personal level. Now I'd like to ask you some questions that will help me to learn more about your professional skills." Sara indicated that she had enjoyed the conversation as well. Marlene continued the meeting.

MARLENE: Tell me about yourself from early childhood through high school.

Sara told Marlene about growing up on the West Coast, being a good student, and enjoying water sports and expressing herself creatively through the arts.

MARLENE: Why did you select UCLA?

The answer focused on proximity to home and it fit the family's financial parameters.

MARLENE: What was your major? Why?

The major in liberal arts and minor in art sprung from her broad interests and the continuing interest in creativity.

MARLENE: Which of your jobs has been your favorite? Why?

This was all making sense to Sara. There was a logical progression from early childhood through high school, college, and now into her career interests. She answered that her last job, a marketing position with an emphasis on the creative side, had been her favorite. Earlier, Sara and Marlene had discussed the fact that Sara's previous employer was moving and that Sara's personal circumstances would not allow her to move at this time.

MARLENE: What was your biggest mistake in that job?

Sara remembered thinking that seemed like an odd question when they had just been talking about how much she had enjoyed the position. When it became apparent that Marlene wanted an answer, Sara said something about a communication issue with a major client. She also told Marlene how they were able to quickly correct the miscommunication.

MARLENE: Describe the characteristics of your best boss and your worst boss.

Sara answered the question by saying that her best boss was intelligent, a visionary, a good manager, consistent, and had an excellent sense of humor. Her worst boss lacked intelligence, was inconsistent and emotional, and did not know how to use resources that could help him to overcome his weaknesses.

MARLENE: What one thing has kept you from progressing faster in your career?

Now red flags were going up all over the place in Sara's mind. Where was this conversation going? Was there a purpose? Was the questioning going to be individual questions that were shotgunned with no direction? Would the conversation continue on such a negative course? What did this have to do with determining Sara's skills to perform effectively? Sara indicated that her career had been progressing exactly as she had hoped.

Marlene then asked the following questions:

- Tell me about a situation you handled involving conflict.
- What are three words that do not describe you?
- If you could only be one animal in the jungle, what would you be and why?
- Could you complete the following number sequence: 3,8,5,10,7, _____ ?
- What's your position in your family (oldest, youngest, etc.) and how does that affect who you are?

By this point, Sara was so turned off that she could not remember other questions that were asked or how the interview ended. She had been quick to realize that Marlene was on an ego trip. While some of her questions were excellent as stand-alone questions, Sara could tell that Marlene was much more interested in phrasing the question than she was in listening to the answer. Far worse was that there was no relationship to anything that had come earlier in the interviewing process. Previous interviewers had discussed Sara's accomplishments as evidence that she could successfully perform in the job and had asked about her management style as evidence of her fit within the culture. That had all made sense. The fact that Marlene was not consistent with the others, did not have a clear picture of the profile, yet would have a close working relationship with Sara if she were to take the job, was enough to convince Sara that she needed to seek employment elsewhere.

PREPARATION

Preparation should be so ingrained in the interviewer's psyche that you might think that it is not worth mentioning. Unfortunately, many interviewers have learned the hard way that a few minutes worth of preparation can make all the difference in conducting a successful interview.

Career Profile

Opening Jitters

Shari had been the top student in the sciences program at Michigan and she was being recruited by a number of pharmaceutical companies for their R & D divisions. Shari had narrowed the search to three of the best-known organizations that were reputed to have highly intelligent people, to be well-organized, to have outstanding resources, and to provide highly competitive salaries and benefits. She had performed well in her first round of interviews and now she was looking forward to the next round, which included her potential boss and other senior managers.

Todd, Shari's potential boss, wasn't looking forward to the interviews that day. It had nothing to do with Shari. He had been traveling for the last 3 days and for 14 of the last 20 business days. That much travel was unusual for him and heightened his immediate problem. He had a major presentation that had to be written, proofed, and practiced that day for delivery the next. Todd knew, as well as anyone, that hiring a new scientist was high on his list of priorities, but not today. The presentation was to senior management and it had to be powerful.

Shari knew her strengths included outstanding intellect, technical skills, and an intense desire to improve the human condition. She also knew that she was often uncomfortable meeting people for the first time and engaging in informal dialogue or chitchat. As much as she had tried to overcome this challenge, she found it difficult. In some encounters, when the conversation was listless or directionless, she became tense or flustered.

Todd wanted to take a few minutes to prepare for the interview with Shari, but it just never happened. Todd pried himself loose from working on the presentation when Shari was waiting outside his office. Todd was somewhat comforted by the fact that he had enough experience and was facile enough to carry off any interview. He was sure that this one would prove no exception.

Todd invited Shari into his office and offered her a seat. He would normally have been relaxed and willing to spend 10 or 15 minutes helping Shari to relax and become comfortable in the interview setting. Perhaps due to his own pressures, he found himself groping for conversation topics. Suddenly, he remembered that Shari's resume had a personal section that listed her interests and activities. He excused himself and went behind his desk to look for her resume. Todd became more embarrassed by the second as he fumbled through the papers but could not locate the resume. Red-faced and uncomfortable, he finally asked Shari if she had an additional copy of her resume. He defended his actions by blurting out that he had just arrived home from a business trip.

Shari was doing her best to remain calm during this episode, but this was the toughest time for her under the best of circumstances. Now she was put on the spot and had to produce a resume. She had not anticipated this request and she wasn't even sure she had an additional copy of her resume. The longer she fumbled in her bag, the more uncomfortable she became. An observer watching the two people could have seen the humor in the situation, but neither Todd nor Shari saw anything funny about what was happening. In the end, neither of them found a copy of the resume.

Todd had no choice but to come back to the interview setting and attempt to resurrect the strained conversation. Now he had a real problem in that Shari had subconsciously retracted to a level deeper within herself during the period of confusion. Todd had to work very hard to draw Shari out; he tried hard and she tried hard but it just never worked. When the interview ended, both people were relieved that it was over, yet were uncomfortable with their behavior. Todd knew that he had blown the interview and was convinced that he never got to know the real Shari (he had received great and glowing reports from earlier interviewers). Shari was angry that she had not had additional resumes with her, that she could not overcome her anxieties when the interview took an unanticipated turn, and that she had been unable to regain a balanced equilibrium. When her interviews went outstandingly well with the other two companies, Shari did not pursue her candidacy with Todd's company despite repeated attempts by Todd.

BUILDING A PARTNERSHIP

Most people who conduct interviews develop their own interview styles that evolve from their personal experience. This is supplemented, if they are lucky, by interview training. Outstanding candidates who have options begin to evaluate the interviewer's ability to build a partnership with them from the first moments of the interview.

Career Profile _____

On the Spot

Carrie was extremely happy in her present position. She had reached the level of vice president at an earlier age than any of her peers and was respected as a key partner on the management team by senior management. She agreed to interview with Jake's company because the executive search professional convinced her that this was one interview she had to accept. He said that the reputation of Jake's company and the outstanding management team were too good to pass up, at least for a conversation. Carrie agreed to the meeting, in part, to test her marketability and to increase her network.

Jake knew that this represented an opportunity for him. His senior management had targeted raising the level of their management depth as a major initiative. In addition, everyone had heard about Carrie because she had been involved in some visible initiatives over the past three years. Jake knew that he needed to conduct a full "buy" interview because no one knew Carrie personally. He wanted to test her technical skills and abilities, intellect and business accomplishments, in addition to her interest, motivation, and her overall ability to fit the culture of the company. He knew that he would also need to sell her on the merits of his company.

When Jake met Carrie she was relaxed and greeted him with a warm smile and a firm handshake. Jake welcomed Carrie, ushered her into his office and asked if she had any difficulty with the directions. "No," Carrie replied, "I have some friends who live in this area and I've had dinner with them at some nearby restaurants." Jake picked up on that comment, turning the conversation to mutual acquaintances, and then transitioned into a discussion of his company.

Jake moved fairly quickly toward his goal of testing her intelligence and technical skills which were the initial tasks he needed to accomplish. As he questioned Carrie about her academic and business experience, including the various positions she had held, he quickly became convinced that she was an excellent candidate. The breadth of her experience at impressive companies qualified her technical skills. As she told Jake about her major accomplishments, her eyes lit up and it was obvious she had great energy and passion for her work. Carrie handled all of Jake's questions with poise and with professional ease and it was clear that he was impressed with her answers.

By this time, 45 to 50 minutes of the hour had passed and Jake transitioned smoothly from "buy" to "sell" by asking Carrie what he could tell her about the company. She had a number of questions and Jake answered them well. At about the hour mark Jake moved competently to the close. Jake told Carrie he really enjoyed meeting her and he thought her background was outstanding; he then indicated that he hoped that Carrie would be willing to come back and meet with others on his staff. Carrie was very pleasant and indicated that she'd like to think about it. She asked Jake about the time frame for filling the job and he indicated that he hoped to have the position filled in six to nine weeks. Carrie thanked Jake and left.

Jake felt great about the interview. He had accomplished everything on his agenda and in a cordial manner. Carrie was an outstanding candidate, one that Jake would love to have on his staff. In addition to her technical skills, interest and drive, she had just the right balance of team player and leader. Jake knew that his people would think Carrie was terrific.

Carrie did not leave the interview feeling the same way. It had taken her time to work her way up the ladder at her present company. She had done it by having outstanding technical skills, working extremely hard, having a positive attitude and passion for her job and being an outstanding team player. Colleagues respected her abilities and her opinions when critical business decisions were being formulated. As she was promoted to larger responsibilities, her leadership skills developed. Overall, her major sense was that she was a partner in the venture.

Carrie felt that there was no interest in partnership during her interview with Jake. He had an agenda that he needed to accomplish and he did it well and efficiently. The content he discussed was fine; it was the right content and it made sense. It's just that she hadn't felt part of the process. From the time she walked into the meeting there was very little discussion about Carrie as a person. The only personal conversation focused on people she knew who worked at Jake's company. Then the conversation turned to her skills in a question and answer format with Jake controlling the meeting. There was little room for interactive conversation and no feeling of partnership in the interview. Carrie was struck by how much she had taken the partnership for granted in her present company and how absent it was in the interview. Those two issues, the concern for her as a person and whether Jake believed in managing by building partnerships were difficult for her to overcome. At the suggestion of the executive search consultant she came back for a series of interviews, but she could not overcome the issues that had surfaced in the first meeting with her potential boss. None of the additional interviews convinced her that her initial feeling was incorrect, and she eventually turned down the job offer.

MANAGING THE SELL

The sell begins the first minute an outstanding candidate walks into the company. Everyone in the organization is part of that sales effort.

Career Profile _____

Singing from the Same Page

Alicia was pleased by the initial reports from her group at the end of the first day of interviews. Everything seemed to be going according to plan. Rafael had met six of her people and the interviews had gone well. They felt as good about Rafael's candidacy as Alicia did. She scheduled Rafael to come back for a second round of interviews the following week.

Rafael was equally impressed; he had enjoyed the initial meeting and was looking forward to the next round of interviews. It was clear to him that his ability to write and develop creative marketing material, and his fluency in Spanish as well as English, were in high demand in the airline industry. Alicia's company presented an interesting opportunity for him, but he was also seriously considering offers from two of her competitors.

Alicia did everything right in preparing her people for the next round of interviews. She personally reviewed the first round of meetings with the next two interviewers and left lengthy notes for Gary, who had been traveling. She reviewed what had taken place with

Sherry, the new recruiter who had been hired for her division. This was Sherry's first assignment since being hired, and she gave Alicia high marks for her preparation.

Rafael arrived early for the next round of interviews. He reported to a new location and announced himself to the receptionist. She called for Debbie, who would be one of his colleagues in the marketing department. Debbie appeared in about five minutes and was apologetic both about making him wait and in informing him that an emergency project had arisen and she would not be able to meet with him. She told him that James, also from the marketing department, would be excited to meet with him. Rafael was a little disappointed but went with Debbie to meet James. James was very pleasant but it was obvious that he was a few levels below Debbie in the organization and was clearly uncomfortable interviewing Rafael. Rafael helped James as much as he could and they had a pleasant conversation for about 40 minutes. Because that was a shorter interview than was anticipated, Rafael waited in the reception area until Alicia came to escort him to meet Gary.

Gary was a salesman and a bit of a loose cannon under normal circumstances. He had never bothered to read the E-mail that Alicia left for him, so he was a very loose cannon on this occasion. Alicia and the other interviewers had indicated the importance of strategic marketing programs as one of their key development objectives. Without really being prompted, Gary gave Rafael his view: We don't need additional marketing programs but we do need larger expense budgets to entertain our clients. Gary went on to explain that in this industry the key to selling was personal relationships, and marketing programs, while helpful, were not as critical to the sale as building the relationship. Gary told Rafael that if he joined the firm, he would help him understand the difference between working for the airline and working for the advertising agency.

The remainder of the day went well and Rafael had an outstanding recap with Alicia. On his way home, however, doubts began to surface about the company. Alicia was great, but there was more to working for the company than one person. Debbie had been pleasant to him, but she hadn't shown him much respect when she asked such a junior person to substitute for her. As Rafael thought about it, she never even offered to meet with him at another time. Gary had presented a view that was the exact opposite of the way Alicia described the corporate goals and direction. What if Rafael signed on and then discovered that the company really didn't care about the marketing expertise he could bring? As time went on, his doubts grew stronger.

Alicia did not know about either of these two incidents. She would find out later that Debbie had asked James to conduct the interview and she had no idea that Gary was saying things that were directly opposite the stated goals of the organization. When she asked Gary about the meeting, he said that it went extremely well and that he liked Rafael.

The more Rafael thought about his interviews with Alicia's company, the more uncomfortable he became. He decided, however, to wait a little longer to see what happened. He received a number of follow-up calls from the two competing companies, from both line executives and high-level recruiting professionals. Rafael did receive a great call from Alicia, but Sherry, the recruiter, did not call. Apparently, she didn't know that she was expected to make follow-up calls to candidates. When Rafael realized that Sherry was the only recruiting professional from the three companies who hadn't contacted him, it added to the warning signals in his head. Alicia was terrific, but he wasn't sure about all the others he had met in her company.

When Alicia called Rafael to find out why he wasn't continuing in the interviewing process, he found himself in a dilemma. He had been taught to leave every situation on the best of terms because you may be working with the person in the future. Consequently, instead of being honest with Alicia, he said that one of his longtime friends was working at one of the other companies and he was excited about working with him. He indicated that he thought Alicia was great (which was true) and he hoped they would have an opportunity to work together in the future. Alicia never knew what happened.

NEGOTIATION

The interviewer, as well as the candidate, often shows her true mettle in the negotiation process. The objective is to come out with a win/win situation, and it takes integrity, finesse, patience, and understanding in addition to an excellent set of skills to accomplish that goal.

Career Profile _____

On the Road

Jean was extremely pleased. She had just received her second offer within 24 hours to be president of a division of a women's apparel company and still had a scheduled meeting with Stephanie, the CEO of yet a third apparel company. Jean had a strong reputation as a division president and she had been considering a possible move within the industry that she knew and understood. She actually enjoyed the negotiation aspect of looking for a new position, because she felt it gave her a great opportunity to learn more about her potential boss. She knew that she would be working extremely long hours, six seasons per year, and she would be considered "as good as her last season." In exchange for that pressure, she had a right to expect an outstanding compensation package.

Stephanie had a reputation for being extremely intelligent, highly successful, and an excellent businesswoman; yet she was also perceived as arrogant, uninterested in details, and very tough to work for. Everyone in the industry knew Stephanie paid her people well. Because she traveled so much and was never in the same spot for very long, it had been difficult to schedule a meeting with Jean.

Jean had heard the stories about Stephanie and part of her agenda was to separate fact from fiction. Another issue was to determine whether working for Stephanie would be fulfilling, given the rumors. Her biggest concern, however, was the mixed reviews she had heard regarding Stephanie's integrity. Jean knew that would be a critical ingredient for her, a game breaker. If she didn't sense integrity, she'd remain in her present company or accept one of the other offers she had received.

When they met, Stephanie was charming; she was clearly a great saleswoman. She spent a good deal of time building rapport, which Jean appreciated. When this introductory phase was completed,

Stephanie spent time talking about women's sportswear. It was a great conversation about the industry, the marketplace and the products in Stephanie's company. They spoke about which products were outstanding, which were weak, and how they could be improved. They clearly seemed to be "on the same page." Stephanie seemed open to Jean's input on the topic. The only thing that was unsettling was the number of interruptions in a short time. Three times they were interrupted in person and twice by telephone. Stephanie apologized but was clearly distracted on at least two occasions.

At the conclusion of the first meeting, Stephanie told Jean that she was impressed. She also said that they would have to move quickly because Stephanie was only in town for a few days. Consequently, they met almost nonstop for the next few days. They discussed all aspects of the business, including spending a good deal of time in the retail stores examining the clothes and talking to clients. They continued to find themselves in sync regarding the future direction of the product.

Jean was impressed with Stephanie's knowledge of the business and her legendary sales abilities, but she was feeling uncomfortable about an issue she felt she needed to discuss. Finally, there was an opportunity at dinner. Jean told Stephanie that she was used to working 10- to 12-hour days and expected to do that, but for personal reasons she had to be home-based in New York. Jean was relieved when Stephanie said that wouldn't be a problem and that the amount of travel the position required was reasonable.

At the conclusion of the second full day, Stephanie spoke about the compensation package she had in mind. She threw out a substantial base salary, talked in percentage terms about the bonus potential, and told Jean there would be stock options. Stephanie went on to offer a clothing allowance of $15,000 (it was necessary to wear the company's clothes to work) as well as an automobile allowance. Jean thanked Stephanie for her consideration, said she was very excited, and said that she'd like to think about the offer for a few days. The meeting ended cordially with Stephanie saying that she would be traveling (she traveled about 80 percent of the time) and if Jean had questions, she should discuss them with Kevin, her vice president for human resources.

Jean left feeling great. The conversations had been terrific, their views on the business had been very much the same, and the offer was outstanding. She knew herself well enough to know that she'd better take a little time for all this to settle down. She clearly had "fallen in love" with Stephanie but wanted to make sure she understood the full scope of the job. In a day or two, something told Jean that she better explore the offer with human resources. She called Kevin and made an appointment to discuss a few issues. When Jean met Kevin he was very cordial and clearly was in a sell mode. He asked about the meetings with Stephanie and seemed pleased when Jean said that they had been great. Kevin asked Jean if she had any outstanding issues. She said that she wanted to learn more about the company and its people. Jean told Kevin that she would like to meet with some other members of the company. Kevin was a little reluctant, saying that Stephanie was the key person. Jean was professionally persistent and eventually Kevin set up meetings with three of the other senior executives in the company.

Over the next two weeks, Jean met with the three senior executives. She was impressed with each of them and felt they had strong apparel backgrounds. Jean was a veteran at asking questions, assimilating information, and filling in the gaps to reach conclusions. It was clear that Stephanie ran the company and that no major decisions were made without her input. That was not always easy to get and that caused major frustration for the executives. Through carefully worded questions, Jean was able to determine that each of the executives traveled over 50 percent of the time, partly to catch up with Stephanie to discuss their business. They indicated that it didn't matter where you were home based, because you would be living out of a suitcase a great deal of the time. Jean expected a fair amount of travel but that was very disappointing news.

After one of the meetings, Jean ran into Kevin. She asked if she could review the terms of the offer with him. The base salary and stock options were exactly as Stephanie had told her, but the bonus potential was five percent less and Kevin reported the clothing allowance would be $10,000. Jean asked Kevin to check on the bonus potential and the clothing allowance because they didn't seem to be what had been discussed. When Kevin called her later he offered explanations for why the bonus potential and clothing allowance needed to be the lesser amounts.

The following week, Jean called to speak with Stephanie. Kevin picked up the phone and apologized, saying that Stephanie's trip had been extended. Jean was polite as she told Kevin that she really appreciated the offer but had decided not to accept it. Kevin was stunned. After she hung up, Jean was relieved. Her thoughts centered on Stephanie's behavior, the conflicting information she had received, and what it would be like to work for her.

The game breaker, just as Jean knew it would be, was whether Stephanie would be a boss with a high integrity level. Jean couldn't satisfy herself that Stephanie measured up. It could be argued that Stephanie intended to honor the "reasonable travel" she had mentioned, yet none of the other senior managers were even close to what Jean considered a reasonable travel schedule. Jean was used to working in partnerships, but it seemed that Stephanie would be a micromanager. Furthermore, although the reduced bonus and clothing allowance were not large amounts of money, they represented red flags to Jean. She decided to move on and Stephanie lost a star.

SUMMARY

The best candidates are intelligent and savvy and have demonstrated that they can make a major impact on the bottom line of a company. They are also impatient and often intolerant of hiring missteps. Companies lose the best candidates when interviewers display weaknesses in:

- Motivation,
- Respectful treatment,
- Interview team consistency,
- Preparation,
- Building a partnership,
- Managing the sell,
- Negotiation.

PART

2

PREPARING FOR THE INTERVIEW

Part 2 deals with the interview preparation that is necessary to compete effectively. The process begins with a senior management that is passionate about the vision to hire truly outstanding talent and communicates it clearly. This includes establishing a sense of urgency with specific goals and timelines. A recruiting model is established that fits the industry and the size and culture of the company. The process begins with the development of the Ideal Success Profile, which describes the ideal candidate. Implementation of the process rests with a highly energized and motivated interview team.

STEP 1

Take Ownership of the Process

The CEO and his two senior vice presidents met to discuss their thoughts on the director-level position they needed to fill. The executive search firm had surfaced five excellent candidates, all of whom could perform successfully. It was the hiring team's view after meeting the candidates, however, that they could not perform any better than Gwen or Ted, the two inside candidates who had knowledge of the people and how to get things done as well as product expertise.

The decision as to which of the internal candidates to hire was difficult, because each brought valuable skills to the table. Ted had a broader base of experience gained in working in a variety of positions in three companies. Gwen was a classic, home-grown product who had advanced through a series of promotions within the company; she had also attained her MBA at night while working. Clearly, there were a number of positive factors about each of the candidates.

As the three executives tried to reach a decision it became clear that they were not in agreement. The CEO, who had remained fairly quiet during the discussion, proposed a possible solution. "You know how much time we have spent trying to communicate my objectives to staff," he asked. The senior vice presidents nodded. "Why don't we use those objectives to help us make this decision? We state the objectives as:

- Having a vision and implementing plans that positively impact the bottom line;
- Hiring outstanding talent who will drive the business; and
- Producing a product that we are proud of and that helps clients accomplish their objectives."

Again, both senior vice presidents nodded in agreement. When the executives examined the candidates' contributions to the bottom line, they were indeed impressed. Both Gwen and Ted had value-adding accomplishments that substantially increased the company's revenue and profitability. After a thorough discussion, it became apparent that this objective did not enable them to differentiate enough to make a selection.

The CEO then suggested that they adjourn until the vice president for human resources could prepare the data they needed to evaluate the second objective. Later, when they reconvened to examine the recruiting, hiring, and development track record of each candidate, they were amazed. Ted had hired four people since he had been with the company; two remained and one was considered someone with high potential. Gwen had hired eight people; seven remained and six were considered outstanding or of high potential. Once into the discussion, the vice president for human resources recalled two instances in which Ted lost a consensus hire, but related that Gwen was known for never losing a key hire. What had been a really difficult process became an easier decision. Gwen won the job and the senior executives were very comfortable with the decision.

The job market is tough, the competition is fierce, and the differences between highly qualified candidates are often miniscule. Making the best selection requires interviewers who are at the top of their form. It is possible to prepare your interview team for all major issues and to prepare them for most tactical considerations, therefore dramatically decreasing the probability of making mistakes.

Hiring the best must be a major initiative of the CEO or division head, or it simply won't happen. The recruiting program must be headed by a senior executive on an ongoing basis, with the goal of constant improvement. The process must be implemented in a manner that will maintain industry competitiveness and be consistent with the size and culture of the company. We examine these issues as they relate to small, mid-size, and large companies in this chapter.

Note to the Reader

Throughout the book we refer to experienced hires and new graduate hires. *Experienced hire* refers to an individual with business experience whom a company is seeking, regardless of whether the position represents a lateral move or a promotion. *New graduate* refers to an individual who is graduating from an undergraduate, professional, or graduate degree program.

THE ROLE OF SENIOR MANAGEMENT

The role of the CEO or division head is to create the vision and the sense of urgency to hire impact players. Establishing a sense of urgency requires specific goals and timelines, or it will be impossible to measure results. This concept seems obvious. But making great hires is extremely hard work, requires resources, and takes tremendous dedication to the task. It's also becoming more difficult each year, due to global and domestic competition.

Credibility is a critical ingredient in the process. Because attracting top candidates is difficult and is accomplished as an additional responsibility to normal duties, staff will watch the leader to see whether there is a strong, ongoing dedication to the goal. If the leader wavers in his or her dedication, then the probability exists that others in the division may waver. The senior executive's behavior will be constantly reassessed by everyone. Does he believe in hiring the best? Is she committed to providing the resources necessary to carry out the goal? Does his own track record indicate that he has been able to attract top-level talent? Does she walk the walk and talk the talk? Does he truly believe in involving the team? Does she respect their input? Does he constantly communicate with staff about the importance of the process? Does she praise those who have done an outstanding job of hiring the best and reward those who accomplish the goals?

One of the best ways to keep the organization focused on hiring the best is for the CEO or division head to remain actively involved. In a small company this may be an absolute necessity, with the CEO interviewing every candidate prior to hire. In a mid-size or large company, a policy may be set that all experienced candidates above a certain level will be interviewed by the senior executive. Beyond the policy, however, the senior executive can randomly become involved in the hiring process at lower levels to show interest and to monitor the recruiting methodology and practice, as well as to remain current regarding the education and experience of the candidates. This is a great opportunity to learn where the company is outstanding, competitive, or weak.

It is easy to say that having the CEO or division head involved in the recruiting process is impractical, that a CEO is just too busy. We disagree. It is a matter of ranking one's objectives by asking, "What are my most important objectives and will I commit the time necessary to carry them out successfully?" We have a friend who is the CEO of a company that he founded some years ago. The company now has thousands of employees and a truly outstanding reputation for managing its human capital. The CEO still insists on interviewing every professional who is being recommended for hire.

In addition to personal involvement, the leader must keep the recruiting process under constant review, because the marketplace is constantly changing. Leaders need to communicate openly with staff about the successes and improvements that are necessary. If they feel that the hiring process has been an outstanding one, then their communication must remind staff how difficult it is to remain at that level and how easy it is to slip. If the hiring process must be improved, staff must be reminded how important it is to improve relative to the competition. The timing is fairly easy to define for new graduates, because the college hiring season normally runs from the end of the summer intern experience through the first month or two of the next year. There is no particular season for experienced hires, which are normally based on expertise that is

not currently in the skill set of those in the organization or the opportunity to hire an "A" player who would not normally be available. However, whenever an experienced hire is made, there is a specific and easily defined time frame that creates its own urgency.

THE PROCESS: MID-SIZE AND LARGE COMPANIES

A major issue in mid-size and large companies is building a motivated, core group of line executives and recruiters with a consistent hiring philosophy who can react quickly and efficiently to maintain competitiveness with their smaller counterparts. In each of the sections that follow, both the integrity of the recruiting process and the speed of reaction time are important considerations.

Head of Recruiting

The Head of Recruiting is our term to represent whoever your company calls the highest empowered recruiting person in the division. This individual must be held in high regard by everyone, clearly an "A" player. He must be totally committed to hiring the best and have the same vision as the CEO or division head in every phase of the recruiting process. He must be personable, positive, and have a high energy level in addition to having a highly developed client service mentality.

This individual must also have additional broad-based skills. At the strategic end of the spectrum, he will need to be a terrific recruiter and salesperson for the organization. He will need to understand the psychology of recruiting "A" players from a technical and intuitive point of view (the subject of later portions of the book). He needs to be a consummate team player and have an understanding of the dynamics of human interaction. With this knowledge he will be able to match staff members and candidates who made a real connection with each other and dramatically increase the organization's chances of landing great candidates.

At the same time he will have to be a coach, mentor, and cheerleader to the members of the recruiting team in an era when top recruits need more attention than ever before. He will have to help members of his own team understand that neither the job market nor candidates are the same as they used to be. Consequently, it is not productive to hold to the past by saying, "When our class was hired there was none of this coddling. We were told that we'd be lucky to have a job at such a great company, and we appreciated being given an offer."

> **INTERVIEW TIP**
>
> **HEAD OF RECRUITING**
>
> The Head of Recruiting must be held in high regard and must understand the psychology of recruiting "A" players from a technical and intuitive point of view.

At the tactical end of the spectrum, the Head of Recruiting needs to be extremely strong in organizational and management skills. This includes the entire range of recruiting activities from summer intern offer letters and follow-up, to campus recruiting meetings, to tracking candidates with offers. As a specific example, imagine the organization necessary to transport 20 to 25 MBA students to the company campus, house them, and schedule a carefully orchestrated set of six or eight interviews for them with middle and senior executives of the division.

Alignment of Staff

The Head of Recruiting can't implement a great hiring process alone. The CEO or division head's executive committee or direct reports must become disciples of the program and they, in turn, must inspire others in the organization. The key is to build a strong, solid core group of key line executives, stars, rising stars, and human resource professionals who are committed to the vision and will successfully implement it.

When recruiting new graduates, the hiring team will include senior management, school managers (head of a team that recruits at a specific college), and recruiting team members. When recruiting new graduates, it can be immensely helpful to have recruiters who are graduates of that college. The team should also be representative of the diversity in the organization or to which the organization aspires. The hiring team, with the help of the Head of Recruiting, will define the list of *target colleges that represent the pool of talent from which you normally recruit.* The list of *stretch colleges represents the pool of talent from which you aspire to recruit.* The stretch colleges represent your "A" candidates. If you are fortunate enough to be recruiting at the absolute top colleges, then your challenge is to figure out how to remain at that level, because the fall is fast and steep if you become arrogant about your lofty position.

Recruiting of experienced professionals occurs as the need arises. If there is a specific position that the organization can't fill from within, then senior management may be using the human resource recruiters or an executive search firm to help source the pool of final candidates. If there is no specific need but the organization has a policy of constantly seeking outstanding talent, then senior managers will constantly be tapping their personal networks in search of potential talent. Once identified, a potential experienced hire will normally meet a series of senior managers selected by the hiring manager. It is not at all unusual for this to be a team of eight to twelve senior managers and recruiters. Scheduling must be done on an as-possible basis due to scheduling issues on each side. If there is an immediate need the process must be compacted. In fast-moving companies this might mean scheduling a series of interviews on a Saturday.

INTERVIEW TIP

**ALIGNMENT
OF STAFF**

A core group of
inspired line execu-
tives and recruiters
who are "A" players
themselves should be
selected to implement
the program.

One final note on staff alignment: it should
be the goal of senior management to select a
recruiting team composed of the company's
top talent, people who are up to the task of
recruiting outstanding candidates. A place on
the recruiting team should be recognized as
an honor and a stepping-stone toward career
advancement. It should be clear that maintaining a spot on the recruiting team is based
on productivity and that there are no lifetime
appointments.

The Hiring Manager: Owner of the Hiring Process

The hiring manager will be the new hire's boss and it is ultimately her decision as to who will join the team. That leaves the
ultimate authority and accountability for the quality of the hire
squarely on her shoulders—in other words, the ownership of the
hiring process. When a hiring manager asks what is the most
important question she should ask herself, we respond, "Assuming your next hire will be the most critical and visible of your
tenure, and will have a major impact on your career progress,
are you totally confident regarding the hiring abilities of every
member of your team?"

Hiring top talent is one of the most important decisions that
any manager has to make. It is also one of the most visible to the
senior management of the division. Clearly, this structure provides
the hiring manager with the accountability as well as the authority, which is as it should be. It is her responsibility to understand
the needs of the company and her area and to require that the recruiting process is handled correctly. This starts with having the
right people on the team. She will undoubtedly want to have
strong, technically trained staff to question the candidates' intelligence, technical skills, and abilities. She will also want those
whom she considers knowledgeable about the professional style

and personal skills that have proven successful to question candidates about those abilities. And she will want other stakeholders to be able to add their expertise.

Incidentally, you may find yourself saying, "I don't know that I agree that ownership is so clean. In our company I see instances of mutual or consensual ownership." There is no doubt that there are outside influences, as we will see in the next section. Those influences, however, don't lessen the hiring manager's authority in making a great hire for her area. If no one in the final pool of candidates meets the organizational and divisional requirements, then the recruiting process should be restarted until a great candidate is found. Great candidates are needed because a major component of the contract between the organization and the entrepreneurial, cross-functional team is that it produces or it loses its mandate.

> **INTERVIEW TIP**
>
> **OWNERSHIP**
>
> Ownership of the process is in the hands of the hiring manager, who holds ultimate authority and accountability for the hiring process.

Composition of the Interview Team: Stakeholders

Complicating the hiring process is the fact that the division or corporation may also add initiatives of concern to the larger organization. These may add additional members to the screening and hiring teams. For example, if a company has been experiencing difficulty with cross-divisional communication, the president or CEO may mandate that at least one interviewer from outside the division join the interview team. Another example might be the case of a licensing agreement whereby the licensor has a right to interview the candidate who will service the business prior to an offer being made by the licensee.

Diversity is another initiative that must come from the corporate level. With more companies becoming global in nature, the ability of candidates to relate to a diverse internal workforce and client base becomes critical. If the individual is being considered for a management position or for a future management position, the ability to hire and manage a diverse, global team will be critical. There may be a head of the diversity initiative who becomes a member of the hiring team.

The hiring manager is expected to welcome this type of input. In almost all instances of multiple interview models, interviewers are collegial in nature and do not hold veto power. The reason is simple. If you have a few or many interviewers and any one of them holds veto power, it might be very difficult to get agreement on any candidate. The role of these stakeholders is to help the hiring manager to make the best selection possible. It is always the hiring manager's final decision, because she is accountable.

INTERVIEW TIP

THE STAKEHOLDERS

The interview team may include stakeholders who represent corporate or client interests, as well as divisional representatives.

Setting the Ground Rules

Having stated the vision, a plan must be put in place. Normally, the Head of Recruiting, together with the recruiting team, writes the draft of a plan that is then discussed and eventually agreed upon by the senior executive and executive committee. There may be different procedures for the new graduate, college recruiting program and for experienced hires, but both will include the following guidelines:

- Job open or need defined for new position and approved.
- Internal recruiter and hiring manager form a team.
- Hiring team identified.
- Job description or ideal success profile written.
- Recruiting sources identified and candidates generated.
- Internal and external candidates interviewed.
- Screening process reduces the number of candidates.
- Final candidates interviewed by team.

- Selection made by hiring manager.
- References checked.
- Offer extended, negotiation (if necessary), and acceptance.
- New hire starts.

Mid-size and large companies normally have considerably more resources than small ones in the form of recruiting assistance and budgets. Indeed, this is necessary given the time and effort it takes to accomplish the process. It is a major task to hire many new associates at the beginning of a year.

INTERVIEW TIP

THE POLICY

Clear, concise recruiting policies and procedures must be in place.

Questions about an Open Position

This is not usually an issue when it comes to new graduates during times of consistent profits. The organization has a track record of the number of hires that have been made and in which areas of the division. The CEO or division head and the executive committee, with the assistance of the Head of Recruiting, will decide how many positions to fill at a staff meeting. At that point the recruiting process, beginning with the summer intern program and fall recruiting, can take place.

Once again, hiring someone experienced is more complex. The first step is for a decision to be made that there is an open position, that the division's approval guidelines have been met, and that there is budgetary authorization. The hiring manager and team then need to ask a number of questions to clarify their thinking. This process has the elements of any planning activity; namely, that time spent in the beginning improves the process and usually leads to a better hire. The complexity increases in the case of a brand new position as opposed to filling a vacated position. The planning activity will also be necessary if the hiring manager is to justify the need for the new hire to the senior executive. Questions that should be asked include:

What is the job that needs to be accomplished and for how long?

Writing a job description or an ideal success profile sounds like a no-brainer, until the team leader asks the question and the discussion begins. One person feels there is an immediate need for a marketing person with strong training skills to communicate with the sales force. Another person feels that the interface with the advertising agencies is an absolute must for a candidate's skill set. Yet another argues that mathematical skills for the analytical part of the job are critical. The team leader and the group need to come to agreement concerning the position needs now and the skill sets needed moving forward.

To what degree is the job the same as previously defined?

The greater the similarity, the more that can be learned from past incumbents. As these strengths and weaknesses are analyzed, the evolution of the job also has to be considered. In the past, for example, the vice president of marketing may not have needed any sales background. After a strategic change, however, it may be imperative that the new vice president of marketing have sales in her background in order to relate better to the sales force.

Can the need best be filled on a full-time, part-time, or consulting basis?

The costs associated with a full-time hire are being scrutinized more carefully than ever due to the base salary, the bonus, and the 25 to 40 percent cost of benefits. The decision often comes down to whether the position in question is in a core function of the business or is in a support area. If it has the function of producing revenue for the company or is a necessary support function, it will be funded. If not, it might be a service performed more efficiently through a shared services vehicle or by part-time or outside assistance.

Is this a developmental assignment that could be filled internally, or is it specialized expertise required from outside the organization?

All organizations have a pipeline of young talent waiting for an opportunity to advance. That need must have an outlet or it will be difficult to maintain talent. One of the major problems facing companies that eliminated layers of middle management is the problem of providing career paths for their rising stars. Often it has become necessary to provide the channels of growth through lateral transfers to new areas to broaden the executive's perspective. It is also important to infuse new blood into an organization to prevent stagnancy and present new ideas. However, this must be done carefully and with a plan.

What are the potential career moves for the individual who fills this position?

Smart candidates for positions today inquire whether it is a short-term or a long-term assignment. They are asking what type of career path they might expect if they accept the position. You need to ask the same question. If, in fact, it is a short-term need, then perhaps you would be better served by hiring a part-timer or a consultant rather than creating a full-time position. If a full-time position is needed, then the issue of potential career moves needs to be addressed.

> **INTERVIEW TIP**
>
> **QUESTIONS ABOUT AN OPEN POSITION**
>
> All questions regarding the position, the duties, the type of position, and the potential career path need to be answered before the interviewing process begins.

Communicating the Vision

There is no doubt that the senior executive's role in communication is critical. Due to the time commitment above and beyond normal duties, members of the staff will seek reinforcement from senior management that hiring the best remains a top initiative.

The CEO or division head and the Head of Recruiting should review the communication agenda often. One of the most powerful tools the senior executive has is holding one-on-one meetings at which discussion about the progress of the recruiting effort can occur during the conversation. A standing agenda item at company or divisional conferences reinforces the initiative. Comments by senior management in company publications are effective. In short, communication needs to come in every way possible.

Another key milestone occurs when the broader recruiting team begins to inspire others in the organization to "catch the passion," and when those staff members become salespeople for the implementation strategies. Once this process begins, there is a real chance that long-term commitment will be developed.

In addition to the senior executive, the Head of Recruiting will want to implement an ongoing communication campaign to inform and educate staff about the importance of making great hires. A standard column in the company newsletter, new marketing materials, and updating the company Web site to better attract candidates are a few examples.

> **INTERVIEW TIP**
>
> **COMMUNICATION**
>
> There simply cannot be too much communication about the organization's commitment to hire the best. Use every means possible.

A friend of ours who is the CEO of a financial services firm emphasizes the excellent work of his hiring teams every time he gives a "state of the company" address. He not only speaks about the accomplishment, but he gives special recognition for accomplishment in targeting an outstanding person or hiring a key individual.

Hiring As Part of the Performance Evaluation

It is not enough to merely talk about being talented at hiring the best. There needs to be a payoff for those who spend hours doing it and prove to the senior executive that they are skilled at recruiting talent. Outstanding ability can be recognized in a number of ways. The individual can be given a commendation, a discretionary bonus, additional vacation time, an evening on the town, or "points" on a performance evaluation or the data used when making decisions for internal promotion. Earlier, we saw Gwen win an important promotion over a very close competitor because she had established a track record and a reputation as an executive skilled at hiring and retaining outstanding talent.

Organizations are becoming more aware of the need to keep data regarding hiring managers' track records in hiring and retention. Outstanding interviewing and retention can be added to the performance evaluation process in an informal way in the beginning. A simple question such as, "Why don't you tell me about the hires you have made in the last three years and how the individuals have progressed?" or, "How much turnover has your department had in the last few years?" adds weight and credibility to the importance of making excellent hires and retaining staff. Interviewing can more formally be addressed in performance evaluations in a second or third cycle.

The ability to hire well should be considered a prerequisite for promotion, as we saw in Gwen's case. When the CEO asked the senior human resource executive to come back with hard data about the results of the hiring process, a new level of importance was realized. You can well imagine how the word spread through the organization that Gwen won the promotion because she was deemed to be outstanding at making key hires and mentoring those people toward continued success.

THE PROCESS: SMALL COMPANIES

A major issue in small companies, professional practices, or consultancies is maintaining consensus and consistency in building an effective interview model as the company grows and a division of labor is necessary. Here we address the growth of the organization until those strategies that were addressed for mid-size and large companies apply.

Early Stage

While the entrepreneur or the original partners control the company and are actively involved in the hiring process, the informal systems that have evolved usually suffice. The issues of communicating and maintaining the vision do not apply because there are very few if any people to keep in the loop. The problem is resources: There may be none to call on. The founder may have to do it all alone.

As the need and the ideal candidate profile have been defined in the hiring process, the founder will normally seek candidates through an industry network, which is often extensive, or through an ad in the newspaper. In some instances, although not as often as in larger companies, the founder will seek the services of a search firm. The founder will normally conduct an initial screening of candidates by reading resumes to identify the smaller pool of candidates who seem to have the necessary professional characteristics.

Because time is limited, the next step is often a telephone screening with the pool of candidates in order to verify the professional characteristics and to begin to ascertain the candidates' personal characteristics. In some instances, the founder may have a second telephone interview with a few candidates as the hiring pool is reduced.

The telephone calls help the executive accomplish some initial steps in a time-efficient and cost-effective manner. The founder can then personally meet those few candidates who remain. The interview process is often reduced to a few meetings if the founder is looking for an employee, or a series of meetings over a number of months if the founder is looking for a senior executive to help lead and grow the business. Part of the process includes reference checks with a number of people the founder knows in the industry prior to making a decision.

Middle Stage

Once the founder makes the decision to expand the company, it usually requires additional stakeholders such as financial partners, the hiring of key executives, or joint venture partners. Each of these stakeholders will have an agenda and goals. As this happens, the organization may experience radical changes in its core values. Because there is a strong possibility that the ranks of senior management will be growing, it is critical for the CEO to attain senior management agreement and buy-in to the mission, vision, and values statements. The CEO must continually "sell" the vision to the growing organization. Life is likely to be moving so fast that hiring the best is a concept that can get lost in the need to hire many people quickly or to maintain a focus on revenue-producing functions.

Therefore, early in the growth process, the organization needs to identify and empower the person who will head the recruiting effort. It may be the founder or an original partner or, if the growth is anticipated to be fast enough, a new hire who is a recruiting specialist. Whoever fills the role must be totally synchronized with the CEO's vision and style and understand the developing company's culture intimately. In this position, having ownership of the human capital will mean that the Head of Recruiting must build a set of policies and procedures that are appropriate for the company at that stage in its existence. It may, for example, mean that everyone in the company is on the recruiting team if there are five people; or the team may be a fraction of the company if there are 50.

As the composition of the recruiting team changes, it is the function of the Head of Recruiting to orient the team not to the current ideal profile, but to the profile of the individual who is needed to help the company achieve its objectives in the future. He or she must also review and change the recruiting model as needed and train the recruiting team in how it is to be implemented.

Whether a company is growing rapidly or slowly, issues will arise regarding the management and deployment of people. The Head of Recruiting, who is also a senior executive, will often be called on to resolve or mediate issues. Small companies face a huge range of potential issues. Our discussion is limited to two examples: one company facing rapid growth and one company facing slower growth.

Rapid-Growth Company

Once a position is authorized, it is easy to identify jurisdictional and territorial issues. Suppose, for example, an Internet company needed to hire software engineers to build a framework monitoring system, and both the technical operations staff and the systems integration staff saw the function as their responsibility. It may fall to the Head of Recruiting to resolve the ownership issue prior to attracting the ideal candidate. When the candidate is hired, he or she is assigned to one area or the other.

An issue facing rapidly growing small companies such as high-tech start-ups is the silo effect, the creation of a closed system in a functional area or a regional office, which can occur in a subtle and quick manner. The partner who heads the newly opened San Francisco office, for example, may feel that candidates for that office need a different set of professional and personal characteristics than are needed in the rest of the company. If this attitude is passed along, then the newly hired professional often feels a loyalty to the San Francisco office and not to the company. The same thing can happen within the marketing, research and development, and operations departments.

It is much easier for the senior executive to stop silo development early than to allow territories to be staked out and then try to change the practice. Certainly there will be some different needs in company offices and departments and they must be addressed. However, the need to achieve the goals of the organization in an efficient, fast, flexible manner has to be everyone's number one priority.

There are many initiatives that the head of recruiting can implement to alleviate the silo effect. Establishing a policy that candidates must meet senior management and representatives of different offices and different departments provides a broader perspective to the candidate and the potential for a better hire for the company. The Head of Recruiting helps the candidate understand the vision and values of the company prior to accepting a position. Once the candidate accepts, the Head of Recruiting is in a position to provide an orientation, preferably at corporate headquarters, that reinforces the culture and values of the larger organization.

Slower-Growth Company

An issue facing a slower-growth manufacturing company might be attracting a key senior executive to a remote location, where she would be expected to partner with the CEO in taking the business in a new direction and to a new level. Suppose the decision has been made that a COO is needed to help with this task. Clearly someone is needed who is a self-starter with a vision for the business and who is an implementer. If the CEO is a great salesman and Mr. Outside, then the partner he needs may be a Ms. Inside to handle the day-to-day operations of the company.

Complicating the picture, however, is the fact that the employees of the company have lived in the town and worked at the company for generations. The management style has always been team-oriented and caring. If an employee has a child with a personal problem, he or she is given time to take care of the problem. Senior management have served on boards of directors of local volunteer organizations and are very much a part of the community.

Consequently, the new COO needs to have vision and a proactive management style, yet be willing to partner with the employees even if it means that tasks will be accomplished a little slower than she would like. In other words, patience will need to be one of her personal characteristics.

In this case it is probable that the CEO is also the Head of Recruiting and will follow the screening procedures that were indicated earlier. Once he had identified two finalists, he would have them to the company on one or more occasions. If at that point one of the two candidates decided that she could not move her family to so remote a location, then the CEO would spend his time with the other candidate. He may have to think creatively and in a partnering manner in order to strike an agreement. The CEO might encourage her to bring her spouse and spend a weekend. He and his wife might take the candidate and her husband to dinner, entertain them, and have them meet some of the people from the company and town. Over the weekend, the CEO might have a real estate agent available to show them housing.

Suppose that after some thought, the candidate calls the CEO and says that she and her husband have loved everything about the community and the solid family values it affords them and because her husband has his own marketing design business it doesn't matter where they live. However, the more she has thought about the business the more concerned she has become about whether she would fit the culture of the company. The CEO might very well have to come back and after telling her that she is the perfect candidate, offer her an opportunity to try the position for three months on a no-fault basis. If she loves it, as he thinks she will, she can stay on and bring her family out sometime thereafter. If she doesn't enjoy the job, she can leave with no strings attached. This kind of flexibility helps the CEO fill a very difficult recruiting assignment.

Late Stage

As the company continues to grow, it is approaching the mid-size company and a new set of problems. Now the Head of Recruiting will have to prepare the organization to address those issues that we discussed earlier in the chapter for the mid-size and larger companies.

SUMMARY

Impact hiring will only take place if senior management creates the vision and the urgency to hire the impact player. The Head of Recruiting must be a highly regarded individual who has the strategic and tactical abilities to create and implement the hiring process as well as the skill to sell "A" players on joining the company. The recruiting model must be appropriate for the industry and for the size and culture of the company. Implementation of the program rests with a highly energized and motivated interview team.

STEP 2

Define the Ideal
Success Profile

Maria, the group president, sat in her office at the end of the day and reviewed the day's events. They centered around filling the position of publisher for one of her major magazines. She and her team had interviewed a number of people and rejected them for various reasons. This week they had been interviewing a new candidate, Stan, whose background seemed interesting. Maria had been out of town earlier in the week so she had her interviewing team start without her. By the time she returned there was a buzz of excitement in the office about Stan. Not only had everyone who had seen him liked him, but they felt he was extremely well-qualified to run the sales and business aspects of the magazine.

Human resources had Stan come back to meet Maria on Thursday, and she could understand why her team had enjoyed Stan so much. He was confident and outgoing without appearing arrogant, and he smiled and laughed easily. It was effortless to have a great conversation with him. Stan spoke with Maria about mutual friends in the industry and it was obvious he networked effectively. He was also clear about his willingness to make a career move, saying that his present company was great but that opportunities for advancement would be blocked by incumbents for some time.

When they transitioned to the business conversation, the discussion remained fluid and exciting. Although Stan's present position was publisher of a magazine, it was not as large and did not have as much responsibility as Maria's position. Still, Stan's job was close enough in size and scope that she felt he could be a viable candidate. They discussed personnel issues and he had dealt with a wide range of issues and problems. She felt it was a real plus that he had been promoted to publisher at such a young age.

Maria knew something about the climate and style of Stan's former and present companies. They were smaller and more entrepreneurial in nature and probably a little less political than her own. As a result, the measurement of one's productivity was important and Stan had proven that he knew the magazine business. What Maria had not realized was the degree of entrepreneurialism under which Stan was mentored. She was surprised, for example, that most of Stan's bonus was based on the profit from his personal objectives. This was different from her company where 40 percent of the bonus was based on individual objectives, 40 percent was dependent on the department reaching its goals, and 20 percent was dependent on the company reaching its goals.

As she recalled the interview, she understood why her people were so excited about Stan. Her emotional side felt the same way. As the group president, however, she had to listen to her logical side as well. That side suggested that she evaluate Stan against the ideal success profile that had been identified at the beginning of the search. The interview team was to identify someone who:

- Is extremely bright and combines mental flexibility, creativity, and good judgment.

- Sets and meets aggressive targets while working effectively in a partnership.

- Has polished interpersonal skills and the charisma to relate to a wide range of successful and accomplished people.

- Demonstrates a large view of life yet takes reasonable risks to attain his goals.

- Thrives in fast-paced environments where success depends on rapid-fire decision making on multiple issues while under stress.

- Has passion for excellence that is manifest in the formation of tightly knit partnerships with clients.

- Builds powerful global teams with sensitivity to diversity and cultural differences.

Maria read the list, but as a savvy, successful manager she also knew the reality. The ideal success profile for this position described an ideal candidate but it had to be understood within the context of the company culture. Her company had a reputation for being one of the best magazine companies. It had a long history of hiring bright, outstanding candidates from great schools and inviting them into the club. Once hired, progress required the ability to meet aggressive targets, but productivity wasn't the only measuring stick. Political integration was important; networking with the "right" people was an absolute must. Being regarded as anything other than a total team player was political suicide.

What also had to be factored in was Patrick, the new president, who had recently come on board with a mission to change the culture of the organization. He was well-regarded by some who were interested in a more entrepreneurial, less political environment. Patrick was clearly focused on bottom-line results more than political connections. Maria also knew that it was early in Patrick's tenure and that while some things would change quickly, the transition would take a number of years.

Maria was concerned that Stan's definition of entrepreneurial would be very different from the current vision in her company. Stan had grown up in companies with a "do it yourself and make it happen" culture. From their conversation, Maria knew that Stan was not accustomed to having strong corporate resources at his disposal. The human resources department was just one example. It would provide services and expect to be involved in decisions regarding people. Maria questioned how he would react to a broader involvement by this type of stakeholder.

As Maria looked at the list, her dilemma was obvious. Some of the key success characteristics were the reasons everyone thought Stan would be terrific. They were:

- Sets and meets aggressive targets.
- Demonstrates a large view of life yet takes reasonable risks to attain his goals.
- Thrives in fast paced environments where success depends on rapid-fire decision-making on multiple issues under stress.
- Has passion for excellence that is manifest in the formation of tightly knit partnerships with clients.

There was no doubt in her mind that Stan would be very successful in meeting objectives.

However, there were the other success characteristics. They were:

- Works effectively in a partnership.
- Has polished interpersonal skills and the charisma to relate to a wide range of successful and accomplished people.
- Builds powerful global teams with sensitivity to diversity and cultural differences.

These characteristics worried Maria. She was concerned that Stan would be able to deal with politics intellectually but in practice would prefer to drive the business forward. This could cause him to miss political signals and get himself into trouble on meaningless issues. If this happened, it would be a small leap for some people in the organization to believe that Stan was not a team player and was only in the job for himself. Maria knew how tough the culture could be when someone was isolated. It was usually a fairly short time before the individual left the firm.

Maria understood the risks, but decided that Stan's strengths were exactly what her organization needed. She allowed the interviewing process to continue until Stan had met the 10 to 12 people on the interviewing team. The consensus was that Stan was the person they had been seeking for some time. Meanwhile, Maria had gone to see Karen, her senior mentor, to review the events and to test her strategy for dealing with Stan. Karen suggested that Stan come back to meet with both of them to have a heart-to-heart talk about the key success characteristics within the culture of this organization. It would be a "buy" interview, with Karen giving Maria candid feedback as to whether she thought Stan understood the message and could succeed in the environment. Both Karen and Maria felt comfortable with the strategy.

The meeting with Stan was a straightforward, no-holds-barred talk about what they thought he could bring to the organization and where they had concerns about the fit issues. When dealing with the entrepreneurial, action-oriented, bottom-line issues, Stan responded quickly and confidently. As they discussed the culture and the necessity of working in concert with a number of people and groups, Stan became pensive. He thought about what he was going to say before responding and he did not immediately say that he would have no difficulties. Rather, he said that he might have some difficulties because in his present situation he had little direction, and help from other groups and political issues were minimal.

Karen told Stan that the organization had experience with terrific people who had risen through the sales ranks but had difficulty understanding that the other stakeholders in this culture were, in fact, internal clients requiring the same sales skills that were effective with external clients. She was blunt in saying that in those instances when people did not get the message, they did not last long. At the end of the discussion Karen asked Stan whether he thought he could make it in an environment where using the word "we" when talking about success was more important than using the word "I." Stan was honest; he said that he was not positive that he could and that he would need help, including some coaching and mentoring. He said that he was really excited about the opportunity and that he appreciated the honesty in dealing with him. He said that he would commit to them that, if they offered him the job, he would do everything in his power to work effectively within the environment.

Maria walked Stan to the elevator and then returned to Karen's office. Karen asked if Stan's behavior at this interview was consistent with what she had heard and seen of his other interviews. Maria said that it was very consistent and that she was anxious to hear Karen's thoughts. Karen did not have to think long. She said, "I think he is great. He is as personable as you said he would be and there is no question about his bottom-line orientation. I was impressed with the way he listened when the discussion turned to culture. He was thoughtful and did not attempt to come out with a quick, glib response. Rather, he asked questions and made comments and was thoughtful about his ability to be successful within the environment. You and I have been in this business a long time and no one can say with absolute certainty whether someone will be successful. In this case, however, Stan seems willing to make the commitment to success. My gut reaction is that he will be an excellent hire." Maria made the commitment to work with Stan personally to ensure his success. He was hired within a few days and on board within the month.

PREPARATION

Did Maria and Karen seem highly aware of what it would take to be successful in the culture of their company, and were they intent upon hiring someone who would be a good match? The answer is a resounding, "Yes." Many interviewers are not as clear about whom they are looking for as Maria and Karen were because they haven't spent the time honestly assessing their own culture and coming to terms with what it takes to be successful. In the absence of a clear profile, the interview process often slips into a concentration on intelligence, knowledge, and skills for new graduates and on whom you know for experienced hires.

Defining an ideal success profile takes more than a concentration on one competency. It needs to focus on the interaction of three core competencies:

- The candidate's intelligence, knowledge, skills, abilities, and necessary experience (professional characteristics) to do the work successfully;

- The interest, motivation, energy, and drive to do it; and

- The "fit" (personal characteristics) necessary to be successful within the culture of your company.

Throughout the book, we use the term *competencies* to relate to the broad abilities necessary to perform work, and *characteristics* as the specific abilities necessary to be successful in your company.

Defining an ideal success profile can seem like a daunting task if it is done alone. But it becomes an exciting learning experience if done with a group of people (usually your interview team). Three data points are useful in building the success profile if the job is essentially the same as a previous position. First is the combined experience of the members of the group. Second is the analysis of the professional and personal characteristics of current stars and rising stars in the position. Third, and equally important, is an analysis of the characteristics and behaviors of individuals who were hired with high expectations but who were not successful and left the company.

If a change in direction is being contemplated and the job will therefore be different than the previous one, then the team writing the ideal profile will face a different challenge. There will be no position history, so a greater effort will be needed to utilize the experience of those in the company. The team will need to focus on the necessary technical skills and abilities and on previous change efforts to understand the professional and personal characteristics necessary to bring about change successfully.

The most common form of profile to assist the interviewer is the job description, which in one form or another is used almost universally. It defines and describes the job. As part of developing the job description, the team defines the threshold characteristics for new graduates, which include the target colleges, major, grade point average, graduate work, and any specific skill training. Threshold characteristics for experienced hires depend upon the job requirements. Threshold characteristics are defined as the minimal set of academic training, skills, abilities, and experience to proceed further in the hiring process.

A second and more sophisticated profile is the job specification, which is composed of the job description plus an additional section. The additional section, entitled Performance Requirement Factors (or another name), identifies professional and personal characteristics deemed critical to success in the organization. These factors *focus on one of the three core competencies* we listed at the beginning of this section (ability to do the job; *OR* interest, motivation, energy; *OR* fit within the culture).

A third, and we feel the best format to use, is the ideal success profile, which is composed of the job description plus a different additional section from that found in the job specification. In this format, the additional section is entitled, Success Characteristics. They are the four to seven most important characteristics for job success, as defined by the interview team. These factors focus on the *interaction of the three core competencies* we addressed (ability to do the job; *AND* interest, motivation, energy; *AND* fit within the culture). Once the Success Characteristics are set, it is possible to identify Defining Questions for each characteristic, which provide additional information to help in the evaluation of the candidate. As you look at examples of each of the three formats in the pages ahead, remember that each format is designed to help interviewers select the best candidate for your company. The one that you choose will depend upon the degree of time and commitment your organization wants to make to the process.

The purpose of the ideal success profile is to assist you in gathering the best data to assess each candidate. The hiring process can be a very scattered process if poorly managed and conducted, or a highly focused process to identify the best if it is well-conceived and well-managed. The more clearly defined the ideal success profile before the process begins, the more consistency between interviewers' assessments and ratings. This means you will hire the best person while building consensus for both the candidate and the organizational goals. This consensus around the candidate dramatically improves the new hire's probability of being successful. Let's look at some examples, beginning with the job description, then the job specification, and finally, the ideal success profile.

The Job Description

The job description is exactly what the title suggests: a description of the job in terms of the duties that need to be performed. It typically deals with some or all of the following: the title of the position and to whom the job reports; a brief overview of the job; the job duties or responsibilities; the position requirements; and the salary and grade level. Let's examine a typical job description. Suppose the organization was looking for a Vice President and Chief Financial Officer for a $600 million division of a manufacturing company. In addition, the division is the company's largest and the successful candidate is expected to have an excellent chance to become the corporate CFO when that individual retires in two or three years.

Vice President and Chief Financial Officer

Reports to: Division President with dotted line to Corporate CFO
   Responsible for division's financial plans and policies, its accounting practices, and the conduct of its relationship with lending institutions and vendors. Directs financial evaluation and analysis, tax, audit, accounting, budgeting, and real estate activities for the division. Partner to the division president in all mergers, acquisitions, and financings of the division. Develops and coordinates necessary and appropriate accounting and statistical data for all departments.

Specific Responsibilities

- Sets overall financial plans, sets policy for the division, and reports division's financial results.

- Acts as controller by providing and directing procedures and systems necessary to maintain proper records and adequate accounting controls and routines.

- Serves as custodian of the cash, funds, securities, and assets of the company.

- Provides due diligence and analysis of potential acquisitions and divestitures.

- Directs, consolidates, and analyzes all cost accounting procedures and other statistical reports, including analysis of monthly departmental reports.

- Provides financial analyses and operating results (to the parent company).

- Appraises the division's financial position and issues periodic financial and operating reports.

- Directs the establishment of budget programs.

- Analyzes and reviews capital equipment requests.

- Works with the vice presidents to coordinate expenditure programs with forecasted cash flows.

- Maintains pricing models and coordinates product pricing with marketing to determine profitability.

Qualifications

- 10 to 15 years of experience in finance and accounting with premier manufacturing companies or divisions of $200 million + as CFO, controller, or senior director.

- Undergraduate degree with MBA or CPA a plus.

- Experience in independent operation with both strategic and operational background in planning, analysis, etc.

- Experience in a complex manufacturing environment, including supply chain management experience.

- Experience as management team member of a business unit.

Compensation

- A competitive salary plus bonus and comprehensive benefits package.

Job descriptions help interviewers and candidates to understand an overview and the specific duties of a job. They also identify the minimal qualifications (threshold competencies) that the
organization requires. As we discuss the Job Specification and
the Ideal Success Profile, remember that they are *in addition to*
the job description. The candidate must pass the threshold competency test in the screening interview to prove he or she has the
skills to perform, before the additional job specification or ideal
success profile become relevant.

The Job Specification (or Job Spec.)

It is a given that a candidate must have the intellect, skills, abilities, and experience to perform. Most people don't succeed,
however, merely because they have the necessary skills. They
thrive because they are excited about the work and they have
a set of professional and personal characteristics that are an excellent fit within the culture of the company. In other words,
they relate to the people in the company, the culture of the
company, and the management style and values that define
the way decisions are made and carried out. These characteristics are examined by getting into the "how and why" of a candidate's background, the way he or she thinks and how he or
she most enjoys accomplishing tasks.

The job specification includes the job description and one
additional section, called Performance Requirement Factors. That
section identifies and brings focus to the personal and professional characteristics that are critical to success in your company. This helps the interviewers create a clearer mental picture
of the ideal candidate than the job description alone provides.
The clearer that mental picture, the more consistency in interviewers' ratings of candidates.

Vice President and Chief Financial Officer

Note: This section is in addition to the job description.

Performance Requirement Factors

- Bright and able to assimilate ideas quickly.
- High-energy, action-oriented person.
- Excellent interpersonal skills.
- Leader in the financial area.
- Strong communication skills.
- Team player.
- Outstanding strategic and analytical skills.
- Well-organized, with strong prioritization ability.
- Able to challenge others with valid business concerns.

Helping the interview team to focus on the attributes that are critical to success in your company is a huge step in the right direction. The issue that the Performance Requirement Factors does not address, however, is the singular focus. Each factor only *focuses on one of the core competencies* (ability to do the job; *OR* interest, motivation, energy, and drive; *OR* fit within the culture). Let's take the first three factors as examples:

- Bright and able to assimilate ideas quickly (Focuses on the intelligence, knowledge, skills, abilities, and experience to do the work.)
- High-energy, action-oriented person (Focuses on the interest, motivation, energy, and drive to do the work.)
- Excellent interpersonal skills (Focuses on the fit necessary to be successful within the culture of the company.)

Just as a homing beacon's accuracy improves when there are multiple data points, the performance requirement factors will be stronger when there is interaction between two or three of the core competencies. What *bright, high-energy, action-oriented,* and *excellent interpersonal skills* mean to one person can be very different to another person. If the interviewers are given more data and the picture becomes clearer, it will be easier to compare candidates.

The Ideal Success Profile

Let's assume that the senior management team of your company is really serious about hiring the best and they are willing to put whatever resources it takes to accomplish the goal because they know that human capital is the company's most important asset. Let's also suppose that you are appointed to head the recruiting team for an important position in the organization.

First, you and your team will need a comprehensive understanding of the job that needs to be accomplished. This will be driven by the company's strategy and will give you clues as to the type of executive you will need. New business ventures, for example, will require different skills than if you are looking at a turnaround. To help you gather information it may be helpful to ask yourselves a set of questions:

- What is an overall statement of the job that needs to be accomplished?
- What are the specific duties that the job entails? (This will become the job description.)
- What specific skills, abilities, and/or experience are needed to accomplish the job effectively?
- What are the key objectives for the first 6 months, 12 months, and 18 months?
- What resources will be needed?
- What are the most successful ways to recruit, lead, motivate, and build a team in our environment?
- If the position requires a new direction, how is the new hire expected to balance the need to get the new system

or direction installed quickly and the need to train and motivate staff to move in the new direction?

- What are the specific criteria on which the executive will be evaluated at the end of the first year on the job?

Another means of gathering information is to think in terms of business situations that the executive will be likely to experience. If the position is similar to that held by previous executives, then they can help to give you examples of situations that may be faced. It may also be possible to interview executives in similar jobs in the company. If the position is a new direction for the organization, then it may be necessary for some of your executives to network with their friends in your industry or even a new industry to understand some key business examples. The importance of this exercise is obvious: developing a set of key competencies expected of the successful candidate. In a marketing position, for example, the major focus over the next two to four years could be:

- The vision to establish an international marketing agenda.

- A series of new product launches domestically.

- Resolving conflicts and building a sense of teamwork among marketing, research and development, and sales.

Once the overall objectives are defined and some business problems that may be faced are analyzed, it will be possible to develop the four to seven key success characteristics you are seeking in the ideal candidate. It is impossible to think about the final list of competencies, however, without analyzing the strengths and weaknesses of the members of your current management team. It is important to think in terms of:

- Superiors.
- Laterals (those at the same level).
- Subordinates.

This analysis of the strengths of current staff members helps you to determine the skills needed in the new executive.

There is one final step that must be agreed upon before compiling the final list of key success characteristics. That issue is consensus. There must be consensus among the members of the team that once the list is complete, everyone on the interview team will evaluate each candidate against those competencies defined by the team. The Ideal Success Profile and the Key Success Characteristics represent the product of your preparation and define the target.

The Ideal Success Profile is the job description plus one additional section called Success Characteristics. It focuses on the interaction between the three core competencies. Once again, they are:

- The knowledge, skills, abilities, and experience to do the work;
- The interest, motivation, energy, and drive to do it; and
- The fit necessary to be successful within the culture of the company.

Success characteristics are the interview team's definition of the four to seven critical characteristics that determine success within the culture of the organization. Each characteristic focuses on the *interaction of the three core competencies* addressed (ability to do the job; *AND* interest, motivation, energy, and drive; *AND* fit within the culture). Let's remain with our example of the divisional CFO and assume that the interview team has determined that there are four critical characteristics necessary for job success.

Vice President and Chief Financial Officer

Note: This section is in addition to the job description.

Success Characteristics

- Demonstrates the presence to command respect and confidence from the highest level of firm management through every level of the organization.

INTERVIEW TIP

SUCCESS CHARACTERISTICS

The interview team defines the four to seven critical characteristics that determine success within the culture of the organization.

- Sets and meets aggressive targets while building partnerships in fast-paced, multi-task environments.

- Solves complex problems through evaluation, analysis, creative solutions, and marshalling resources to implement the adopted plan.

- Builds powerful global teams with sensitivity to diversity and cultural differences.

The Success Characteristics give the interviewers the clearest picture of the ideal candidate, which becomes the standard for evaluating each of the outstanding candidates.

Defining Questions

We are often asked, "Is it possible to give the interview team even greater assistance in creating the picture of the ideal candidate?" Our response is, "Yes; it depends upon how deeply your organization wants assistance in identifying candidates who can have an impact on your business." An even more sophisticated level is to provide your interviewers with questions they can ask themselves about the candidate's abilities. This, in turn, will provide better information with which to evaluate the candidates and to make the best hiring decision. Let's take each of the example success characteristics and see how this process might be implemented.

VICE PRESIDENT, CHIEF FINANCIAL OFFICER

Success Characteristics with Defining Questions

- Demonstrates the presence to command respect and confidence from the highest level of firm management through every level of the organization.

- Is he highly intelligent, yet diplomatic?

- Does she have polished interpersonal skills and relate to a wide range of successful people?

- Does he build strong networks based on trust and confidence?

- Does she talk in terms of the team's success rather than her own?

- Sets and meets aggressive targets while building partnerships in fast-paced, multitask environments.

  - Does he set and meet aggressive targets, always with unyielding integrity?

  - Does she have passion for ownership, accountability, and commitment?

  - Does he have enormous energy and an "act now, can do" attitude?

  - Do customers verify that they remain loyal to her?

- Solves complex problems through evaluation, analysis, creative solutions, and marshalling resources to implement the adopted plan.

  - Does he have merger and acquisition and sophisticated financing skills?

  - Does she seek creative and imaginative solutions?

  - Is he acutely aware of the balance between profit and risk?

  - Does she seek win/win solutions?

- Builds powerful global teams with sensitivity to diversity and cultural differences.

  - Does he foster commitment, collaboration, and mutual trust among team members?

> **INTERVIEW TIP**
>
> **EVALUATION**
>
> To make the best hiring decision, rate each of the final candidates on every success characteristic.

- Does she recruit a diverse workforce and develop them through coaching and mentoring?

- Does he lead by example and have outstanding credibility?

- Do her people understand clearly the job to be done, the resources available, the degree of autonomy, and exactly how performance will be measured?

A Message to the Interview Team Leader

Defining the key success characteristics and then creating questions that probe for those characteristics aren't difficult tasks, but they take some time and dedication. Therefore, it is not a surprise that this type of planning is not always undertaken. It requires the leader's commitment to hire the best. Here are some points to keep in mind.

1. *Leadership and management:* The leader of the interview team must have a vision for the position the group is trying to fill. She must sell the importance of a great hire to the group, including how an outstanding hire will benefit them, which will justify the resources (time and effort) that it will take to complete the task. In addition, she must make it as easy as possible for members of the team to carry out their tasks efficiently.

2. *Honesty and objectivity:* The success characteristics are only as effective as they are honest. The key is to describe the ideal candidate for the culture of your organization. If you are in the process of changing the culture, then you must be realistic as to the timetable for the change and the possible interim steps that may be needed. Otherwise you will lose credibility with the hiring team and will risk hiring the wrong person.

3. *Team-orientation:* It is easier, faster, and more efficient to have one or two people define success characteristics and

to implement the interview process. However, that misses the great opportunity to demonstrate your commitment to hiring the best, to empower all the people on your team to have full involvement, and to build positive morale as you experience success.

SUMMARY

Time spent in preparing for interviewing will result in the reward of hiring the candidate who most closely fits your ideal success profile. The job description is universal. It provides an overview, the specific job duties, and the qualifications of the job. The interview team must go beyond the job description, however, to view the interaction of the following competencies:

- The intelligence, knowledge, skills, abilities, and necessary experience (professional characteristics) to do the work successfully;
- The interest, motivation, energy, and drive to do it; and
- The "fit" (personal characteristics) necessary to be successful within the culture of your company.

Success characteristics, or statements that describe the way that successful people act in your environment, help the interviewers develop a clear picture of the ideal success profile. Candidates can then be compared with the ideal. Defining questions help to further clarify the image and thereby reduce variance from interviewer to interviewer, encouraging consensus on the candidate who most closely fits the success profile. Achieving consensus on the candidate dramatically increases the probability that the individual will have a long and successful career at the company.

STEP

Develop the Competitive Edge

One of our all-time favorite interviewing stories is about a situation that occurred a few years ago when a friend of ours, a senior executive, was being recruited for positions at two well-respected companies. Ben had been through 10 interviews at one company and was clearly approaching the end of the interview process. He was then asked to meet a few of the key executives of the organization; these promised to be the "sell" interviews.

When Ben stopped in to see us a few days after the interviews, we could tell immediately that something was up. When we asked him how he did, he responded, "I don't think I did very well." The quizzical look on our faces prompted Ben to tell us the story.

Career Profile

The Dinosaur Sleeps

The second of Ben's three interviews was with Keith, a senior member of the company about whom Ben had heard mixed reviews. Earlier in his career Keith had been regarded as a productive member of the company. More recently, however, there were reports that time had passed him by and some unkind reports used the term dinosaur.

When Ben first met Keith he liked him, as he had been told that he would. Keith was a big man, outgoing and friendly, who communicated easily; Ben felt relaxed in no time. The rapport building was great as they found that they had a number of similar interests, and when the conversation turned to networking they found they had numerous friends in common. During that part of the conversation, Ben knew that he passed all of Keith's tests because he had successfully worked with people whom Keith respected.

When Keith closed the rapport building, his manner changed completely. From that point, Keith took over the conversation. Ben soon realized that Keith had been designated to take him through the history of the company and to sell him on working with the senior management team. Yet Keith began talking and did not involve Ben at all; it was 100 percent Keith. Actually, Keith didn't need anyone for this monologue. He was wound up and he was going to start at the beginning and take Ben through every step of the history. Ben wondered why Keith hadn't bothered to find out how much he already knew (70 to 80 percent), but he wasn't too concerned because he figured there was always more he could learn.

About 10 minutes into Keith's monologue, Ben noticed that Keith was beginning to slow down. Ben hadn't wanted to meet Keith in the middle of the afternoon when everyone's energy is at its lowest point, but it hadn't been his decision to make. A few minutes later, Keith was leaning on his elbow and a few minutes after that he was almost asleep, in the middle of his own monologue. Ben was dumbfounded. Should he try to inject life into the conversation or just wait it out? Ben was a veteran of the senior executive ranks, and he had often seen people lose energy, yet even he hadn't seen anything like this before. He decided to wait it out and see what happened. In a short time Keith snapped back to alertness and, without missing a beat, completed his remarks. He didn't ask if Ben had any questions and, by that time, Ben was very happy to be ushered to his next interview.

When we asked Ben why he felt that he had done poorly, he said, "Well, I almost put Keith to sleep, didn't I?" We each laughed, but it was a sad commentary on the situation. Ben didn't know whether Keith had a medical condition that caused him to be that drowsy or whether he was in poor enough shape or had had a drink at lunch to cause him to become tired. What Ben did know is that it put a damper on his evaluation of the company. Ben couldn't imagine how the head of the hiring team (whom Ben thought was a first-class individual) could ever have made the decision to allow Keith to remain on the team. Ultimately, Ben's decision was a very close call but he decided to select the second company that was recruiting him with equal fervor. Ben couldn't positively say that he selected the other company because of the incident with Keith, but it certainly was one of the contributing factors to his decision. Ben was a motivated and driven individual who worked hard to achieve his goals and he expected everyone else to do the same. He couldn't shake his experience with Keith. Ben did not feel that it was his place to tell the head of the interview team about his meeting with Keith when he was asked why he did not join the firm. He just let it pass and said something innocuous like, "I felt there was a closer match between my skills and the needs of the other company."

We're sure you're saying, "That's such an extreme example." You're right; however, interviewers who show a lack of energy, drive, and motivation are far too commonplace. They leave indelible impressions on candidates.

Candidates understand that it is critical to demonstrate motivation, energy, and drive in the job interview. But what about the interviewer? The first thing that the great candidate observes, before the interview gets under way, is presence. Presence includes warmth, confidence, fitness, grooming, and choice of dress in addition to enthusiasm, interest, energy, and mental alertness. The initial value judgment the candidate makes is whether the interviewer projects presence or does not. When candidates feel warmth and confidence from the interviewer, it helps them to adjust quickly and allows bonding to begin sooner.

Do these value judgments actually occur to candidates? Absolutely. Do they affect the decision-making process? Yes. Presence is part of an important first impression.

> **INTERVIEW TIP**
>
> **PRESENCE**
>
> Each person's presence is observed early in an interview. It includes warmth, confidence, fitness, grooming, and choice of dress in addition to enthusiasm, interest, energy, and mental alertness.

Career Profile _____

Appearance, Energy, and Fitness

Rick was athletic and fit and he knew that he was in excellent shape as he went for his interviews. He was surprised, however, that in each of his eight interviews he had been asked about his four years of college soccer and the fitness involved in the program. There was a lot of interest in the fact that he had been recruited as part of a group of six men whom the new coach hoped would turn the program around. The college had suffered through a number of years of losing seasons. Rick told the interviewers with some pride that the team was 8–8 the first two years, and then the program took off. They won the Ivy League championship and reached the quarterfinals of the NCAA Division I championships their junior and senior years.

When Rick met Ned again at the end of the second day of interviewing, Ned had a few more questions. Ned asked Rick to describe what an average day was like at school. Rick told Ned that he would be up before class to do his weight lifting then spend the day in class, followed by two hours at practice, dinner, and studying. Ned also asked about fitness in preparation for the following season. Rick responded, "Coach would establish for each player an individual plan that was expected to be accomplished over the summer. He would indicate the expected increase in each of the various exercises in weight training. In addition, we knew that we would have the Cooper Test on the first day back in the fall. That involved a two-mile run followed by a short rest and another mile that had to be accomplished in 17.5 minutes. In order to pass that test you had to run combinations of sprints, middle distances, and long distances every day in the summer. If you didn't pass the Cooper, you weren't on the team."

Ned thanked Rick for coming in and indicated they'd like him to come back for one more round of interviews the following day. Ned asked Rick if he could be there at eight in the morning. The next morning Ned started Rick on a series of six interviews plus a lunch with three associates. The day ended at 6:30 P.M. Throughout the interviews there were many more questions about Rick's fitness training and interests.

At the end of the day, Rick saw Ned again. This time he didn't hold back. Rick asked, "Ned, why has there been so much interest in my college soccer experience and fitness program?" Ned responded, "Rick, we know that you are smart enough to work with us. We have checked you out academically in every way possible. But you have no idea what it takes to be successful here. We have had many very smart people come here with great expectations and quit within six months to a year." "Why?" Rick asked. Ned went on, "Appearance is important in our business. Maybe it shouldn't be, but it is. You're fine on that count. The next thing we need is energy that is beyond belief. You can try to describe it to someone but even then it isn't real until you are in the job for a while. As you know, we work under great pressure. When we are interested in buying or selling one of the companies in our inventory, there is usually a very tight time frame. The deal will be done either quickly or not at all. Consequently, you'll be working seven days a week for extremely long days, often 18 hours at a clip. Sometimes you'll be working straight through the night. This rigorous pace could go on for a number of weeks. As you can imagine, it takes incredible energy to keep up that pace, much more than most people can, or would want to, commit."

Ned continued, "The reason we spent so much time on fitness is that it is an indication of your energy level to commit to something you believe in. Frankly, the regimen that you followed for four years of college soccer is way beyond what most people would be able or willing to do. We have found that success in college athletics has a high correlation with success at our company. Almost everyone here competed in college sports."

Ned went on, "One thing I forgot to mention. We will often fly home from halfway around the world on a Sunday and need to be back in the office on Monday. Each person has his or her own way of adjusting to jet lag, but a number of us have determined that the fastest way to shake the time adjustment is to take a 10- or 15-mile run. We often do it together."

Rick wasn't surprised when Ned continued his train of thought. Ned said, "There is another consideration that is incredibly important to us: teamwork. We are very apolitical in this company. We are focused on determining and reaching our goals and not on internal politics. We are also very thinly staffed. Consequently, having each person pull his or her own weight is critical. We are literally right next to one another in cramped quarters for hours at a time, and we require cooperation and good humor in working with one another. It is obvious that we need to love our work. Do you understand now why we have spent so much time on your soccer experience? Oh, one last thing. We are more interested in you because most of your time was spent as a halfback and marking back rather than as a striker. Team player, right?"

Rick was silent for what seemed like a long time. Then he responded, "I see what you mean. This is a huge commitment but I'm willing to make it. If I'm offered a position, I think I'll do a great job." Ned responded, "I think you will, too." Shortly thereafter Rick was offered a position and accepted it with full knowledge of the expectations and the rewards involved.

INTERVIEW TIP
ENERGY
An energetic and enthusiastic interviewer emits a positive, can-do attitude.

An aerobic conditioning program can help you to develop fitness, generate more energy, and project positively. Let's review what an aerobic exercise program might include.

Aerobic Exercise

To achieve fitness, the best systems are aerobic exercise programs and the best exercises are swimming, bicycling, walking, or jogging. This is not a haphazard, once-in-awhile program, but a systematic, three to six times a week regimen. As with any exercise plan, it is important to build up slowly until you reach full strength. Exercise more times per week rather than fewer. The schedule should start immediately and become a part of your weekly schedule. (*Note:* Any exercise program should be conducted under the direction of your doctor.)

Your routine helps you to be in outstanding physical shape for all your activities. It will also bring benefits on those long days of interviewing multiple candidates. Working out on the day of the interview can help you to relax and remain focused. How much should you exercise on that day? Certainly you should do no more than you have been doing in your regular program. You want to do enough to relax but not so much that you tire yourself. With the appropriate amount of exercise, your head is clearer and you keep the interviews in perspective. These are, after all, of critical importance to the new hires who want to work for you.

The notion of fitness as important to a career is not new. In acting, for example, it is commonplace. A new female lead had been hired for a highly successful Broadway play and it was her first night. She was so nervous that she was almost ill and she was afraid that she wouldn't be able to perform. Instinctively, she began to walk. She found herself in the deep shadows behind the stage. As her eyes adjusted to the dark she thought she saw a person in the corner. It was the star of the show; his legs were spread apart, hands pressed up against the wall, and he was doing exercises. He stopped when he saw her and, realizing how upset she was, he insisted that she join him. No one ever said "No" to this huge star, so she nervously began. Soon the physical exercises relaxed her to the point that she could do her normal breathing exercises. Her first performance was outstanding.

> **INTERVIEW TIP**
>
> **FITNESS**
>
> Exercising on the day of an interview enables you to relax and gives you a chance to focus. Exercise at a level of 75 to 100 percent of a normal workout.

Building in time to exercise on an interview day offers other potential benefits. The additional time it takes allows you to forget the pressures of your present job or activities and to focus on the candidates and the potential value they bring to your group and company. Taking this time often pays large dividends.

Mental Alertness

Along with fitness, mental alertness is another benefit of an exercise program. Fitness and mental alertness go hand in hand. You must be as physically prepared and as mentally alert at the end of your last interview (perhaps at five o'clock on a Friday afternoon) as you were at the beginning of your first interview. Mental alertness furnishes the energy and stamina required to remain positive and focused through one or more interviews.

A major component of mental alertness is the ability to listen. University studies show that most adults stay plugged in attentively to a conversation for less than a minute before their attention is diverted. Be honest. Don't you find that when a family member or friend starts to speak, you either tune in or tune out, depending on your interest in the subject? Remember being in a class at college and realizing that your mind was wandering? You had no idea what the professor had been lecturing about for several minutes (or even longer if the subject matter wasn't very high on your list of favorites).

In interviewing, you can't do that. Instead of listening selectively, you must remain focused as close to 100 percent of the time as possible. Active listening is required to determine whether candidates are truly motivated and interested in working in your firm and industry. There are times when the most compelling personality isn't the right person for your position, and you've got to sort through the issues.

Career Profile _____

The Budding Politician

John, the wily veteran of his Washington, D.C.–based law firm, was the next interviewer to see Tim. John had heard great things about Tim from the dozen interviewers who had seen him previously. Tim had great credentials. He had graduated from UCLA and had a law degree from the University of Virginia. He was extremely personable, made a great appearance, and dressed well. In addition, his personality was charismatic and he loved interacting with people.

As was his style, John spent a great deal of time on the "What do you like to do outside of work?" question. Tim indicated a passionate interest in politics; he had worked on political campaigns since he was in his teens in his native California and had loved being close to the political networks when he held several summer government intern jobs in Washington. Tim also expressed interest in outdoor activities such as white water rafting with friends.

The interviewer focused first on the white water rafting, asking Tim to describe a typical trip that might interest him. Once Tim told him the basics of the trip, John had a series of questions. His questions focused primarily on the relationships Tim developed on the trip. Questions included, "What were the dynamics of the group at the beginning and the end?"; "Did you deepen any friendships?"; "Did you lose any friends?" John spent significant time following up each question with additional probing questions and listening carefully to Tim's responses.

When they had exhausted that topic, John moved on to Tim's political and government interests. He asked specific questions, such as "Why did you first become interested in politics?" and then followed up with additional questions that sprung from the conversation. John was particularly interested in what drew Tim back to campaign after campaign. The move to Washington, D.C. seemed to make a lot of sense given Tim's interest in politics. John learned that every summer since coming to Washington Tim had worked either on a campaign or for a government agency. This, as Tim and John agreed, was great preparation for a career in law.

Tim recalled being amazed at John's ability to listen for detail, recall those details later, and then bring them back into the conversation in the form of a question that was penetrating and made a lot of sense. John spent some more time on the motivators that drove and excited Tim, and then they concluded the interview.

The next day a group of senior people in John's firm got together to discuss their reactions to the candidates they had seen. When it came to Tim, the reactions were positive around the room. John waited to speak and listened carefully to the comments. When he did speak he surprised his colleagues by saying, "I really liked Tim a lot. He has a great academic background and he is a very personable young man. He just doesn't want to be a lawyer; he wants to be a politician and that is fine. When each of you has discussed his strengths, you mentioned them in connection with his political or government activities, and you were right. He continually selected those activities out of the choices that were available to him because that is where his interests lie. Did you notice how his eyes lit up when he discussed the theater atmosphere of a political campaign, the rush that it causes, and the second-by-second decisions that have to be made? Do you think that this young man is going to be happy working on analysis gathering for a corporate litigation case? How long do you think he would remain with us if we hire him? I think the answer is, until the next political campaign calls him. I don't think hiring Tim is a wise investment of time or resources when we know it takes five to seven years to produce an outstanding attorney."

There was silence in the room until one of John's senior colleagues looked up, smiled, and said, "You know, John, that is what makes you so outstanding. We go through this process every year and each year we believe that we will get a higher percentage of right calls than we did the year before. And every year we make the same percentage of mistakes or more than the year before. The reason we make the mistakes is that we don't listen to what the candidates have to say about what drives and motivates them. I was sold on Tim because he has a great personality, but when you ask me what excites him, you're right, it is politics. Maybe we won't make a wrong choice on this call." Tim went on to have a great career in politics.

SUMMARY

The interviewer's presence is observed early in an interview by an outstanding candidate. It includes warmth, confidence, fitness, grooming, and choice of dress in addition to enthusiasm, interest, energy, and mental alertness. An important component of presence is fitness. One of the best ways to enhance fitness is through an aerobic exercise program (walking, swimming, bicycling, or jogging). A program should be undertaken as soon as possible (under the direction of your doctor) and should include exercising three to six times per week. The benefits include:

- Excellent fitness to withstand the rigors of interviewing;
- Increases in energy and stamina; and
- Added ability to focus and listen.

INTERVIEW TIP

LISTENING ABILITY

The ability to listen carefully is critical for evaluating the candidate and learning what it will take to land him or her.

3

BUILDING A PARTNERSHIP

In Part 3 we analyze the content portion of the interview from the interviewer's and the candidate's perspective. Building a Partnership is the process of conducting the interview. It involves personal bonding followed by a stimulating, interactive business conversation focused on the business goals. Interview strategy and tactics are based on the interviewer's need to gather clues about the candidate's passion and motivation for the work and his or her ability to fit within the culture of the company.

STEP

Understand the Interviewer's Agenda

In this chapter we examine the content portion of the interview from the interviewer's perspective. Step 5 examines content from the candidate's perspective. The goal is to understand what the interviewer and the candidate need to do in order to walk away from the meeting feeling that they have achieved their objectives. We discuss the interview process in Step 6.

Although there are some obvious differences in emphasis for screening and hiring interviewers, we ignore them at this time. The reason is that screening interviewers emphasize professional skills (intellect, skills, and abilities) a little more and hiring interviewers emphasize personal skills (ability to interact, motivation, and overall fit) a little more; but each interview focuses on both. We have chosen to deal with personal characteristics first because building rapport, hence personal characteristics, is normally the first thing that happens in an interview. (Note: We will come back to a detailed discussion of the screening and hiring interview in Step 7.)

As part of rapport building, the interviewer conducts an informal evaluation called the "normalcy" test to determine whether actual behavior matches expected behavior. We start here and

Adapted from *Killer Interviews* by Frederick W. Ball and Barbara B. Ball (McGraw-Hill, 1988). Reproduced with permission of The McGraw-Hill Companies.

then go on to deal with the personal and professional skills of importance to the interviewer.

THE "NORMALCY" TEST

Interviewers play Solomon. On the one hand, they want to give candidates an opportunity to sell themselves; on the other hand, they need to fill a position with the best person they can identify within the time constraints. To accomplish the task quickly and efficiently, balancing tests and scoring systems are devised.

Interviewers engage in their own personal "normalcy" test. We say their own test because there is no one style or format. In most cases the test begins at the start of the interview, is informal and conversational in tone, and is broad and general rather than specific. The test is part of, and impossible to distinguish from, the rapport building that people conduct at the beginning of an interview.

In the nonverbal portion the interviewer observes the candidate. The interviewer seeks data concerning overall personality, dress, fitness, demeanor, and mannerisms. A series of mental questions helps the interviewer keep track of the data required.

- Does the candidate make a good appearance?
- Is his dress appropriate?
- Does she appear confident and friendly?
- Does he smile?
- Does she have any unusual mannerisms?

Interviewers are looking for deviations from their concept of ideal behavior for someone at the level of the open position. Glenn, who has just graduated from college, would not be expected to have the same quality of dress as Susan, a proven senior executive. However, Glenn would be expected to wear a conservative, dark suit and tie if that's the company culture.

The verbal portion of the "normalcy" test begins during the "get to know you" or rapport building mode. The key question is the same as in the nonverbal check: Does the interviewer find differences between actual and expected behavior? Rapport building is a critical time for both the interviewer and the candidate. The introductory period lasts as long as the interviewer feels it is productive or time constraints allow. Most theory indicates that an interviewer discovers a lot about a job seeker, including attitudes, values, behavior, and management style, by helping the individual to relax and become comfortable.

Most interviewers spend time focusing on the candidate's personal interests or mutual interests. This time normally gives the candidate a chance to relax and become comfortable in the new surroundings.

Suppose, for example, the interviewer and Kristina were having a conversation about skiing.

INTERVIEWER: Kristina, I see that you have an interest in skiing.

KRISTINA: Yes. I really enjoy it.

INTERVIEWER: Have you been interested in skiing for long?

KRISTINA: All my life. My father was on the United States downhill ski team and he started my brother and me on skis at the age of three.

INTERVIEWER: Have you skied competitively?

KRISTINA: Yes, I have won numerous championships; but unfortunately there isn't enough money in the sport to make it a full-time occupation.

INTERVIEWER: You seem a little sad about that.

KRISTINA: Well, I guess I am. It has been a big part of my life.

INTERVIEWER: Are you able to keep up with your skiing now that you've graduated and have been working full-time?

KRISTINA: Absolutely. I go to Vermont every weekend from October to March or April.

Those are simple enough statements: "Unfortunately there isn't enough money . . . to make it a full-time occupation" and "I go to Vermont every weekend from October to March or April." They seem to be speaking, however, about considerable time commitments. Kristina didn't say "a few weekends" or "a number of weekends" or even "most weekends." She made it clear that she skis "every weekend." Now the issue to be addressed on the interviewer's normalcy balancing scale is, Has the interest gone past "normal" or "reasonable" and into a red-flag zone?

On one hand, Kristina has every right to her personal life, interests, and passions. Passions may even indicate energy, excitement, and zest for life. Indeed, many employers look for employees who have participated in competitive sports because those employees know about dedication, commitment, and how to win.

On the other hand, what about the company and its needs? If hired, will Kristina come to work on Mondays and Fridays with enthusiasm for her job? Or will those days be mental extensions of her weekend? What happens when there is an emergency project that requires evening or weekend work? How about the two corporate planning weekends that take place each year in October and April?

How the interviewer weighs that short dialogue may well be the critical determinant in whether Kristina's candidacy continues or ends. The normalcy test continues just as it did in our example throughout the interview, with the interviewer making value judgments that reject or propel a candidacy.

At the conclusion of the initial "get to know you" time, the interviewer normally throws a signal to indicate that it is time to move on. It can be framed in many different ways. For example:

- Would you tell me about your career path?
- I've enjoyed getting to know you and now I'd like to ask you some questions.
- I'd like to spend some time talking about your business career (or plans).

Every good interviewer knows that, while the emphasis may have shifted to business, rapport building and the "normalcy" test will be important throughout the interview. Think of the number of times that you ask a question and the answer that comes back indicates an interest, person, or outside activity that is important to the candidate.

As the conversation shifts, the interviewer should use finesse in asking questions about personal background, level of education, and career history, including specific case studies, strengths and weaknesses, and outside interests, to gather the data needed. The information generally fits into two categories: personal or professional characteristics. Personal characteristics are addressed first because the "normalcy" test is the first aspect of an interview.

> **INTERVIEW TIP**
>
> **THE "NORMALCY" TEST**
>
> This test determines whether there are differences between a candidate's actual and expected behavior that go past "normal" or "reasonable" and into a red-flag zone.

PERSONAL CHARACTERISTICS

Personal characteristics provide evidence that the candidate's interpersonal skills, management style, attitudes, and values are consistent with those of others in the organization. The areas of concern to the interviewer are:

- Interpersonal skills,
- Style,
- Attitudes and values,
- Motivation, and
- Outside interests.

Interpersonal Skills

While the interviewer could attempt to observe many individual skills, she normally limits herself to the interaction of a few critical ones:

1. She wants to get a feel for the candidate's general understanding of human behavior, of what makes other people tick.

2. Next, she wants to discover the candidate's understanding of tact and diplomacy or politics, as well as his ability to read between the lines and understand hidden agendas.

3. Finally, she'll evaluate the candidate's empathy level, or the ability and willingness to take the time to understand and deal with the underlying motivations of others.

The interaction of these three skill clusters is of real interest to the interviewer. What may be good in one situation may be less appropriate or even bad in another. Someone who is strong in all three areas may be an excellent candidate to work in a highly political organization where politics is as important to getting ahead as productivity. Other individuals who have a strong task orientation may score high on general understanding of human behavior, but low on tact and diplomacy or empathy. This does not mean that they don't care about other people or their problems, but their desire to complete the task successfully is so overriding that they don't take the time and effort that tact and empathy require.

The interviewer usually presents different scenarios of possible interactions at the appropriate level for the candidate and then determines whether you have to think very hard about your response. She evaluates the strength of your answer. The interviewer's evaluation goes beyond a generic rating to a function-specific examination. In this regard, individuals who are in sales almost always must be viewed as having high levels of empathy to function effectively.

For the executive, on the other hand, high levels of empathy may not always be viewed as positive. While there needs to be a balance in terms of empathetic response to others, too low a score indicates a task motivation or task orientation that could interfere with effective management techniques. Too high a score can indicate that the individual may be too concerned with or sensitive to the underlying motivations of others and therefore will not be as effective in getting the job done. In fact, when compared with successful executives, high-empathy people are likely to be described as too soft or too concerned about other people's feelings to get the task accomplished.

Style

Style is the combination of temperament, interpersonal skills, and understanding as well as intellect and problem-solving approaches. The issue for the interviewer is to determine how these skills will come together in a working or management style. On the personal side, for example, the interviewer needs to know if the candidate is aggressive or laid back, outgoing or introverted, flexible or rigid, direct or circuitous, and scheduled or spontaneous. On the professional side, the issues might be whether the candidate prefers autocratic or participative decision making, a team-oriented or individualistic work atmosphere, an intuitive or logical approach to problem solving, and a strong concern for the logic of a decision or a focus on the impact of that decision on people.

The best way to obtain data regarding style is by firsthand observation. This method is often impossible, but the interviewer may be able to talk to former superiors or subordinates in addition to the candidate. The interviewer typically discusses actual case studies with the candidate to gather information. A wise interviewer discusses how and why the candidate made decisions and how he interacts with superiors, peers, and subordinates, because it is common for individuals to exhibit different styles when working with different levels within the organization.

Another variable in style is stress. People behave differently under varying degrees of stress. A few interviewers still like to conduct stress interviews, which are designed to put a person under considerable tension and push them to behave in ways that would only occur in high-pressure situations. This is not a well-regarded hiring technique today, but it has been used in the past. All people going through a selection interview are likely to experience some levels of stress (usually self-generated).

Perhaps the most important consideration relating to style is not what the candidate does, but rather what the company itself

does. The organization needs to be sure that the screening interviewers are in sync with the success characteristics that are developed. You would be surprised how many times the full
interviewing team either is not in agreement or has an incorrect
perception of successful style in their own organization.

Another variable is management edict. A senior executive can
say, "We need a hardnosed, no-nonsense, take-charge kind of individual. I'm sick and tired of not getting results and having no
one accept responsibility for the failure." What typically happens
is that the interview team finds that type of person whose style is
tough, autocratic, and individualistic. What the senior executive,
in a moment of frustration, fails to realize is that the organization
is built on teamwork and participative management. This is obviously not fair to the executive or to the organization.

Attitudes and Values

Many interviewers feel that attitudes and values are the most important areas aside from skills. These are an individual's beliefs
about other people, about the world, about the business; they
are the values that individuals bring to a job on both a personal
and interpersonal level. They dictate how people are likely to interact with others and their effectiveness in present or potential
management roles. If the candidate's attitudes and values match
the organization's, then there is likely to be a good fit.

The interviewer's goal is to go beyond the basics to understand what attitudes and values drive the candidate. How strongly,
for example, does the candidate value family and time with the
family? Are activities that support the family unit important, such
as coach, church volunteer or scout leader? Issues such as valuing
relationships with people must be explored. Is the candidate, for
example, used to spending time with people at work and socializing with people from the organization on the weekends? What is
the candidate's attitude toward quality work? The range extends
from "Get the product out the door, even if there are returns," to
"Meet the deadline," to "The product will leave only when it is

perfect, regardless of time constraints." Where does the candidate stand on the issue of personal achievement versus organizational achievement? A candidate with a strong personal achievement orientation typically has a very difficult time in a company that values organizational achievement above personal achievement.

These are a few of the many issues that are important to the interviewer. The list depends on the environment of the organization. Other possibilities include:

- What is the candidate's attitude toward the relationship between management and labor?
- Does the candidate like to be managed? How is it best to do that?
- What recognition and approach does the candidate have toward internal politics?

There are times when savvy interviewers can save a candidate from a situation that is not in his or her best interest. David helped Kevin think through his attitudes and values and saved him from making a wrong career move.

Career Profile _____

Family Values

Kevin had been a contributing member of his very aggressive organization for about ten years. He had worked hard, had been successful from both an interpersonal and a productivity point of view, and had been promoted in accord with his productivity. His fine reputation had spread to other divisions of the company.

Kevin was also known in the company as being a strong family man and a pillar of his community. He had a wife and two children and he served on a number of community boards that supported activities of interest to members of his family.

One day he received a call from a close friend in another division of the company, telling him of an opening in his department and asking Kevin if he was interested. It represented a very large promotion.

Kevin was stunned, but he indicated a definite interest. His friend, David, indicated that Kevin was not the only candidate and that he would have to interview for the position. That did not bother Kevin, and he accepted. Kevin knew that David was aware of his strengths; he was sure he would be a good candidate.

The interview went smoothly, in a conversational style. There was no need for David to probe too deeply because he knew Kevin so well. The crux of the conversation came down to the following dialogue:

DAVID: Kevin, there is only one concern I have about your candidacy: your ability to balance work and the aspects of your personal life.

KEVIN: Why is that a concern, David? You know that I work hard and am always willing to do extra for the organization.

DAVID: What about weekend work?

KEVIN: I don't have a problem with coming in once in a while on the weekend.

DAVID: How old are your children now?

KEVIN: Thirteen and nine.

DAVID: Those are very impressionable ages.

KEVIN: I agree; what is your point?

DAVID: In your present responsibility, don't you normally leave about 5:30 P.M. to go home?

KEVIN: Yes, but as I indicated, I am willing to stay late when work calls.

DAVID: Listen to me. You are a great candidate for this job and, if you want it, I will hire you. But you need to recognize and focus on the fact that your family life is going to change radically if you take this job. You will not leave at 5:30 P.M.; it will more likely be 8:30 P.M. or later, all the time. And you will work on the weekend on a much more regular basis; not every weekend, but two or three per month. Have you discussed this with your wife and family?

KEVIN: No, I haven't. You're right, David. I need to think about that issue. Thanks.

Ultimately, Kevin did not take the job. After discussions with his wife and family, he called David and declined. His attitudes and values placed a higher worth on time with his family than on a large promotion including a great deal more money. David was an interviewer who knew and understood the job needs and the culture of his organization better than most, and was kind enough to help Kevin focus on the key issue.

Motivation

Motivation can be somewhat difficult to identify in the selection process. The interviewer has to dig into the candidate's past history and get examples of actions taken, successes, failures, and what was important about a given situation that led to success or failure. The interviewer knows that more proof is needed than candidates' stating they are highly motivated. The interviewer is trying to determine whether money, success, achievement, or the opportunity to work in a creative mode, for example, is the candidate's principal motivation.

It is also important for the interviewer to determine how motivated candidates are by one of the many social reinforcers. If, for example, an individual is strongly motivated by positive regard, recognition, and pats on the back, then money alone may not be a sufficient reward to keep motivational levels high. In this situation a team-oriented environment is an important ingredient in the success quotient. If, on the other hand, the components that are most important in the motivational picture are an opportunity to work in a creative mode or personal achievement, then these need to be taken into consideration in assessing a person's suitability for a particular position.

Many successful salespeople, for example, are not highly motivated by the interpersonal interaction side of the equation. Rather, they have very short reinforcement links. In other words, they need immediate reinforcement for their actions and frequently the best measure of success is the number of dollars that they can accrue over a short period of time. For this individual, motivation needs to be focused around how he or she can, in fact, generate more dollars in a short amount of time rather than "how great it's going to be to interact with these people."

One piece of the motivation picture is energy. The knowledgeable interviewer seeks evidence of energy (or lack thereof) throughout the interview, and not just in portions of the meeting that are specifically designed to seek evidence about energy. Energy, as every interviewer knows, is an attitudinal variable and is not age-related.

Career Profile

Fire in the Belly

Amelia had been on a search for the head of her firm's legal department for some time. Unfortunately, she had a string of bad luck. When she had found a candidate she was excited about, the person was unable or unwilling to continue in the interviewing process. Then she uncovered Jim, who had been the head of the legal department in his $4 billion firm. Jim was soon to be out of work because his firm had been sold. She felt that she was extremely lucky that both firms were in the same Midwestern city; if there was a match, she would not have to face relocation costs.

Amelia's major concern was that Jim was in his mid-50s and she wasn't sure that he would display the energy and drive that would be required to be successful in her environment. When they first met, Amelia liked Jim. He answered all her initial questions regarding education and work history with enthusiasm and poise. He was extremely positive when talking about building and managing the legal department from its inception, through its growth, and to its current size. He seemed to enjoy the challenge of a complex problem, such as the process he followed in recruiting an attorney who functioned in a highly specialized discipline. He told Amelia the number of hours per week he averaged at work and demonstrated a knowledge of selecting creative solutions to difficult problems. Overall, his demeanor was very confident and upbeat and, together with his answers, was viewed positively by Amelia. All indications were that Jim was a candidate with high motivation and energy levels.

Amelia left her focus on motivation, interest, and energy. She had learned, after years of interviewing, that she would learn more about Jim when she discussed his interests outside of work. About 20 minutes later she addressed the subject. She asked, "What civic or volunteer activities do you most enjoy?" Jim removed any of Amelia's concerns about his energy with his response. He said, "Amelia, my interests have been aligned with the needs of my children. I was a leader in the Indian Guides, then in Boy Scouts, while simultaneously being a soccer, basketball and baseball coach. When the children graduated from high school and went on to college, my wife and I served on the parents' advisory council at the college. Now that they are young adults, we are able to pursue our own interests, which include a state advisory committee." That was all Amelia needed to hear. Jim was recommended to the selection interviewing team and was soon offered (and accepted) a position as the head of the legal team.

Screening interviewers are particularly concerned with energy as a key factor for entry-level candidates. These candidates do not have loads of experience; so they must sell enthusiasm, motivation, and energy. Many firms look at the candidate's ability to balance a number of activities as evidence of their energy and enthusiasm. From the interviewer's point of view, if entry-level candidates with little or no experience don't bring energy, enthusiasm, and motivation to the organization, then they might not be good hires.

Outside Interests

Outside interests are of concern to the interviewer because they provide information about style, values, and motivation as well as showing breadth of interest. They also give the interviewer an idea of how candidates are likely to use their time and whether or not they are going to be well-balanced with respect to work versus play. One of the most important activities that bridges work and outside interests is involvement in professional associations. Not only does this activity have the

> **INTERVIEW TIP**
>
> **INTEREST**
>
> The candidate must have the interest, motivation, energy, and drive to join the team.

potential to increase your professional skill set, but the networking can be valuable.

Certainly there is a need to find someone who will work hard, but there is also the desire for a colleague who is interesting and fun to be around, someone with whom folks would like to spend time outside of work, someone with a sense of humor. In addition, there is mounting evidence that working extremely long hours, day after day, leads to a loss of efficiency in the workplace. So balance matters a great deal to the interviewer. Once again, it varies a great deal, depending upon the culture of the organization.

Many organizations want leaders and potential leaders who are involved in the community. First, volunteerism reflects well on the company whose people are giving something back to the community. Second, it may teach new and important skills to executives, rising stars, and future leaders. The need for cultural diversity is a reality and will continue to be important in the 21st century. Community service is a laboratory for a candidate to learn the skills of managing individuals who come from diverse backgrounds. Add to this the issue of motivating volunteers, whose agendas sometimes differ from the stated goals of the organization. Many people believe that volunteer positions are among the most difficult of management assignments and, consequently, teach many valuable skills.

Career Profile

Volunteer Work

Community service can sometimes be turned into a significant advantage in the workplace. Susan had been a captain in her local United Way chapter for a number of years. Her volunteer work gave her a great sense of pride and satisfaction. When it came time for her to look for a new job, she was asked if she had supervisory experience. She responded, "Yes, I have been a captain in the United Way for the last eight years." Not only did that experience put her in a different category from the other candidates, but her potential boss was also a United Way volunteer. Susan won the job.

PROFESSIONAL CHARACTERISTICS

Professional characteristics give evidence of the candidate's educational background, professional credentials, and business experience that provides the background for successful performance. Communication, leadership and management abilities offer information concerning the candidate's ability to fit comfortably within the organizational setting and to produce. The areas of concern to the interviewer are:

- Intelligence and technical skills,
- Experience,
- Communication,
- Leadership and management abilities, and
- Organizational fit.

Intelligence and Technical Skills

Intelligence is one measure of potential job success. Because intelligence can be defined in many ways depending on the point of view, interviewers look for as many objective hooks as possible to defend their evaluation. High school grades, SAT scores, college attended, college grades, graduate school attended, and graduate school grades are all data that give evidence of intelligence.

The college and course of study are most important to the interviewer when this is the candidate's first job. The stronger the college program is, the more it can be used as evidence of intelligence and the fewer questions the interviewer needs to ask. Interviewers also know, however, that students choose colleges for a variety of reasons, many of which are beyond their control. Examples are cost, proximity to home, or restrictions imposed by parents. The interviewer should probe these issues to understand high school interests, the college selection process, why the major was selected, the degree of enjoyment and satisfaction with the major, and grades in and out of the major, for each college attended.

The interviewer also likes to be able to quantify the candidate's technical skills via a professional degree or license from a highly accredited school. An engineering degree from Purdue University with a 3.5 grade point average is a strong indicator that the candidate has the necessary technical skills to perform. Interviewers may also want to delve into the specifics of the program. Many highly recognized schools throughout the country confer MBAs. Some are general in nature, some specialize in marketing or finance and some are heavily quantitative. The job specification may call for an emphasis in one area or another.

Career Profile

Following Interests

Another means for the interviewer to gain evidence of intelligence and technical skills is to follow interests to see where they lead. Richard didn't want to attend college after graduating from high school. He got a job as an automobile mechanic working on sophisticated foreign sports cars and quickly received a number of promotions, becoming the service manager of the dealership at the age of 20. He was probably the youngest service manager in the country. His interests also turned to servicing airplane engines, and he earned a pilot's license. Then, at the age of 22, he decided to go to college. He earned an engineering degree and now develops sophisticated financial products on Wall Street.

The savvy interviewer will understand what it takes to be successful in the industry, company, and job function. It isn't always possible to quantify intelligence and technical skills because everyone doesn't need credentials such as an MBA, Ph.D., M.D., or D.D.S. Consequently, the interviewer may need to follow the candidate's progress, as was done with Richard's, to tell whether there are strong sales skills, merchandising skills, finance skills, or whatever additional skill base is required.

Experience

Job experience and career direction are of great interest to the interviewer. The reasons a candidate selected a career path can give many signals about interests and aptitude. With a recent graduate, career direction has to be the interviewer's focus. With an experienced candidate, the interviewer wants to understand the motivation for taking and leaving each job and carefully evaluate whether the career is progressing in a steadily upward direction. Given recent trends to remove layers of middle management, there are more lateral moves than in the past. The interviewer must understand the challenges in each job; otherwise, a lateral move could be perceived as a negative.

As the interviewer tries to understand the career overview, those candidates who have more predictable career paths (such as assistant product manager to product manager to group product manager) are easier to understand. If the candidate has had a successful stint with a well-established, blue chip firm such as Procter & Gamble, that gives the interviewer greater confidence in the candidate's abilities. The interviewer can then focus on variables like the actual time to promotion versus the expected time to promotion.

When the candidate is from the same industry, the interviewer can compare accomplishments directly. Suppose, however, an organization wants someone from another industry, but needs someone who has experience making rapid-fire, clear decisions. As an example, a candidate who has successfully managed an airport should have an easy time convincing an interviewer in this regard.

The more diversified the experience, the more the interviewer may have to test to be sure the skills and abilities are appropriate to the job. For example, when interviewing the candidate for a talk show host position, the interviewer would have to be sold on the candidate's persuasive skills, which were developed while previously employed as a TV evangelist, consumer products salesperson, or school board member. A recent graduate or career changer is judged on potential. Lifetime skills and accomplishments become important in these situations because of their general nature.

With the overview clearly in mind, the interviewer usually starts with the "what," "when," and "where" questions. Although the questions may be asked in interesting or creative ways, the underlying intent is to get at:

- "What did you do?"
- "When did you do it?"
- "Where did you do it?"

Depending on the direction set by the interviewer, a greater or lesser degree of detail is requested for each job. As the interviewer senses an important point in the candidate's career or one that is important to the new position, the questioning usually becomes more complex and includes the "how" and "why" questions. These questions are designed to examine interpersonal skills, attitudes and values, and management style. They give the interviewer clues regarding organizational fit. To kick off the questioning, the interviewer might ask:

- "Why did you decide to reorganize your department?"
- "How did you implement the decision?"
- "What was the impact on the professional staff?"
- "How did the decision impact net profits?"

This might lead to a full discussion of a job assignment, project, or problem that needed to be solved, with an entire series of how and why questions. The interviewer typically spends

INTERVIEW TIP

INTELLIGENCE, SKILLS AND ABILITIES, AND EXPERIENCE

The candidate must have the intellectual background, skills and abilities, and experience necessary to perform successfully.

a good deal of the interview time talking about the candidate's experiences and asking how various situations were handled. The interviewer is able to gather a great deal of information about all the professional characteristics from the candidate's answers to the questions.

Communication

Communication skills are in evidence during the interview for the interviewer to observe firsthand. Because each person in an organization must be a salesperson for ideas, products, or services, communication skills are vital. It is surprising how many times the interviewer only has to observe the candidate's behavior, and the candidate torpedoes an opportunity through poor communication.

Career Profile

Unprofessional Behavior

The interview should have been merely a formality. Mike, a bright young administrator, was one of two finalists for a promotion in a large suburban hospital with a national reputation for excellence. He was the candidate from inside the organization, and his track record had been impressive during the four years he'd been employed there. He was respected and popular, known both for his ability to get the job done and for his warm, easy manner. Ted, the hospital administrator, liked him very much; in fact, he had hired Mike originally and continued to be impressed by him.

Mike knew that a group of his colleagues would be among the interviewers, and he more or less knew the questions. He was even familiar with the board conference room where the interviewing would take place. Nothing should go wrong. But his interview blew him out of the water and out of contention for the promotion. He had no one to blame but himself.

When Ted brought Mike into the interview and began to introduce him to the group, Mike smiled and interrupted the administrator. "I think I already know everybody." He looked around the group, waved his hand, and breezily said, "Hi, guys." As he sat down, he pushed his chair away from the table a bit and leaned back, crossing his legs. Throughout the 45-minute interview, he frequently made joking, sarcastic remarks. To be conversational, he used phrases like "a hell of a good idea" and "a damn fine plan." Once, when he didn't have a ready response, he allowed, "I don't want to BS you by making up an answer."

Mike interrupted two different interviewers when he thought he understood their line of questioning. In response to one question about crisis management, he chuckled and responded, "Well, you know, it can be a zoo around here at certain times." Toward the end of the interview, Ted asked Mike if he had any questions of the group. "Nope," he replied, "I pretty much know everything I need to know about the position and the hospital."

The interviewing team was polite in thanking Mike for meeting with them, but when he left the room, there was total silence. Finally, the chairman of the hospital's board of trustees spoke to the hospital administrator. "Ted, I know you're really high on Mike's abilities," he said, "and I respect your judgment. I also am willing to admit that what we just witnessed might not be a true indication of who Mike really is and what he can do. But whether this was a fluke or not, it happened. Mike was unprofessional and inappropriate during this interview, and we can't run the risk of having him be unprofessional when he represents this hospital. Despite the fact that I like Mike personally, I cannot vote to promote him." The rest of the group, including Ted, agreed, and Mike lost his opportunity to advance.

The interview team was correct in eliminating Mike. They were conducting a formal business meeting, which demanded a formal, businesslike manner. They were expecting to see a relaxed and confident but totally professional Mike, and certainly not the informal side of him that might be found on the golf course or at a party with close friends.

The team expected Mike to greet each person with a smile and a handshake and to sit in a relaxed but alert position. They expected him to listen closely to a question in its entirety and to answer concisely. Good eye contact with each member of the team was expected over the course of the interview, with specific eye contact given to the interviewer who asked the last question. Mike was expected to speak clearly. Since most people speed up their rate of speaking when they're nervous, it was important for Mike to be aware that the pace might need to be slowed a bit.

Furthermore, the interview team expected Mike to be organized, specific and logical in his delivery. They would not have been concerned if Mike had been silent for several seconds to consider a question and prepare his answer. That behavior, however, would not have been acceptable had Mike taken time before every answer. Then it might have been taken as a sign that he was unsure or unprepared.

Finally, the team had some very specific "don'ts" in interviewing that could end a candidacy very fast.

- Don't ever interrupt. The interviewer is in charge. It is her or his interview. The candidate can always ask for clarification if a question is too long or involved or difficult to understand.
- Don't use slang or even mild cursing; neither is professional.
- Don't use sarcastic humor. It's never certain how it will be interpreted.
- Don't ever put down a current boss or company.
- Don't pass up the opportunity to ask a question. Intelligent, thoughtful questions can show grasp of a situation or the research that's been done to prepare for the interview.

Leadership and Management Abilities

Leadership is defined as "showing the way by going in front of" or "one who starts something." Management is defined as "the skillful handling of people and details so as to get results" or "supervising the action of a group working together." In today's world where small, quick, action-oriented teams or individuals make decisions at lower and lower levels in the organization, leadership skills are more necessary than ever. Leadership is one of those nebulous qualities that drives interviewers crazy. The CEO of a major consumer products company once told us, "I don't know how to define it, or tell if a candidate has it, but I sure know leadership when I see it exhibited in a business setting." Analogies such as "The leader knows where to place the ladder" and "The manager knows how to climb the ladder" abound in professional literature.

It is also clear, however, that with less middle management and other administrative support, corporate teams must possess a blend of leadership and management skills. It is not enough to devise creative solutions to problems; the team must also be able to implement the program effectively. Leadership skills and management skills can be compared in these ways:

Leader	*Manager*
Conceptualizes	Analyzes
Invisions or inspires	Plans or implements the game plan
Takes risks	Solves problems
Produces change	Produces order
Relies on people	Relies on systems

At times, the interviewer needs to fill a position that is heavily focused on leadership skills or management skills. In other cases, the position may require both types of skills, as in the next case study. In this situation, the interviewer wants to understand whether Marian has developed leadership skills, management skills, or both, and has asked Marian to explain a complex problem and her behavior.

Career Profile

Leadership and Management

Marian was the superintendent of schools in a system with two large high schools. One was regarded as more desirable by better-educated, more articulate parents, but it was overcrowded. The less desirable school had abundant space. Marian explained to the community the process she followed in gathering data in order to re-district the school system. She also explained all the steps she followed in public awareness and input. Plans were formulated, following all the steps that logic would dictate. (Note the management skills.) However, the issue was more emotional than logical. At this point she had no choice: Marian made the decision to redistrict some students, recommended it, and the school board approved her recommendation. (Note the leadership skills.) It was an extremely unpopular decision with those who felt that they were negatively affected.

It would have been easy for Marian to move on to other pressing issues. Instead, she met with the press and spoke on local cable TV stations to explain the reasons for the changes. (Note the leadership skills.) She made sure that nothing fell between the cracks. Orientation sessions for the redistricted students made them feel more comfortable. In addition, faculty of both schools met with parents. In short, Marian did everything possible to provide a smooth transition. (Note the management skills.) Despite her best efforts, a small group of parents chose to file suit. One year later, after litigation, Marian's position had been 100 percent upheld from a legal and policy standpoint by the State Commissioner of Education. Marian's case study demonstrated her ability to plan as a manager and presented an excellent example of her leadership skills as well.

Leadership and management potential can be assessed in the same manner. It isn't acceptable for the candidate to say, for example, that he hasn't yet had the opportunity to assume a leadership position. Instead of focusing on work experiences, an outstanding interviewer focuses on the nonwork experiences, which include athletics, school experiences, and personal life.

Suppose, for example, the candidate was discussing his interest in children's theater and how he had directed plays involving 15 volunteers from the theater guild, 30 child actors, and 50 parents of those children. The discussion could include the leadership issues of determining the leads or calming parents who thought their children should be the "stars." The management issues could include handling the funds or putting together a rehearsal schedule. Preparation is the key. The interviewer asks about leadership and management and the candidate must have outstanding examples with specific details.

Organizational Fit

All the personal and professional characteristics are aimed at addressing the question, "Assuming the candidate has the necessary talent and skill to do the job, will he or she fit comfortably within the organizational setting and as a result be able to produce at high levels?" However, to understand the total fit issue, the hiring interviewer needs to have a very good understanding of the organization itself and its culture. Two people with many common factors can be entirely different in terms of their fit. Fit in an organization tends to be something that is too often neglected until there is a problem. Then there is great concern with it.

Career Profile _____

Lack of Fit

A consumer products company with an excellent reputation was in trouble for the first time. After wrestling with the options, the board of directors, on the advice of the CEO, hired a professional manager from the outside to be the president of the company. The new president, with a reputation as a hard-driving manager with a consumer products background, knew how to turn a company around.

His style was individualistic and dictatorial. He had been through turnarounds before and he knew what to do. He didn't need input. The results spoke for themselves: higher sales and profits and a five-year plan in place. In 24 months he had accomplished every financial objective targeted for him.

Yet internally there was turmoil. For years the organization had embraced a decision-making style that encouraged staff involvement and team building. Although there was respect for what the president had done, there was no rapport between the president and his direct reports or anyone else in the organization.

Within 30 months the president was dismissed. The publicly stated reason, his weakness in developing a succession plan, had nothing to do with the reality. His leadership and management philosophy was so different from the company's customary culture that it ultimately created an organizational chasm that even off-the-charts production figures couldn't bridge.

In this case, the issue hinged on professional characteristics and the president's philosophy of managing an organization and the people in it. Personal characteristics are equally important in achieving success within an organization.

From year to year, TV sitcoms change characters dramatically, or they don't return for the new season due to a conflict between the producer and one of the stars of the show. Even if the stars clearly have the right professional credentials (usually the ability to make an audience laugh), their personalities and style may make life difficult for those around them.

If the star's ego and demands grow at the same rate as the show's success and popularity, then the working conditions for the cast and crew can deteriorate just as rapidly until there is complete chaos. Finally, decision time comes when the producer fires the star in the interest of the show.

> **INTERVIEW TIP**
>
> **FIT**
>
> The candidate must demonstrate the interpersonal skills that result in an outstanding fit within the culture of the company.

CLOSE

The close is an important part of the interview. The interviewer signals the end of the interview once she has attained all the needed information. She normally tells the candidate that it has been an enjoyable and productive meeting. Human nature is such that, if the interview has been terrific in the interviewer's mind, the candidate has a much greater chance of receiving additional information about the interview process, when the next round of interviews will be held, and when the final decision will be made. In addition, any last questions from the candidate are likely to be answered. (Note: We deal with this topic in more detail in Step 7.)

The manager of the interview team has the responsibility of polling the team to get a consensus of opinion concerning each of the candidates. The results of this poll determines whether a candidate continues in the process or is eliminated from further consideration.

SUMMARY

Interviewers need to have a clear concept of the success characteristics they are looking for. They then need to learn about candidates' personal and professional characteristics to make a fair, objective assessment of their potential for success in the organization.

Personal characteristics are defined as:

- Interpersonal skills,
- Style,
- Attitudes and values,
- Motivation, and
- Outside interests.

Professional characteristics are defined as:

- Intelligence and technical skills,
- Experience,
- Communication,
- Leadership and management abilities, and
- Organizational fit.

STEP

Know the
Candidate's Agenda

There is a commonly held point of view that in an effective interview, the interviewer is in control and directs the meeting's agenda like a maestro. To do well, therefore, candidates need to demonstrate their capabilities by being composed, quick, and facile with their answers to questions.

Any hiring manager whose career depends upon hiring "A" players would be well advised to keep the person who subscribes to that philosophy off of the hiring team. One individual out of a team of eight to twelve or more interviewers, as we have seen from some of the case studies, can single-handedly torpedo the team's efforts to hire the best.

The purpose of this chapter is to give you an understanding of the agendas of the best candidates. It presents the ideal interview from the candidate's perspective. In the same way that an excellent negotiator should be able to represent either side, an outstanding interviewer should understand what the candidate is trying to accomplish and why. Having greater knowledge of each role prepares you for any eventuality and prevents surprises. In addition, understanding the candidate's agenda helps you with one of your most important tasks: helping the candidates achieve their objectives.

Adapted from *Killer Interviews* by Frederick W. Ball and Barbara B. Ball (McGraw-Hill, 1988). Reproduced with permission of The McGraw-Hill Companies.

NOTE TO THE READER

Since the chapter focuses on the candidate's agenda, we have chosen to speak to the candidate (*"YOU" REFERS TO THE CANDIDATE*) so you will understand what the candidate is trying to accomplish. The only exceptions are the Interview Tips which are written to the interviewer. With knowledge of the interviewer's agenda (Step 4) and the candidate's agenda (this chapter), we will be able to concentrate on forming a partnership in the interview (Step 6).

INTRODUCTION

Companies are looking for self-starters who can take the ball and run with it. A relationship with a company begins with the first interview, so it behooves candidates to be proactive and involved throughout the interview. Granted, the interviewer leads more than the candidate; but the responsibility for a successful interview rests with the candidate just as much as with the interviewer.

This chapter offers new ways for a candidate to approach an upcoming job interview. We encourage you to assume the roles of:

- Active partners in the discussion;
- Business consultants establishing needs and indicating how you can help to satisfy them; and
- Salespersons attempting to close a deal.

If doing this seems difficult, it is only because the approach is new. To act as a business consultant, you must discover the needs of the customer (the interviewer) before selling your competencies to help the organization solve its problems. An easy way to think of this is "needs sell." The importance of building rapport cannot be overstated in this approach, because if the customer isn't comfortable, then the real problems may not be revealed. You will discover the interviewer's needs by asking appropriate questions that draw out the issues. The more the customer talks and you listen, the better. Customers may absolutely know what they need, may have no idea, or may be somewhere between these two extremes. Once the needs are defined, you sell the products (your skills and abilities) that can satisfy the customer's needs or solve the problems.

In this role you are acting as a consultant who both sells and delivers the service. Present your skills and abilities in the best possible light, or you will not make the sale. Likewise, it is important not to oversell what you can do, because you will need to show you can produce. Give an honest answer relative to your abilities, along with examples of your most successful accomplishments, such as:

- The best system you created.
- The largest contribution you made to the bottom line.
- The greatest sale you completed.

If you are a recent graduate, the theory still applies. Use lifetime or school accomplishments as examples.

As a consultant conducting a successful interview, you will need to accomplish a number of objectives. They are:

- Building rapport.
- Questioning (gathering information).
- Developing and clarifying needs.
- Presenting skills and abilities.
- Testing the strength of your candidacy.
- Overcoming concerns.
- Closing.

Prior to examining these steps, let's look at the preparations you need to make before the interview.

BEFORE THE INTERVIEW

To be an effective, needs-oriented salesperson, you need to obtain sufficient background information about the company and

its people to allow you to conduct a meaningful business discussion by asking the
most intelligent questions. Your additional
tasks before the interview are 1) to review
your strongest skills and abilities and 2) to
get physical exercise on the day of the interview. Finally, your dress should be professional and on the conservative side, yet
appropriate for the industry and company.

DURING THE INTERVIEW

The importance of exhibiting strong interpersonal skills from the
moment you meet or speak with someone in the organization
cannot be overemphasized. Often you are so focused on the interview itself that you lose sight of what happens from the moment you arrive on site until you leave. Obviously, the way you
conduct yourself outside the interview situation should be an extension of your interview behavior.

Rapport Building

Establishing rapport with the interviewer is critical for the candidate. During the first moments of the interview, initial impressions are established. As much as interviewers are trained not to
make snap judgments, suspending an opinion is difficult. How
you dress, your physical appearance, the way you greet them,
whether you smile and make eye contact, the firmness of your
handshake, and your walk all meld into that initial composite.

Once in the office, you and the interviewer need to spend
time getting to know one another. This also gives you a chance to
become accustomed to the new environment. Candidates who are
geared to the content part of the interview comment that this part
of the interview is difficult because they want to get right to the
meat of the interview. You must remind yourself that rapport

building is critical. Forget content for now. If you establish a bond, then content becomes important. If you don't, you are mentally eliminated before you ever mention your skills. The chances are that everyone who has been invited for an interview has the skills to do the job and they are probably at about the same level. But are they all alike in terms of personal characteristics, attitudes, values, and management style?

We are sure that they are not. Most of the outstanding interviewers we have met say that if they meet one candidate who is a pleasant person and is head and shoulders above the rest of the candidates in terms of skills and abilities, it is no contest. They hire that individual. They are also quick to point out that in most instances, it doesn't happen like that. With candidates in the same general range, the choice comes down to the personal factors. Interviewers will all tell you that fit is more important than skills at that point. The best technical candidate is often not the one to whom the offer is extended, because another candidate is deemed a better fit in the organization.

The key to effectiveness in this stage of the interview is to take your cues from the interviewer. If the interviewer seems to be relaxed, open, and comfortable with meeting someone new, then your job is easier. You become comfortable fairly quickly and you probably volunteer information about your past and present interests and activities. It becomes easy to keep an interesting and stimulating conversation going, even if you don't feel that you are naturally outgoing.

If, however, the interviewer is not comfortable with himself or the interviewing process, then your job is much tougher, but certainly not impossible. It may fall to you to keep the conversation going. Whether or not you have reached a comfort level is irrelevant, because this is your one, and perhaps only, shot to meet with the interviewer.

Rapport building is not as difficult as it sounds. Starting with a smile is tremendously disarming. Be prepared to converse in such a

> **INTERVIEW TIP**
>
> **INITIAL GREETING**
>
> A warm smile and a firm handshake make a strong first impression.

way that you are willing to give a little more detail in your answers. Volunteer some personal information such as where you grew up, your family background, or personal interests and activities. If you help the interviewer to accomplish the task easily and effectively, you'll reap rewards.

Career Profile _____

Interpersonal Skills

Rebecca instinctively did the right thing. She had always been able to determine the most uncomfortable person in a room. Her friends admired her ability to involve that person in conversation and help him feel comfortable. By the time she left the room, Rebecca had learned intimate details about the person that even close personal friends hadn't known.

When her children reached high school, Rebecca decided to reenter the workforce. She was concerned about her marketability due to her 15-year absence, but she had not taken into account the tremendous interpersonal skills that she had gained through her life experiences. She interviewed with three organizations and, before long, received two job offers.

Once in the position she chose, Rebecca was called into her new boss's office. Carol told Rebecca that the interviewing team had been impressed with her interpersonal skills; in fact, they told Carol they had never met anyone with such strong skills. Carol was curious; she wanted to know where Rebecca had learned such powerful techniques. Rebecca thanked Carol and then laughed. "I haven't had any formal training. In all the volunteer work I've done, and as the mother of two teenagers, I've learned to be both a good listener and persuasive. I've discovered that if you ask a few open-ended questions and genuinely care about what the person has to say, almost everyone will open up." Is it any wonder that Rebecca was hired?

If you can learn something about the interviewer's background prior to the interview, it can be a huge help. Clint never interviews without doing all the homework possible on personal background. Somewhere in the history Clint is almost always able to find some common educational bond or mutual friend or interest. This information often helps Clint to cut through numerous layers of surface rapport building to reach a deeper, personal level. When discussing mutual friends, the interviewer is able to reach a faster comfort level through association. The thought process is, "If Clint is Peter's friend (someone the interviewer knows), then he must be okay." If Peter also happens to be bright, successful, hardworking, and easy to get along with, then so much the better.

In terms of fit, this may translate to, "Peter is our kind of guy, so you may be our kind of person as well." You can see that, even at this early stage of the interview, fit is becoming important. As we have discussed, it remains extremely important throughout the interview.

In some situations, however, you are not able to ascertain any information about the interviewer or other key individuals in the organization. This doesn't mean that you will not be successful. It means that you are probably in the same position as the other candidates and you have to develop rapport from the initial conversation.

In summary, the candidate should go into this segment of an interview keeping one cardinal rule in mind: Do not cut the rapport building short. You cannot control what the interviewer does, but you can control what you do. The key is to follow the interviewer's lead while keeping your own agenda in mind. This introductory phase of the interview helps to create an easy conversational exchange. How do you know that the other person isn't a scout leader, jogger, coach, or traveler just like you? If the two of you share the same interests, it makes for an interesting dialogue rather than a one-way monologue. So relax, smile, and go with the flow.

Questioning (Gathering Information)

At the conclusion of the rapport building, a transition is needed to move to the business portion of the meeting. As we have indicated, this is done by the interviewer, who might say something like, "I've really enjoyed getting

> **INTERVIEW TIP**
>
> **RAPPORT BUILDING**
>
> Rapport building is the first step in forming a bond with the candidate.

to know about your personal background and interests. Now I'd like to learn something about your professional background," or, "I'm interested in hearing about your career and how it has developed."

No matter what the interviewer's method, the message is that a change is being made. The focus changes from personal background to business background, from "getting to know you" to interview content. Rapport building and fit issues do not go away, though. They continue to be important throughout the interview.

As you prepare to move into questioning, the information that you have gathered about the company and its people becomes crucial. It gives you enough background to conduct a meaningful business discussion. Now you need the interviewer to help put that information into the right context and continue to educate you. The objective is to learn more about the condition of the company, including prospects for short- and long-term growth, the future direction of the company, some definition of how the organization expects the successful candidate to assist in attaining its goals, and the ideal personal and professional skills needed to fill the role successfully.

The better the rapport you have established, the easier it is to ask the questions you need to ask. The best way to get a positive and enthusiastic response is to help the interviewer see the benefit. You might say, for example, "Mr. Jones, I've received some background from reading your annual report. I'd really appreciate some additional information about the organization, your business goals, and the specific position, because then I can target my skills and abilities to assist you in achieving your goals." Imagine how clear this sounds to a bottom-line business executive who wants to cut straight to the core. The answer is almost certainly, "Sure, how can I help you?"

Incidentally, if you don't like the way the question is phrased, change it. The style of this question (or any other one) is not as important as the sincerity and enthusiasm you show when asking it. Any question can be asked hundreds of different ways.

Having attained permission to ask the questions, it is important to know where you are trying to go with your questioning. Typically, you lead from the general to the specific:

- Company and its external environment;
- Internal environment;
- Goals and objectives;
- Department;
- Specifics on the job.

The final level of exploration is the specific skills necessary to do the job. This question can be worded in many different ways. You might ask, "Can you describe the ideal candidate?" Or "Will you describe the personal and professional skills in an ideal candidate?" This information may prove invaluable later. Through an initial understanding of how the position fits into the total company puzzle, you gain knowledge of the specific needs in some sort of priority order. (Note: This data helps to determine which of your skills to present later on.)

Developing and Clarifying Needs and Presenting Skills and Abilities

As your questions begin to generate information, you discover seeds of the organization's needs or even a clearer definition of them. This process is called needs development. Patience is a virtue at this point. Needs can be misinterpreted if you jump to conclusions. The way the company has tried to deal with a problem is as important as the problem itself. Ask how the proposed solutions have turned out. Understand where there have been successes and failures. Ask why.

It is also important to understand the subtleties of the problem. Do the key managers all see the problem in the same way? If they don't, try to understand why not, because it is possible they may have different objectives for the individual to be hired. This can be a politically awkward situation. It can also be a real opportunity for a well-prepared job seeker, since a focus on the issues can help an organization clarify its thinking and obtain management consensus prior to hiring a candidate.

Needs clarifying occurs when you think you understand one or more needs. This may seem redundant, but it's not. Perception is a funny thing. You are quite sure that you have heard what has been said, but you need a final test to be sure. You might say, "In light of our discussion, is it fair to say that the three critical objectives for the first few years are 1, 2, and 3?" Or "If I heard correctly, sales forecasting and assuming the responsibility for reaching the objectives are important. Is that correct?" If the response is that you are correct, then you have the information you need.

Let's take an example to see how the interaction might flow. Suppose you have some experience in sales and are interviewing for a sales management position for a high-end, sophisticated product in the health care industry. The interviewer seems to be vague about needs, but at one point says, "We have been too passive. We need a take-charge type of person as we move forward." You have now been given a seed of information that should be developed. Why is the interviewer raising this issue? Is the interviewer concerned about the sales forecast? Was the prior manager weak in the fundamentals of the function? Is there concern about the management of people or resources? Is it a management style issue?

In moving the conversation forward, you might ask, "Could you be a little more specific about taking charge?" Suppose the response was, "Certainly; managing the numbers is one concern." Now there is more than a seed; there is real substance. The conversation might move forward as follows:

CANDIDATE: Is the concern sales forecasting or ownership of the numbers?

INTERVIEWER: The real concern is ownership of the numbers.

CANDIDATE: Has that been a problem?

INTERVIEWER: The previous two sales managers have forecast revenue dollars, but then did not produce.

CANDIDATE: Were there extenuating circumstances?

INTERVIEWER: No.

CANDIDATE: Unrealistic forecasting?

INTERVIEWER: That, we feel, was part of the problem. The situation was compounded by the lack of willingness to accept responsibility for the forecast. The sales manager always had an excuse if the numbers were not met.

As a need is identified, you may have a strong desire to jump in with the various ways that you can help the company to solve the problem. Resist the urge. This is most difficult in areas where you have previously accomplished what is being sought. You must first be sure that you understand the need as it exists in this company. Ask additional questions to further define the need. Sometimes there are major differences between your first impression and the actual need, and sometimes subtle but important refinements have to be made in your first impressions. Suppose, for example, the candidate continued, "Can you tell me the process by which the revenue forecasts are determined?"

The answer to this question may further clarify the situation. Is senior management being unreasonable and perhaps autocratic in the establishment of the revenue forecast, or has a reasonable process been employed? Once the need has been defined and clarified, the interviewer normally expects you to respond with how you would react in the situation. Although this is jumping ahead to product presentation (how your skills and abilities can help to solve the problem), it is the natural flow of the conversation. Consequently, there are usually a series of leaps back and forth from need definition and clarification to product presentation, and then back again to develop another need.

In theory, there is some question as to whether this is a better progression for the candidate or whether it would be wiser to draw out all the needs and then indicate how your skills could help to solve the organization's problems. In reality, however, it usually doesn't matter. Most interviewers simply don't have the patience to wait until all the needs are developed. They become irritated and that affects you negatively. The interviewer needs to complete an agenda in a timely manner by moving from topic to topic, completing a discussion, and then moving on to a new issue.

Let's assume that the sales forecasting has been done in a reasonable manner and that market conditions appear to be acceptable. As you mentally prepare to respond to the need, you draw on the experiences that give evidence of your abilities to perform successfully and provide proof of your abilities by offering verifiable examples of your successes. If you do not have experience in the area, the alternative is to tell the interviewer how your skills and abilities have prepared you to perform successfully. Let's see how the example might continue.

CANDIDATE: The process you've described in arriving at the sales forecasting sounds reasonable to me. That's approximately the method I use to forecast. We also had a second set of numbers that were our stretch objectives as a challenge to shoot for. But we were evaluated based on reaching our primary objectives.

INTERVIEWER: What responsibility did you bear for reaching those objectives?

CANDIDATE: Prior to being hired, I was told they were mine. I owned them. If I made them, I was successful. If I didn't, I failed for that cycle. The organization felt that strongly because my numbers were fed into the CEO's earning forecast, and his success was dependent on my success. The balance was to create a set of numbers that were challenging yet realistic in relation to industry and market conditions. Needless to say, I had input from others on the management team.

INTERVIEWER: How successful were you?

CANDIDATE: I'm proud to say we hit our numbers in seven out of eight years. And there were clear reasons, beyond our control, that caused the one loss.

INTERVIEWER: That's impressive. Were the numbers enough of a challenge?

CANDIDATE: The business grew 15 percent per year over that period of time. In addition, we hit our stretch objectives four of the eight years.

During the discussion, the interviewer gives verbal signals concerning his interest in pursuing this line of questioning. Suppose, for the sake of our case study, that you want the conversation to move to a discussion of the sales force.

CANDIDATE: Are there any areas where you have had concerns or faced specific frustrations with the sales force?

INTERVIEWER: We have experienced frustrations in a number of areas.

CANDIDATE: Have you been able to identify one or two key concerns?

INTERVIEWER: Our track record is extremely inconsistent in hiring quality staff.

Another need may have been identified. It takes some more development and clarifying to be sure.

CANDIDATE: Are you able to offer a competitive salary and benefit package?

INTERVIEWER: Yes. That's not an issue.

Note: That's good information for you to have if you reach the salary negotiation stage.

CANDIDATE: Is there consistency in your recruiting and hiring guidelines?

INTERVIEWER: Can you give me an example?

CANDIDATE: Have you come to grips with the technical ability versus selling ability debate?

INTERVIEWER: No, that is an ongoing issue. Some regional managers believe one thing, some believe another. One of our problems is that each manager acts autonomously.

CANDIDATE: How about the characteristics that you look for in a candidate?

INTERVIEWER: Unfortunately, we don't have consistency there either. Can you tell me what you look for in a candidate and how successful you have been with hires you have made?

Now it's the candidate's turn. The interviewer has been patient, has identified a need, and has begun to clarify the need. Now there is a strong desire to hear from the job applicant. Any effort by the candidate to raise other needs at this time could easily be seen as an effort to stall because the candidate has no position on the issue or no experience in that area.

CANDIDATE: Certainly. Let me start with the technical ability versus selling ability debate as an overview. If I can find an ideal candidate who has technical ability and sales ability, it's simple. I hire the person. If I don't have the ideal, then my experience has taught me to make my trade-off on the side of the sales ability or potential.

INTERVIEWER: So you would hire the one with the stronger selling skills.

CANDIDATE: Yes. I've had greater success leaning that way.

INTERVIEWER: Good. That's the CEO's experience as well. What characteristics do you look for?

A little good news in an interview doesn't hurt now and then. The CEO agrees with your position!

CANDIDATE: In terms of a sales profile, I look for certain general characteristics and certain specific ones. General characteristics would include someone who understands the customer and what it takes to make a sale; is hungry for commissions; has familiarity with the territory; is intelligent and organized; and makes an excellent appearance and communicates well.

INTERVIEWER: Which of these is most important?

CANDIDATE: Hungry for commissions. The drive to sell.

INTERVIEWER: I agree. I will want to talk about that some more. But you said that you look for certain specific criteria as well. Can you tell me about some of those?

CANDIDATE: The very nature of the high-ticket item dictates that the sale has to be approved at a high level in the client organization. The salesperson needs business sophistication equal to the task. Consequently, I look for a number of specifics: an understanding of the various buying groups; a track record selling capital equipment to hospitals or a lot of sales potential; an ability to converse technically and financially; skills in life-cycle costing; and an understanding and ability to sell the technical benefits of new equipment versus present equipment.

INTERVIEWER: Do you place any priority order on these?

CANDIDATE: I think that these fall into the category of must have or must learn. They are all important.

INTERVIEWER: I agree. What kind of track record have you had with the retention of sales staff?

CANDIDATE: We averaged approximately 10 hires per year over eight years, and 70 are still with the company.

The candidate (unless redirected by the interviewer) could continue to pursue this line of questioning, or go back to the issue of how to find a hungry salesperson, or move to a new topic. The candidate has learned about two needs: a take-charge sales manager and the hiring of staff. In each instance the need has been developed without exhausting the interviewer's patience, and the candidate was able to target skills and accomplishments that demonstrated her ability to perform successfully in the areas where the company needed assistance.

Let's follow one more trail from need development to candidate presentation. Suppose the interviewer volunteered that he had a specific interest in the evaluation of the sales force.

INTERVIEWER: Can you tell me how you evaluate a sales force?

CANDIDATE: I'm used to setting quantitative and qualitative objectives with sales personnel. Would you like to discuss both or focus on one area?

INTERVIEWER: I'm more interested in quantitative objectives.

Note: The last question helps to define the interviewer's interest and allows the candidate to remain focused.

CANDIDATE: If I could ask just a few questions about your present procedures, it will help me to focus my answer.

INTERVIEWER: Sure.

CANDIDATE: Do you presently rank sales personnel?

INTERVIEWER: Yes, we do.

CANDIDATE: Are they then compared to a median sales level?

INTERVIEWER: Yes.

CANDIDATE: Is there a weighted average, taking account of such things as difficulty of the territory?

INTERVIEWER: No, we haven't given any weighting to those kinds of factors.

CANDIDATE: Is it a matter of time before someone in the lowest 10 percent is discharged?

INTERVIEWER: Not necessarily; it depends on the individual regional manager. Some protect all their people, some protect their friends, and some don't protect anyone. But tell me how you would handle the situation.

CANDIDATE: One last question. What remedial process is employed before the low-producing employee is released?

INTERVIEWER: That is hard to say. It really depends solely on the goodwill of the regional manager.

That's it. The candidate's time is up. It is time to respond. Anything less turns the interviewer into an unhappy camper.

CANDIDATE: It's a difficult process to recruit, hire, and train an effective salesperson. Consequently, evaluation decisions should follow policy and be professional and logical. I believe you have to track progress and compare it across the board. I also think the comparison must be based on a weighted score that takes into account the difficulty of the territory and a series of other variables. When an individual is in the lowest 10 percent, I think an analysis should be undertaken to find out why. If there are extenuating circumstances, they should be noted. If there is no apparent reason, I believe there should be a remedial plan.

INTERVIEWER: A remedial plan? Tell me more.

CANDIDATE: The plan should be positive, with the goal of assisting the employee to improve. While in a remedial situation, there should be monthly monitoring. However, if the same trend continues even with assistance, then the employee should be notified that his job could be in jeopardy. Any decisions regarding an employee should be made with input from all the managers who interact with that person.

INTERVIEWER: Has that type of program proven effective for you?

CANDIDATE: Yes, it has. Employees like it because it is designed to be helpful and fair for as long as possible, and senior management likes it because the focus is on upgrading staff continually.

INTERVIEWER: But isn't that too long a time to keep a weak performer?

CANDIDATE: The process sounds longer than it really is. It was actually necessary to put approximately 20 people into the remedial procedure. In six of the cases, the procedure was probably unnecessary because it appeared, in hindsight, that the low performance was due to circumstances beyond the control of the salesperson (economic conditions). Of the remaining 14, eight left shortly after they were put in the remedial plan, four of the remaining six improved and the other two were asked to leave.

INTERVIEWER: That's very interesting. Did the individuals feel the process was fair?

CANDIDATE: No one ever likes to hear bad news. But from all we could gather, they felt they had been informed and given an honest chance to improve. And, perhaps more important, it seemed to have a positive effect on the remaining sales force.

A third need has now been developed and addressed. Before going much further and making mistaken assumptions, the candidate should clarify that the needs just discussed are the critical needs. Logic would dictate that they should be the key needs, but once in a while the conversation drifts away from the interviewer and secondary needs are discussed first.

CANDIDATE: Is it reasonable for me to assume that hiring a take-charge sales manager, the recruitment and hiring of quality staff, and effective evaluation, especially as it relates to meeting revenue objectives, are critical objectives to the organization?

INTERVIEWER: Yes, that's right.

CANDIDATE: Are there others?

INTERVIEWER: There are, but they're not as important as the three you just mentioned.

INTERVIEW TIP

**NEEDS
DEVELOPMENT**

Allow the candidate
to develop and con-
firm your business
needs and to sell his
or her ability to
accomplish the goals.

This is an important step. Now the candidate has surpassed conjecture, by requesting confirmation and receiving it. This information helps for the remainder of the interview and the thank-you letter. The candidate would never have been sure had she not asked.

This information could also be helpful in future interviews if the next interviewer holds to the same order of critical objectives, but that has to be tested carefully when the next interview comes. Incidentally, this is an excellent way for you to test the organization to see if there is consistency from one manager to another. Finding consistency usually builds confidence and a sense that the organization is well-managed and knows where it is going.

Testing the Strength of Your Candidacy and Overcoming Concerns

As the conversation progresses, the interviewer accumulates additional information about the applicant. The better the preparation and the fit of the candidate, the higher the interviewer's comfort level will be. No matter how successful the candidate is, however, the interviewer has questions or concerns about the candidate's skills and abilities relative to the specific job needs in one or more areas. The concerns may be caused by something that was (or was not) discussed, or by a word here or a phrase there. There may have been misunderstanding of a question asked or an answer given or a nonverbal sign.

Frankly, this is natural. Part of this relates to the fact that seldom does a candidate fill the job specification 100 percent. Another part relates to the role of the interviewer in the negatively oriented screening process. The very nature of the process is to find the things that are wrong so that another person can be screened out. The candidate must be prepared to counter that thought process.

A concern surfacing in the mind of the interviewer is not fatal. It can often be corrected, sometimes easily, especially if it is a misunderstanding. What can be fatal is a concern that is not addressed by the end of the interview. It then becomes a damning statement when the interview team is reviewing each candidate and one interviewer says, "You know I really liked Susan; there was just one thing she said. . . ." That is often the end of a candidacy. The need to deal with concerns, then, should be clear and obvious. Yet the interviewer does not introduce the subject and the vast majority of job seekers won't touch the issue. Why not?

Dealing with concerns or potential weakness in any form is difficult under the best of circumstances. When the concerns deal with your skills, abilities, or personality, it is that much tougher. But we ask you to balance the difficulty of this task with the need to have the information out on the table, where you can deal with it and perhaps make it go away. To us, it's no contest. Having the information is crucial.

The issue, then, becomes finding the best method to test this area while maintaining your comfort level and that of the interviewer. The best method, perhaps, is to return to a previous discussion and request a comparison between the targeted professional and personal characteristics and your own. You might ask:

"Mr. Jones (or Scott if the person has introduced himself by his first name), earlier I asked you to define the targeted professional and personal characteristics for this position. Now that you know a little more about me, can you compare my characteristics with the targeted ones?"

Or, "Mr. Jones, now that we have had an opportunity to talk about the position, I feel more confident than ever that I can be of assistance to your organization. Do you have any concerns about my abilities to do the job or fit into the organization?"

Having asked the question, the job applicant must now be ready for the response and how to deal with it. The candidate has asked a very direct question that requires an open, direct response. Some interviewers are able to deal with the question openly and some have problems with it. If you hear a vague response like, "Oh, I think your skills are fine" or, "You certainly could do the job," you are probably not being given the information you requested. You might come back and say, "I appreciate those kind words. I am feeling good about the fit as well. What I was trying to do was to see if you had any concerns about my ability in any specific area so that I could address them while we're together." This again lays the issue right out there.

At this point either there is response and a dialogue, or not. If you sense that the interviewer is incapable of dealing with the issue directly or is too uncomfortable to deal with it, then you have no choice but to move on. However, take heart, because many interviewers are able to deal with this discussion more

openly and honestly than you think. Remember that if job seekers don't get these issues out on the table, it is usually not because of the interviewer, but because they don't ask.

Let's suppose that the interviewer is willing to deal with
your question. The response to your question can be varied. At
the positive end the interviewer may say, "I'm feeling very good
about your background and abilities. I am comfortable with
what I've heard." You may want to come back to ask about concerns in specific areas or, if your intuition tells you the comments were genuine, you may accept them at face value. A
response totally at the negative end is highly unlikely, since the
organization has spent time and money attempting to screen
out individuals who do not have the technical skills before they
reached the interview process.

What you are most likely to hear is something in the middle that gives positive feedback yet raises a legitimate concern. Let's go
back to the example of the candidate seeking
the sales management position. In response
to the question about the ability to do the
job, the interviewer might respond, "I am
very comfortable with your responses to my
questions. My concern lies in your ability to

> **INTERVIEW TIP**
>
> **EYE CONTACT**
>
> Make eye contact
> throughout the inter-
> view, particularly
> when the candidate
> asks about perceived
> weaknesses of your
> company.

manage and grow a large sales force. Your largest previous experience is with a sales force of 200 people, isn't it?"

Okay, a concern has been raised. Now your preparation is
put to the real test. The question in front of you demands a
response, and you don't have a lot of time to prepare your response. Yet this needs to be your best prepared and presented
response. You would spend a weekend on it if you had the
time, but the reality is that you have only a few seconds to
gather your thoughts. However, you've spent the time prior to
the interview identifying strengths and weaknesses and preparing answers to questions about potential weaknesses. You're
ready. You say:

Mr. Jones, I did say that I had responsibility for 200 people as a regional sales manager. What we haven't had an opportunity to discuss is the experience I had replacing Sonya Hopkins when she was out for one year with her heart condition. I was selected from among ten regional managers to replace her while she was ill. For the first few months I was merely holding the fort, but once it became apparent that Sonya was going to be out for a long time, my role changed. I was given full resources and assumed all of her functions and responsibilities, including supervising a 500-person sales force.

The conversation might continue as follows:

INTERVIEWER: That's interesting. What happened when Sonya returned to work?

CANDIDATE: I was asked to assume responsibility for the largest, most profitable, yet troubled territory in the region.

INTERVIEWER: What territory did the company assign you?

CANDIDATE: The New York area. The office had been off its numbers for five straight years and had terrible morale problems and a huge turnover. I can honestly say that in the two years I have been in the New York metropolitan region, I learned a great deal and have had almost every problem imaginable.

INTERVIEWER: Give me an example.

CANDIDATE: I had a salesman who was a 25-year employee and had been one of the company's most effective salespeople until his wife became ill and died. He then began to drink and his productivity level slipped to an unacceptable level.

INTERVIEWER: Were you able to help him?

CANDIDATE: I believe so. He was a valued employee whom the company wanted to save. We certainly had our ups and downs while we were trying to correct the problem, but we had a remedial plan in place and needed to implement it.

INTERVIEWER: How did it end up?

CANDIDATE: His life started to get back on track and he eventually reached a solid level of productivity. He did not reach his former level, but was three times higher than when he was having problems.

The conversation should continue for as long as the interviewer finds that it is productive and until all of the concerns are raised and addressed.

Does this exchange guarantee that the interviewer's concerns are overcome? Absolutely not. But it defines the concerns, gets them out in the open, and gives you the best shot at resolving them. In the example, you not only had a chance to resolve the interviewer's concerns, but also had an opportunity to reinforce a number of your skills and abilities. You may also have the opportunity to present additional skills that will help to continue the business dialogue. This extends the time you are with the interviewer, which increases the probability of success.

> **INTERVIEW TIP**
>
> **RAISING CONCERNS**
>
> Observe whether the candidate draws out concerns you have about his or her candidacy and attempts to overcome them.

Closing

It is the interviewer's responsibility to close the meeting. What many job seekers forget or are reluctant to do, however, is to determine what happens next regarding their candidacy. Rather, there is a tendency to sit passively and wait until the company initiates contact. By employing the passive strategy, the candidate loses the opportunity to understand what is happening.

Suppose, for example, you receive a job offer from another company with a defined time frame to let the organization know whether you accept. And suppose that this most recent interview is with the company in which you have the greatest interest. It suddenly becomes critical for you to know when a decision will be made. Let's go back and follow our sample interview through to a possible conclusion.

INTERVIEWER: I've enjoyed meeting you and learning about your background. I think I have all the information I need. I'd like to thank you for coming in.

CANDIDATE: I've enjoyed the time as well. I feel that you are doing some really exciting things and I'd love to help you move forward with your objectives. Can you tell me how the process will move from here?

INTERVIEWER: Let's see. I believe that I'm the fourth person you've met. Is that correct?

CANDIDATE: Yes, that's right.

INTERVIEWER: There will be one more round of two to four interviews with the executive vice presidents and president.

CANDIDATE: Can you tell me whether I'll be recommended for that round of interviews?

INTERVIEWER: You are the last person I'm interviewing and I'm impressed. You will be moving to the next round.

CANDIDATE: Thank you. I'm excited about that. Can you tell me how many other candidates will be moving to the final round and when those interviews will be held?

INTERVIEWER: There are two other candidates and we are going to try to schedule the interviews for next week.

CANDIDATE: Will the final decision be made soon?

INTERVIEWER: Probably within three weeks.

CANDIDATE: Is there any additional information that I should have to prepare for the interviews?

INTERVIEWER: I don't think so. Frankly, I'm surprised that you have been able to obtain as much information as you have about the organization. That's impressive.

CANDIDATE: You were extremely helpful in my preparation and I wanted you to know how much I appreciate your help.

INTERVIEWER: You're welcome. You'll hear from me toward the end of next week. Can you find your way out?

CANDIDATE: Yes. Thanks for your time.

INTERVIEWER: Good-bye.

Do you know everything there is to know going forward? No, but you have learned some important information. You are going to the final round of interviews with two other candidates in about a week. The final decision should be made in about three weeks. Furthermore, your efforts at preparation regarding the company and its people seem to have been successful. This is all excellent feedback and indicates that you have handled yourself in a professional manner. You are also managing your job campaign, because you know when and under what conditions the decision will be made.

A final point: By reaching the finals, you have successfully handled all aspects of the interviewing process that are within your control. From this point, personal chemistry and the interviewer's definition of fit are the determining factors, unless one of the candidates "shoots herself in the foot." These things are out of your control. Your goal in the final round is to relax, be yourself, and in-

> **INTERVIEW TIP**
>
> **TIMETABLE**
>
> Let the candidate know about the interview and decision-making timetable, to allow for adequate planning on his or her part.

terview in the same way you have previously. If you receive the offer, great. If you don't, then move forward confidently. Your interviewing technique is effective. The same personal and professional characteristics demonstrated in the next interview may well help you to secure the offer.

AFTER THE INTERVIEW: THE THANK-YOU LETTER

A thank-you letter to each interviewer should be considered an extension of the interview, and an absolute necessity. It can be in letter form or through E-mail followed by a letter. Few job applicants do this, and it really makes a difference. The thank-you letter is usually a few paragraphs in length, with each paragraph covering a different topic. The letter should not be more than one side of a page. The initial sentence should refer to something specific from your conversation, so that it becomes a personal rather than a business letter. You might say: "I enjoyed meeting you and learning about your objectives" or "Thank you for meeting with me and sharing your thoughts on the direction of the company." Then indicate your interest in the position and the company.

The second paragraph is an opportunity to reinforce those of your beliefs that correspond with the company's direction or methodology. It's a way to continue bonding with the interviewer and to indicate that you are in sync with the company. This can include ways that your skills could be helpful going forward.

The third paragraph is the place to mention the skills and abilities that were not discussed during the interview but that you feel will further your candidacy. Sometimes a critical skill or ability was not discussed due to time constraints or due to the direction of the conversation. This is an opportunity to rectify the oversight.

The final paragraph is a review of the next steps and a closing. You might end, for example, with "I look forward to hearing from you in a week to schedule the next interviews" or "I really feel the fit was strong and I would enjoy working with you."

Occasionally, a candidate is given an assignment to complete as part of the evaluation process. Assignments should be of the highest quality, presented in a professional style, and completed on time.

SUMMARY

The best way for candidates to accomplish their agendas is to approach the interview as a sales call. The sales call involves:

- Building rapport;
- Questioning (gathering information);
- Developing and clarifying needs;
- Presenting skills and abilities;
- Testing the strength of your candidacy;
- Overcoming concerns; and
- Closing.

Build a Partnership

As he stood in the seemingly endless line for his daughter's soccer registration on a crisp September Saturday, Mike wondered again how he had drawn this family duty. Meg usually functioned as family registrar, but she had managed a client call at exactly the right moment and had waved cheerfully to him and their 10-year-old, grinning as she stuffed a handful of papers in his hand, pushing him out the door. "You'll be fine," she had mouthed, but now he wasn't so sure. Did he have Serena's photo id, her birth certificate, order form for socks and shorts, parent volunteer check-off list, and the all-important notarized medical release form?

"It was easier to register for business school than for this," he muttered, not realizing he had articulated the thought loudly enough for the person behind him to hear it. A chuckle confirmed that he had been overheard. Turning somewhat apologetically, he faced another equally burdened dad who said, "My wife is going to owe me some major league favors; this is my third registration today and all our kids, being in different age brackets, have different registration lines. You're right; B school was a piece of cake compared to this." Dave extended his hand and introduced himself to Mike.

After each identified their daughters on a nearby lawn amid the jumble of flying ponytails and somewhat erratic but highly energetic ball juggling, Mike said, "What business school did you attend?" "I was at Sloan," offered Dave. "You're kidding," replied Mike. "MIT was my home for the MBA program too." Neither of them noticed the painfully slow crawl of the registration line as

they discovered that Mike had been enrolled only a year behind
Dave and they had had many of the same professors. They thoroughly enjoyed exchanging stories of impossible deadlines, inter-
minable case studies, and the idiosyncracies of the dentures of
one particular professor. They even found that they had practi-
cally lived at the same favorite Italian restaurant in South Boston.
By the time they reached the head of the line, they had exchanged
business cards and volunteered to set up the nets together on one
of the fields each Sunday. What had been an onerous task became
one of the highlights of the weekend for both men.

Dave and Mike's conversation had several key components
that contributed to its success. They both:

■ Established a rapport.

■ Enjoyed the conversation.

■ Found a topic that was stimulating and interesting.

■ Participated actively in the conversation.

■ Talked approximately the same amount.

COMPLEXITIES IN JOB INTERVIEWING

In previous chapters we identified three basic objectives that
must be met for you to be successful in an interview:

Objective 1: Recognize the importance of building rapport.
Bonding with the candidate is a critical ingredient in determining fit within the culture and environment of your organization.

Objective 2: Complete the interviewer's agenda. The purpose
of the interview is for you to determine if the candidate has
the right skills and abilities, interest, motivation and energy,
and fit within your culture.

Objective 3: Complete the candidate's agenda. The candidate
would like to identify the major goals of the organization and
sell his or her ability to achieve them.

Achieving these three objectives is no small task, but there's more. The job is complicated by the personality, style, and expectations of the interviewer, none of which can be ignored. The interviewer:

- Is in a favored position;
- Can control the interview; and
- Is the buyer.

It is important to examine these conventions because they dictate, to some degree, your behavior in the interview. You, the interviewer, are clearly in a favored position because you have something the candidate wants: a job.

That the interviewer controls the interview is a time-honored convention. In virtually all interview training (and intuitively if there has been no training), the interviewer is taught that, once the rapport building portion of the interview is completed, she should take control of the interview. This allows her to determine whether the candidate's professional skills and abilities, interests, and personal characteristics make him or her an outstanding fit within the culture of the organization. This is accomplished, in most cases, by the interviewer asking short, open-ended questions that seek long, complete answers. This keeps the control of the interview firmly in the hands of the interviewer.

Conventional wisdom dictates that interviewing is a negatively oriented screening out process from its early stages through the selection of the final few candidates. It's like a multilayered sieve that refines flour to its finest state. The interviewer doesn't want to spend time selling a candidate on the merits of the company if there is no chance the candidate will make it to the later stages of the interview process. Consequently, the interviewer would rather spend time evaluating fit issues and determining where the candidate stands in the priority ranking.

If the interviewing process worked that way, there would be no complexity. It would be easy and would be carried out however the interviewer wanted. Actually, the model may be fine for a "B" or "C" level candidate who needs a job and is trying to sell skills. The outstanding "A" candidate, however, is as much a buyer as a seller. In addition, he comes to the interview with an agenda of his own, which is to determine the needs of the organization and to sell his skills and abilities in being able to fill them. Furthermore, the great candidate is evaluating the interviewer to determine whether he would want to be a business partner with her. It is the candidate's agenda and the willingness of the outstanding candidate to implement it that makes the interviewer's task more complex.

COMMUNICATIONS FLOW

The key to your success in the interview is to become a partner with the candidate in managing the communications flow; that is, the percentage of talk by each participant. This task is more important with the outstanding candidate because he will be attuned to whether you are treating him as a respected partner throughout the interview. Although it is a deviation from the conventional means of interviewing, making a change from a question and answer format to an open, interactive dialogue is well worth the effort because it makes the interview more exciting, stimulating, and challenging; it also dramatically increases your chances to land the candidate.

> **INTERVIEW TIP**
>
> **FORMING A PARTNERSHIP**
>
> The partnership (buy/sell) model allows you to gain the information you need while building a strong relationship.

The same lively exchange the soccer dads we met earlier had can occur in a dynamic, stimulating interview situation. The candidate gives the interviewer all the data she needs to make a decision, and the interviewer challenges and excites the candidate about the possibility of working for the company. Sure, it's more complicated because you are adding a business conversation to the meeting; but the basics are the same.

INTERVIEW FRAMEWORK

A simple framework can help us visualize the communication flow during various phases of the interview. Let's examine the pattern that most interviewers have been taught, which starts with interactive rapport building, each participant talking about 50 percent of the time. Once the interviewer makes the transition to the business portion, she likes to ask short, open-ended questions and have the candidate talk 85 to 90 percent of the time. She is clearly a buyer at this time. If the candidate's answers satisfy her and hit the mark, she allows a gradual change to closer to 50 percent talk each in the last third of the business portion of the interview. Assuming the candidate is viable, she does some selling during this time.

Figure 6-1 graphs the communication flow as the interview progresses from phase 1 (on the left), the rapport building phase, through phase 5 (on the right), the close. The communication flow, which identifies the percentages of candidate and interviewer talk, is shown as line A.

The pattern the ideal candidate would like to follow starts with the same interactive rapport building (50 percent talk each) as the interviewer pattern. The difference comes in the business portion, where the candidate would like to continue the same pattern throughout the interview. This, the candidate feels, allows him to identify the company's needs, to clarify them, and to present his skills and abilities to accomplish the needs. Then the candidate can test his candidacy with the interviewer, overcome any concerns, and accomplish additional rapport building while the interviewer is closing the meeting.

Figure 6-2 graphs the candidate's ideal communication flow, shown by line B. The phases of the interview describe the candidate's agenda.

Figure 6-3 merges the communication flow of the model many interviewers are taught to follow (Figure 6-1) and the ideal candidate's model (Figure 6-2). The communication flow is shown as line A (the conventional interviewer's model) and line B (the

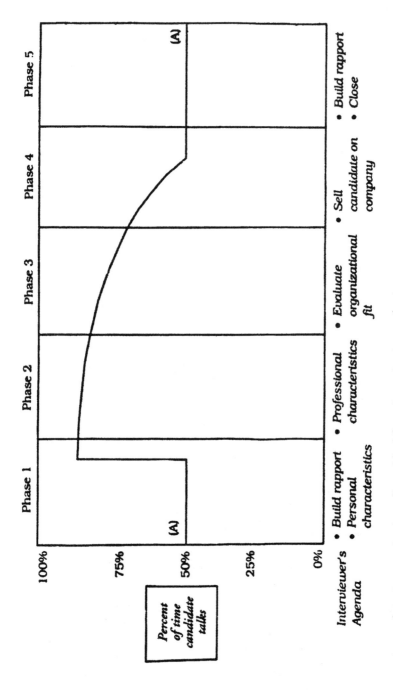

Figure 6-1. Communications flow: Ideal from interview's standpoint
Adapted from *Killer Interviews* by Frederick W. Ball and Barbara B. Ball (McGraw-Hill, 1988). Reproduced with permission of The McGraw-Hill Companies.

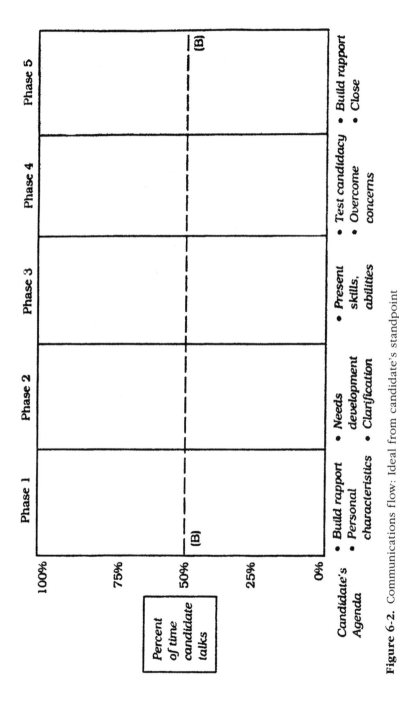

Figure 6-2. Communications flow: Ideal from candidate's standpoint

Adapted from *Killer Interviews* by Frederick W. Ball and Barbara B. Ball (McGraw-Hill, 1988). Reproduced with permission of The McGraw-Hill Companies.

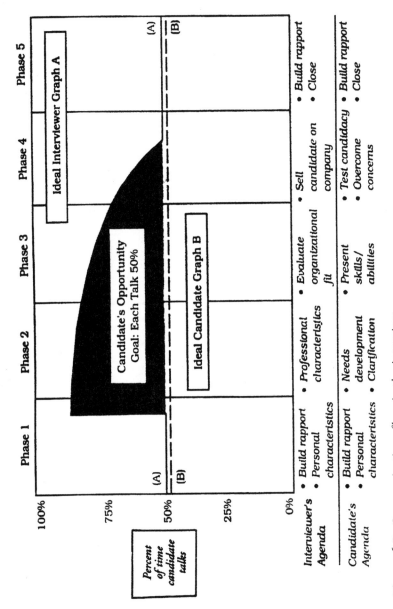

Figure 6-3. Communications flow in the interview

candidate's model). The gray area represents the divergence. The interviewer's and candidate's agendas are identified at the bottom of the graph.

It is clear that the agendas are parallel in phases 1, 4, and 5 and divergent in phases 2 and 3. The divergence (gray area) represents an opportunity for the interviewer and the candidate to change the communication flow from a candidate-dominated pattern (talking 85 to 90 percent of the time) to one that approaches 50 percent talk each.

> **INTERVIEW TIP**
>
> **BUSINESS CONVERSATION**
>
> The goal is to create an exciting, stimulating, 50–50 business conversation throughout the interview.

BUILDING A PARTNERSHIP

To summarize, the argument for building a partnership with the outstanding candidate is overwhelming. You cannot expect to enter the interview, build rapport, and then start firing questions at the candidate to see if any of your favorite questions become "gotcha" questions for the candidate. What will happen is simple. The candidate will decide you are someone who doesn't have the skills to be a true business partner and he will eliminate you (and your company) from his target list, because he will have other great offers from which to select.

The partnership model is simple and straightforward. As in the soccer dad story at the beginning of the chapter, two people meet and establish rapport. Typically, rapport building is established by having mutual friends, interests, activities, educational background, functional expertise, or industry experience. Through the rapport building, a mutual respect begins to develop. As the conversation shifts to the available position or the perceived need to create a position, the interviewer's agenda is to help the candidate present himself in the best possible light. (Note: If all candidates do this, the interviewer will have created a level playing field and will be able to select the best candidate for her company.) The most effective means of helping the candidate present well is to examine the candidate's skills, abilities, and experience, together with interest, motivation, energy, and overall fit, within the context of an open, stimulating, challenging business conversation. This requires a give and take in which each participant talks approximately 50 percent of the time. This style is equally effective if the candidate is savvy enough to draw out the company's needs and goals so he can present his ability to achieve the goals.

The advantage this style gives the interviewer is that from the very beginning, the interview is interactive and shows the candidate the utmost respect. An interactive style, as we have seen in the case studies, encourages bonding at a much deeper level than the question and answer format. This becomes evident as the interview proceeds and the candidate is much more receptive to the interviewer's sell because of the rapport that has been built.

> **INTERVIEW TIP**
>
> **RESPECT**
>
> Engaging in interactive conversation shows the candidate you care about his or her thoughts and ideas and demonstrates the utmost respect.

KEY PERSONAL CHARACTERISTICS

At first, the skills to be an outstanding partner seem to be part of each person's natural skill set. Studies show that the vast majority of us think that we relate to others easily and naturally. Many of us, however, do not have the strong relationship building skills we think we have. Those who partner well are able to "get outside themselves" and really focus on the other person. Being an excellent partner requires both intellect and a cluster of highly important personal characteristics. Thomas Jefferson, of all the presidents, is often credited with the best blend of intellect and personal characteristics. There is relatively little disagreement on representations

> **INTERVIEW TIP**
>
> **PROFESSIONAL AND PERSONAL CHARACTERISTICS**
>
> Professional characteristics (intelligence, skills and abilities, and experience) are the threshold competencies. Personal characteristics (strong people skills) represent long-term potential. Both are extremely important in an outstanding candidate.

of intellect. We can look at things like SAT scores, college attended, grades, or intelligence tests (or in Jefferson's case, inventions and writings).

Recently, social science has concentrated on defining and reaching agreement on the key elements that make people effective at connecting with others. Those characteristics are necessary to be an outstanding partner in an interview; they are especially necessary for the interviewer. Before examining these characteristics, let's look at what type of learning some people need to experience before they realize the importance of being an excellent partner.

Career Profile _____

The Big Ego

Jake was a big ego, hard-driving, goal-oriented, highly successful producer who had been promoted to a management position. Outside the office, he was excellent with customers and was highly regarded for his client service. Inside the office, however, he was brash and outspoken. While some people related to his style, others were totally turned off by it. Jake was convinced that he could "turn on the charm" any time he needed it. For a period of time Jake did not realize that anything was wrong. He was able to hire men and women to join his team. As business got tougher, however, Jake began to do some soul-searching and he had to admit that his hires were "B" and "C" players, not "A" players. His concern was confirmed one day when he was talking to a close friend about his problem. His friend indicated that he knew someone (an "A" player) who had interviewed with Jake. Jake asked whether his friend would ask the person about the interview. The report that came back to Jake was not encouraging. The woman's assessment was that under no circumstances would she work for him. She was succinct:

- I don't care how smart, well-educated, or successful you are. I want to work for a boss who treats me fairly and with respect.

- I want to work for a boss who believes that leadership is not domination, but the act of persuading people to work toward a common goal.

- I want to work for a boss who has a proven track record and is respected by senior management, peers, subordinates, and clients.

- I want to work for a boss who believes that he can be more successful if his people are highly successful and who believes in coaching, mentoring, and championing them.

Jake's friend suggested that he get some coaching on his management and interviewing styles.

What Jake learned through the process strengthened him immensely. Initially, it was difficult for him to understand that although concepts such as character, integrity, and fairness are not discussed openly in an interview, the outstanding candidate is perceptive enough to rate the interviewer on those traits by the time the interview is completed. The ratings are based on clusters of words (often a throwaway or offhand comment) and nonverbal signals (a look, shrug, or smile). The initial impression, if negative, is very difficult to overcome, just as interviewer's first impressions of a candidate are often difficult to overcome.

> **INTERVIEW TIP**
>
> **PARTNERSHIP POTENTIAL**
>
> Demonstrate character, integrity, and fairness through your interview behavior. The outstanding candidate will evaluate whether you have the potential to be an excellent business partner.

Let's now turn to what Jake learned. Social science research points to a set of characteristics that enable outstanding interviewers to form partnerships with great candidates. They are:

1. Highest character-integrity and maturity.

2. Self-awareness—being observant about what we feel and exercising self-control.

3. Being centered—balanced with strong business ethics and values.

4. Strong people skills—empathy, graciousness, and the ability to read a social situation.

5. Team oriented—respects others and builds mutual trust; develops partnerships by helping others grow and develop.

6. Consultative—listens for understanding and problem solving and articulates visions clearly; seeks creative and imaginative solutions.

7. Optimism—positive, self-confident and persuasive; has enormous energy and the ability to energize and invigorate others.

8. Leadership—remarkable people orientation; intelligent, decisive, known to set and meet aggressive targets; client-centered with a passion for excellence.

The characteristics cannot be turned on and off but represent the fiber of the person. You'll see in the next section that it is a word here or a look there that makes the difference. As you read about the characteristics you might ask yourself, "When I have to make a critical hire, one that will have a major impact on my career, who do I want on my interview team?"

> **INTERVIEW TIP**
>
> **CREDIBILITY**
>
> Think carefully about the answer to this question: "When I have to make a critical hire, one that will have a major impact on my career, who do I want on my interview team?"

THE EIGHT CHARACTERISTICS OF OUTSTANDING INTERVIEWERS

1. Highest Character-Integrity and Maturity

Sandy had been interviewing for some time with a small, highly regarded executive search firm. She and Chuck, the owner of the firm, had known each other for years. They had done business together and gained respect for one another and now Chuck wanted her to join as a partner of the firm. Two critical issues remained in Sandy's mind: her overall comfort with the executive search industry and whether Chuck was really ready to enter a partnership and give up some of the equity in his firm. The negotiations were reaching the critical stage when Sandy would have to resolve the first issue and Chuck, the second.

Sandy and Chuck set another meeting to discuss their thoughts. During the social conversation when they first sat down, they began to talk about the philosophy of filling a search. Chuck said, "I've always thought about search as a puzzle. We are trying to help organizations fill a critical need with the best person available, and help the individual find a career niche that is the right fit to drive his or her career." That comment was a perfect opening for Sandy. She asked Chuck if that wasn't a very idealized view of the process and mentioned a few horror stories she had heard of people who were railroaded into positions that sidetracked their careers.

"Yes, I guess it is," said Chuck. "But I absolutely believe that is the mission. The business is like any other in that you try to hit a home run every time you come up to bat, but it doesn't always happen." Sandy asked how Chuck's firm tried to prevent poor matches. Chuck told Sandy that their philosophy was based on quality service, and not quantity, which required understanding the organization's needs in detail, then deciding whether it was a realistic search before the firm would accept the assignment. Once accepted, they worked until they found the agreed-upon quality candidates, even if it took longer than anticipated. Sandy again asked about the firm's responsibility for placing a candidate in the wrong job. Chuck's response was straightforward, "We do the best job we can, but we only meet a candidate for a limited time. We can't know as much as the individual does about his or her own career goals. All candidates need to do the due diligence to decide if a position is right for them." Sandy was very comfortable with Chuck's philosophy.

Sandy and Chuck still needed to resolve the percentage of ownership issue. At one point Chuck admitted to Sandy that he was having a very difficult time with the issue. Sandy told Chuck that she appreciated his concern and understood that it was a difficult issue, but that she was not prepared to leave her job unless Chuck was willing to give up some ownership. She asked if Chuck needed more time to decide if he really wanted to move forward with her. His answer was an unqualified "No"; he was ready.

At that point Sandy made the suggestion that Chuck call his attorney, Ralph, to see if he would be willing to help them talk through the issues. Sandy had met Ralph once and found him to be an excellent businessman as well as attorney and thought that he might be able to remove the emotion from the situation. Ralph helped them to value the business, examine the added value that Sandy could bring by managing another office, and eventually discuss all their issues. In three meetings they were able to come to a resolution. Chuck handled himself with great integrity and maturity throughout the negotiation, eliminating any last doubts that Sandy had about his willingness to accept and work with a partner. She excitedly accepted the job.

2. Self-Awareness—Being Observant about What We Feel and Exercising Self-Control

Tony knew that as a teenager he had had problems with self-control when he was under great pressure. While he had learned to control a lot of that behavior as he got older, some traces still remained. This carried over to interviews, where he found himself becoming combative if he felt he was being challenged by a candidate. Instead of giving the candidate the benefit of the doubt by assuming a missed communication, he would respond as someone who had been backed into a corner. Candidates would then pull back into a shell and merely respond to his questions rather than react in a proactive manner. There would be no further risk taking on the candidate's part and the interactive flow of the meeting would be changed markedly. Over time,

Tony was proud that he had learned to curb this behavior. His maturity had led to three promotions and, recently, to a director title. Tony also knew, however, that he had to remain aware of the old tendencies; he tried to take steps to prevent problems from surfacing.

As Tony looked at his calendar he realized that the next day he was scheduled to meet Ahmad, a candidate his firm had been trying to recruit for about five months. That night one of his direct reports called with an emergency in his business unit. It took time that night and the next morning to straighten out the problem. By that time, Tony was late getting started to work and he had a number of issues to resolve to help his direct report when he arrived at work. In addition, he hadn't had an opportunity to study Ahmad's candidate profile. The interview team did an excellent job of building a candidate profile that was extremely helpful when evaluating a candidate's potential.

In prior years, Tony would have hurried to arrive as close to the scheduled time as possible and would have struggled through the interview while his mind was on other issues. Typically under those circumstances, Tony would fall back into the old pattern of causing one of two problems. First, he might feel challenged and react as he had previously. Second, he might be preoccupied and unable to listen attentively and then blame the lack of fit on the candidate. When Tony first recognized this pattern in his behavior, he was able to gather information about his interviewing record with prior candidates. He discovered that no candidate who had the misfortune of interviewing with him under those circumstances had ever progressed further.

Armed with this knowledge, he called ahead to see if the interview schedule could be adjusted. Indeed, due to the fact that Ahmad was to see four interviewers that day, it was possible for him to meet Ahmad at 2 P.M. By then Tony had a chance to review Ahmad's credentials, speak with the other interviewers (they liked him a lot), and catch up on his business affairs. Tony and Ahmad had a great meeting. Shortly thereafter Ahmad was offered and accepted a job.

3. Being Centered—Balanced with Strong Business Ethics and Values

Ralph and Michelle were completing an hour-long interview, the twelfth that Michelle had at the law firm. She was clearly in demand, the number one student at one of the nation's best law schools. In addition, she was personable and seemed to have great potential in business development. Before she left Ralph's office she asked him a question: "Would you mind telling me why you spent so much time on the subject of how I would evaluate the success of my work?" Ralph smiled and told Michelle she was astute in recognizing what he was doing. He explained there were two reasons.

First, it gave him insight into the person's intellect and the motivations and drive they bring to the legal profession. Michelle looked at him. Ralph said, "How people evaluate their success gives insight into their personal motivations. For example, one person may say that she wants to be the highest gross revenue producer in the firm and make a lot of money; a second person may say that he wants to service client's needs and help them to achieve their objectives; and a third person may say that he is an excellent account manager with the ability to cross-sell the firm's products and he has the ability to manage a law firm with over one hundred lawyers."

Michelle then asked Ralph about the second reason. Ralph told Michelle, "When you begin to examine with people what motivates and drives them, you can't help but gain insight into their ethics and values." Michelle was obviously intrigued by Ralph's approach. She asked, "But isn't it difficult to get at someone's ethics or values in a one-hour interview?" "You bet," he responded, "but it is better to do your best and find out all you can. Interviewing isn't a perfect science, but you can find out a lot with a few probing questions, followed by the willingness to listen carefully to the candidate's answers and to use your intuitive abilities to look for the many verbal and nonverbal signs that tell you what you need to know."

Michelle forgot about the interview and was intrigued by the question. "How do you get at that information?" she asked. Ralph responded, "I tried to give you a few thought-provoking questions, such as: 1. How would you handle a dispute in which a client directly challenged the number of billable hours you charged? 2. Under what circumstances would you turn down a piece of profitable business? 3. Can you give me an instance when your goals and your client's goals might differ and how you would go about attempting to resolve the situation?"

Michelle asked Ralph what he had learned about her. Ralph laughed and said, "You clearly have the ethics and values upon which our firm was built. You are interested in building a reputation based on outstanding service to clients, and that is what we look for in entry-level associates. You are certainly the kind of associate we are looking for, and I think you could have a long and successful career with our organization." Michelle was impressed. No one else spent that kind of time on the subject of ethics and values. That discussion was critical in helping her to decide that she wanted to work with Ralph and Ralph's firm.

4. Strong People Skills—Empathy, Graciousness, and the Ability to Read a Social Situation

Kumiko was Gwen's sponsor in the interview process and she was confident that Gwen would do as well in her tenth, eleventh, and twelfth interviews as she had done in the first nine. She knew that these interviews represented the last round and that they were with individuals who would be keys to Gwen's success. Kumiko greeted Gwen and walked her to the interview with Malcolm. As Kumiko left she felt a twinge. Gwen seemed a little more quiet and reserved than on previous meetings. The feeling left quickly as Kumiko faced the tasks of the day. An hour later she headed back to take Gwen to her next interview.

As Gwen and Malcolm finished their conversation, Malcolm asked if he could see Kumiko for a moment. Kumiko asked

Gwen to wait for her in reception and she went to see Malcolm. He was blunt and told Kumiko, "You were thorough in giving us the summary of Gwen's background, skills, and abilities and a brief personality sketch. I must tell you that I did not see the person you described. She was shy and quiet, definitely not extroverted and outgoing, as has proven successful in our sales representatives." Kumiko remembered the sensation she had an hour earlier. Her intuition, and Malcolm's comments, told her that something was up.

She thanked Malcolm and went back to Gwen. She sat down and asked if everything was okay. Gwen responded, "Sure, why?" Kumiko told her about her initial feeling and then about Malcolm's comments. As Gwen looked at Kumiko her eyes filled with tears. She explained that her father had died five years ago and last night her mother, who had been feeling ill, was diagnosed with cancer. She had been at the hospital most of the night checking her in and establishing a game plan with the doctors.

Kumiko didn't hesitate in telling Gwen she was sorry about her mother and that she should be with her. "But I need the job," Gwen protested. Kumiko responded, "You'll have plenty of time to win a job. I'll retrigger your round of interviews once you get your personal responsibilities under control. Now go and be with your mother." Initially, Gwen didn't want to go, but with Kumiko's gentle insistence she left to be with her mother. Kumiko did exactly what she said she would. She explained what had happened to Malcolm and he immediately said, "Just forget about today. Have her come back to see me when she is ready." The other interviewers were equally willing to reschedule. When Gwen came back, she was the person Kumiko described. She exhibited the outgoing, positive personality the earlier interviewers had met. Everyone thought she was great and an offer was made shortly after the interviews. Gwen never forgot the kindness. When she had three excellent offers from outstanding organizations in front of her, she had no difficulty deciding that she wanted to work for Kumiko.

5. Team Oriented—Respects Others and Builds Mutual Trust; Develops Partnerships by Helping Others Grow and Develop

As Beth interviewed for the position, she knew that the head of client service for global custody products would have to be able to build, train, and motivate a strong global team, because many of the firm's largest clients needed to be serviced around the world. She also knew that this firm had a reputation as a difficult place to enter from the outside. These represented red flags to her.

Beth found herself evaluating Dave's management style every chance she got, because Dave would be her potential boss, his office would be next to hers at headquarters, and he would be her guide. She knew that her relationship with him would be critical, especially in the beginning, until she could get her feet on the ground. If he was a team player who would mentor her as she learned the job territory and help her to learn the strengths and weaknesses of her direct reports around the world, then she would have a chance to succeed. If he had a sink-or-swim mentality, then she could fail.

The critical interaction came during their fourth meeting, when they really got into management style. When Beth asked Dave how he characterized his style, he said, "Beth, I view the relationship we would have as a team venture. You could not be successful here without a lot of help and mentoring in the beginning. You'd have to learn the personalities and how to deal with them internally while learning about the clients and their needs externally. You also know how lean an organization we are.

Consequently, I'd expect you to assimilate information quickly, learn where and how you could add value, and become independent as quickly as possible. Our relationship would then be one of partners. I'd expect you to run the area, and to know when to involve me and to what degree. I need strong business-people on my team, not 'yes' people. And I'd expect you to handle your own people in the same way."

Beth liked what Dave had to say and it seemed to fit with the reference checks she had received. She knew she would have to continue to test what Dave was telling her about his management style with the reality of what it was like to work for him on a day-to-day basis. This could only be done by interviewing with Dave's direct and indirect reports. Fortunately, Dave's company believed in holding numerous interviews before making a decision about a candidate.

By the time Beth had been through the 14 required interviews she had convinced herself that Dave was for real. The interviews gave her an opportunity to test what Dave had told her about his management style with people who reported to him. His reports gave him high marks. Beth believed that there was an excellent chance that she could be successful and find a new home with Dave's company. She accepted Dave's offer and eagerly joined his team.

6. Consultative—Listens for Understanding and Problem Solving and Articulates Visions Clearly; Seeks Creative and Imaginative Solutions

Suzanne couldn't have been happier with her career. Two years ago she had been promoted to chief information officer for a major insurance company in the Northwest. She had over 1,000 people in her group and she got along outstandingly well with her boss, her direct reports, and her staff. In addition, she had developed a great reputation in the industry, was well paid, received excellent bonuses, and had outstanding stock options, retirement, and other benefits.

When the executive search consultant called, Suzanne was polite but short, telling him that she was not interested. The consultant asked if he could just tell her about the job in case she knew someone who might be interested. He described a job that was much like her own except for two things: the business that she would service had more breadth than her current situation, and it was in Dallas. Suzanne was born and raised in Dallas; her parents and all of her brothers and sisters and their families lived there. Suzanne's work had taken her to various cities throughout the country, but none even close to home. Suzanne thought about it for a few days and then called the consultant back to say she would like to have exploratory conversations.

Ted, the chief financial officer, couldn't have been happier. He had been trying for months to recruit a successor to the current chief information officer so he could retire, and Suzanne had all the credentials. The search consultant was candid when he told Ted that this represented a long shot at best. Ted formed his best interview team and prepared them extremely well before Suzanne came. When she visited it took no time for mutual respect to develop. After the first day of interviewing, Suzanne told Ted she was intrigued by the opportunity and the chance to come home, but that she really had difficulty thinking about leaving her current team. In addition, there would be a number of personal issues. Ted asked what they were and Suzanne told him the key issues would be:

- her compensation, and what would happen to her stock options;
- her husband had a good job in financial services;
- her children were 14 and 10 and she was concerned about moving the 14-year-old at this time.

Suzanne did indicate, however, that she would be willing to come back to meet the CEO and others in the organization.

In the time between meetings, Ted worked feverishly on each of the three issues Suzanne had identified. He spoke with the CEO and eventually reached agreement that if he thought Suzanne was as outstanding as he had been told, he would offer her an increase over her current compensation and would negotiate to pay her for some portion of her lost stock options as well as keep her pension whole. Ted mobilized his staff to identify the best career consulting firm in Dallas and paid them up front to do some research on the most likely targets in financial services together with the names, addresses, and telephone numbers of those people. He also put them on notice that they might have a candidate. He had his relocation team identify communities with outstanding public school systems and they lined up top real estate brokers in each town. They also identified the top three to five private schools for Suzanne's consideration and notified them that they might have a visitor.

After a series of meetings, all of which went extremely well, Suzanne and Ted sat down to talk about the possibility of reaching an agreement. The CEO thought Suzanne was perfect, so Ted had no problem offering a large increase in base salary, a bonus potential, and a buyout for three-quarters of her stock options. A generous relocation package was offered. Suzanne was shocked at the amount of work Ted's team was able to do for her husband and appreciated the offer for career transition services. She was also thankful for the information about the schools, although she knew that she would want to live in the same town as her parents. The kindness that most impressed Suzanne, however, was none of these. When Ted offered to send her two children back to the Northwest to see their friends two times each of the first two years, it showed an amazing sensitivity to what Suzanne perceived as an important issue. The fact that Ted listened, heard the concern, and tried to help in a creative manner was a major consideration in helping Suzanne decide this was the job for her.

7. Optimism—Positive, Self-Confident, and Persuasive; Has Enormous Energy and the Ability to Energize and Invigorate Others

George was excited about the magnitude and scope of the job that was being offered to him, the chief operating officer of the U.S. office of a well-known German financial services firm. On one hand, he was proud and flattered that he was regarded so highly; on the other hand, he was apprehensive about his ability to be successful. His concern was not with his own skills but whether it would be possible to work with the CEO. Don had been in his CEO role for about one year. He was positive, outgoing, charismatic, and an absolute dynamo, with worldwide responsibility for two businesses in addition to full responsibility for all the business in the U.S. His duties had increased dramatically in the last year. In addition to his normal responsibilities he was engaged in a major culture change, helping the organization transition from an old-line, somewhat stodgy, reactive organization to a more proactive, aggressive one. George knew that his role would require him to be right behind Don, understanding his vision and implementing the plans.

George and Don genuinely liked one another, which was a great starting point. George agreed in principle with what Don was trying to accomplish and the manner in which he was enacting his plans. He had always been acclaimed to have incredible energy, but he wasn't sure it would be possible to accomplish the agenda that Don had defined for his organization. George's logical side told him that he better do significantly more due diligence, so he asked Don if he could meet his direct reports and some other members of the staff.

Each time George met a new person, he heard much the same story. He was told that when Don first joined the company, the person was highly skeptical of him and his agenda. Soon Don was leading the charge and everyone was drawn along. Don was so positive, so optimistic, and so energized that it invigorated everyone else. During each meeting, George would be told that old-timers in the organization couldn't believe what Don had been able to accomplish. The reaction of senior executives in Germany was to heap more responsibility upon Don. Those meetings convinced George that Don was positive and a real leader, but he still wasn't convinced that they could partner together.

Don was as astute and intuitive as he was positive and outgoing, and he sensed that George still was not totally convinced, so he asked him to work on a project with him. Don had some work to do with the sales force in Asia that would take about a week. George was relieved and thought it would be a great way for him to see Don in action; he eagerly accepted the assignment.

On the plane, Don laid out his agenda for George. He gave George little direction in how he could add value. The agenda and the objectives were ambitious for one week. As soon as they arrived, Don was like a whirling dervish, moving from project to project at the speed of light. He created positive energy, excitement, and enthusiasm wherever he went, but left many of the details unfinished. George quickly assessed that it was in this area that Don needed the most assistance. His style was proactive, so he worked hard and had a great deal of fun. On the way home Don told him he had done a great job. There were one or two things that Don would have done differently but, in general, he was highly complimentary. George didn't need to wait until he got home to make a decision. He told Don that his positive, outgoing, can-do personality was an absolute pleasure and he looked forward to working with him.

8. Leadership—Remarkable People Orientation; Intelligent, Decisive, Known to Set and Meet Aggressive Targets; Client-Centered with a Passion for Excellence

Frank knew the score as he sat in front of the master. Charlie was only a few years from retirement and he had almost become a legend during his working career. He was, purely and simply, the best salesman in the computer industry. Charlie knew the marketplace better than anyone and was intimately involved with the products, having full knowledge of their strengths and weaknesses. What separated him from the rest, however, was his incredible passion for product excellence and client service. This reputation, built over four decades, enabled Charlie to transact the most complex and profitable business for his firm.

Given what Frank knew, this interview seemed like a no-brainer. Charlie only accepted two associates a year to work in his group, and Frank was clearly on the way to an offer. He would be the envy of his graduating class at the University of Chicago if he landed this assignment. But Frank knew it wasn't going to be that easy. The remarkable people orientation that Charlie demonstrated when he was in front of a client was well known. Indeed, friend and foe alike indicated that Charlie had no peer in this situation. His market knowledge combined with his intelligence and problem-solving abilities were unmatched.

Once he sold the business, however, and came back to put a delivery team together, there was a different Charlie. Off came the sales hat and on went the general's hat, along with incredible time and energy demands on his associates. He often had associates work seven days a week or 24 hours a day during peak demand for a project. This part did not bother Frank in the least. He didn't finish number one in his class because he was afraid to work. Quite the opposite; in fact, he had to pull all-nighters for his studies as often as he might have to for Charlie's projects.

Frank's concern had more to do with his personality and Charlie's style. Charlie was known to be a tyrant with his associates. He ordered them around as if they were indentured servants and barked and shouted at them like he was an officer dealing with his troops during battle. To make matters worse, rather than mellowing as he got older, he was becoming more cantankerous. Frank had learned during his 26 years that that was not the best work style for him. He had learned the hard way that asking for justification or even a "why" sometimes had dire consequences for him with some professors during his academic experience. Frank knew that he sometimes issued the challenge prior to his internal governor stopping him, and that could be a serious problem with this boss.

Charlie couldn't have been more charming during the interview. He clearly had on the sales hat and he knew that Frank was a prize catch. Afterward, Frank did a great deal of due diligence. He spoke with a number of Charlie's former associates. What he discovered corroborated what he had learned previously. Charlie was even more difficult to live with now than he had been some years ago. Frank also learned, however, that in terms of his abilities, Charlie was still as formidable as ever. What Frank could learn would be invaluable for the rest of his career. The "calling card" of having worked for Charlie would be worthwhile in itself.

Frank understood his dilemma. He contacted a former University of Chicago classmate and Charlie's current associate and asked if they could have coffee. At the critical point in the discussion, Vanessa said to him, "Look, I wasn't comfortable with his style either. I had the background to be able to select a boss whose interpersonal style would be more enjoyable for me. But when I looked at everything he had to offer, I convinced myself that once in a while someone is so successful that person is worth the negatives. Besides, I decided I would give it one or two years and then, if it didn't work out, I would leave, yet still be stronger for the experience. To my amazement, he has been much more pleasant than anything I had heard. The other associates and I are asking each other whether he has secretly mellowed or whether we were so well-prepared that almost any behavior would seem better than we expected. We think that we have the best of all worlds." Frank thanked Vanessa and as he thought about her comments, he decided it was the right decision for him as well. That meeting, more than any other, helped him decide to accept the offer.

> **INTERVIEW TIP**
>
> **CHALLENGING WORK**
>
> A great candidate must be offered work that is challenging and visible and that will increase his or her skills, abilities, and marketability.

SUMMARY

The key components in building a partnership and creating a win/win approach with the best candidates are:

- Build rapport with the candidate (the "falling in love" process). If the interviewer and candidate "fall in love," all aspects of the interview are viewed more positively and the chances of landing the outstanding candidate dramatically increase.

- Establish an interactive, stimulating (50 percent talk each) conversation. An interview is the most exciting, stimulating, and fun when it remains interactive from start to finish.

This style shows great respect for the candidate and establishes the best framework for the sell.

■ Evaluate the candidate's skills and abilities, interest and motivation, and fit. Gather enough information to decide whether the candidate's overall package is an excellent fit with the culture of your company.

■ Allow the candidate to test his or her candidacy and overcome any objections you have. Discussing your concerns while you are together levels the playing field by giving each candidate an opportunity to present at his or her best. It allows you to make the best choice for your organization.

■ Select interview team members who demonstrate the characteristics of a great partner. The characteristics include:

- ■ highest character,
- ■ self-awareness,
- ■ being centered,
- ■ strong people skills,
- ■ team-oriented,
- ■ consultative,
- ■ optimistic,
- ■ leadership skills.

STEP

Create Effective Interview Strategy and Tactics

"Will this conversation go any better than the last?" Peter wondered as he paused to pick up the stick that the dog had enthusiastically dumped at his feet. When he and Sheila had tried to deal with the topic 10 days ago, she had become prickly as she nailed him with a barrage of questions, and then silence. Now, as the two of them walked along Long Island Sound on this February afternoon, Peter acknowledged that she had reason to be prickly. She had worked hard to establish herself in the architectural firm she joined five years ago and, just in the last year, the firm's partners had recognized her talent for innovative design. The assignments that had begun to come her way were exciting, especially the project for a new wing in a local museum. It mattered greatly to both of them that Sam and Ali were doing well in school and that Sam was reaching impressive levels in his junior development hockey program, thanks to a spectacular coach.

However, there seemed to be somewhat of a truce as Sheila offered him a small smile when she said, "Why don't you try again to explain why you want this new job so badly?" She listened intently as he delineated the reasons why the prospects of being the first outsider to head up a family-owned winery in California was such a provocative challenge. It intrigued her when he said, "Within five years the ownership I receive will guarantee our family security throughout our retirement and create some wealth for Sam and Ali." As they walked back toward the car, Peter and Sheila had come to an agreement that if the search firm continued their conversation with Peter, Sheila would keep an open mind about the potential changes in their lives.

Five days later, Peter was sitting in an airport restaurant, open to a concourse that surged with passengers and airport personnel. Hardly the perfect environment for an in-depth, critical interview, Peter mused wryly. Yet his two-hour meeting with Hank had been great, for a number of reasons. Within the first few minutes of the interview, Peter had totally forgotten the surroundings because Hank had been masterful at creating a relaxed atmosphere. He sat close to Peter without invading his personal space, leaned slightly forward in his seat, and listened intently as Peter spoke. Almost immediately, they began to speak about people they knew in common in the wine and spirits industry, giving Peter a sense that Hank really knew the industry. Hank was very comfortable to remain in this mode for some time and Peter realized later that Hank was evaluating him by asking who mentored him, who befriended him, and who reported to him.

When Hank wanted to change the direction of the meeting to a more traditional business discussion, he did it seamlessly. He waited until they were talking about an individual whom they both respected and who was incredibly accomplished at handling people. At an appropriate time Hank said, "Tell me about an accomplishment in your business life in the last three years that shows how you deal with people, Peter."

Peter gave what he thought was a very credible answer that involved changing the culture of his division. Hank listened attentively as Peter described the circumstances and the new programs that he initiated. Hank asked about the effect of the program on individuals in the organization and how Peter dealt with each person. He wanted to know, in detail, how Peter knew enough about each key person to understand which parts of the cultural change he or she embraced and which parts troubled them. Peter told Hank that he enjoyed learning about people and interacting with them. He remembered telling Hank that he thought that psychology had been an excellent major for him in learning to deal with diverse people. He knew that the reason Hank was spending so much time on this subject was that there were vast personality differences among the members of the family at the California winery.

When it was appropriate, Peter said, "Hank, this has been an interesting dialogue and you have been kind enough to tell me that I clearly have the skills to perform successfully. But my question is, What are the chances that an outsider will be able to come in and survive as the first professional CEO in this family-owned business?" Hank looked at Peter for a long moment and then responded, "I don't know." At that moment Hank's credibility rose dramatically in Peter's mind. That question led to a wonderful discussion about the family and how the patriarch and each of the key family members realized they were going to need help if they were to take the business to the next level. Peter could bring skills they just didn't have. It was also fortuitous that Peter, at 42 years old, fell right between the patriarch's age and the age of the children who might have a desire to run the business.

Since Peter was well aware of the problems in taking the company to the next level, was aware of the potential problems in working in a family-owned business, and had a wife and family who weren't at all sure they wanted to move, he pulled no punches with Hank. He told him that his accepting the job was a long shot at best and that he needed to establish a plan to do a significant amount of due diligence on the company and the family. To his surprise, Hank said, "This is not a traditional search. I can tell you that the California family is very interested in you. You can do all the due diligence you want because it will give them a chance to interact with you and evaluate the fit as well. Obviously, Sheila is going to need to spend some time in California to see if she could be happy there." They agreed upon a plan at the meeting.

When Peter accepted the position three months later, he credited Hank with doing an outstanding job of facilitating the business partnership. Hank had:

- Created optimum situations for Peter and each member of the family to meet, get to know one another, build rapport, and eventually bond.

- Staged Peter's meetings with screening and hiring interviewers in a way that Peter and each family member felt equally valued.

- Provided each family member with a complete profile and some interview training before they met Peter.

- Treated Peter with the utmost respect during their meetings.

- Formed a partnership in the interviews that felt like two senior executives conducting a business discussion and not a question-and-answer grilling.

- Closed each meeting professionally by outlining the next steps that would take place and implementing the plan.

- Informed the family of each of Peter's major concerns and made sure they were addressed.

- Negotiated professionally on behalf of the family while treating Peter fairly.

INTRODUCTION

To this point, we have been analyzing and evaluating the job interview strategically to understand your goals and how to achieve them. We have taken a macro view to focus on your need to determine which candidate demonstrates:

- The best skills and abilities to complete the job successfully;

- Passion for the job, including the energy to perform at the necessary level; and

- The highest probability of fitting in with your people.

Since great interviewing is about forging partnerships, we have also focused on the softer issues of concern to both you and the candidate. They include:

- Showing the candidate respect is critical to your success.
- Developing rapport needs to occur throughout the relationship.
- Creating a stimulating and enjoyable interview by making it interactive is important.
- Enabling each of you to accomplish your goals through an interactive interview is critical.
- Selling effectively so that when the candidate joins the firm she is excited to be your partner.

In this chapter we examine successful ways to accomplish these tasks at a tactical, as well as strategic, level. We begin by looking at the screening and hiring interview, to understand some of the challenges that face each set of interviewers and how the partnership model can be applied in each instance. We have discussed that one of your responsibilities as the interviewer is to help each candidate achieve peak performance.

In both screening and hiring interviews, rapport building, the job content phase, and the close are wonderful opportunities for the savvy interviewer. Rapport building sets the stage for the entire interview. It is a great opportunity for you to help level the playing field for candidates who are less comfortable at the beginning of the interview. In the job content phase, questioning is the engine that opens the doors to stimulating conversation and draws out information for decision making. The level of conversation is directly attributable to the interviewer. The close provides opportunities for the interviewer to observe the candidate's behavior in overcoming organizational concerns and to evaluate the thoughtfulness of the questions she asks about the organization.

The answers to the candidate's questions also become a challenge to the interview team. They need to be well-conceived and consistent. Consistency is a function of preparation, which means that the interview team has to have prepared answers in advance of the interviews. Finally, there are many tactical considerations around the topics of the number of interviews a candidate should have, the maximum in one day, the time of day, and the day of the week.

SCREENING INTERVIEWS

The screening process is sometimes incorrectly viewed as preliminary to, and less important than, the hiring process. This is simply not the case. The hiring process is predicated on having a highly talented pool of candidates. While screening is often conducted by a different team of interviewers, they play a crucial role in the ultimate quality of the successful hire. Think of the process of filling a role in a play. Rather than merely seeking a female actress who has a beautiful singing voice, the fully prepared screener knows that the director needs a female actress between 20 and 30 years old with a beautiful singing voice, who is an excellent dancer with great stamina, who is a team player with her fellow actors, and who can convince an audience that she is deeply in love with the leading male. Obviously, the producer can make a better selection in a shorter period of time if the five final candidates all have the full set of qualifications.

The screening interview is clearly a preliminary step, one in which the candidate must prove herself, but there are some significant obligations on the part of the organization. If the interviews involve students about to graduate, the college expects that the administration of the program will be handled professionally, the students will be treated well and valued, there will be communication quickly as to whether they will receive a company interview, and the college rules regarding recruiting will be followed.

The interview is usually conducted on the college campus (for BA and advanced degree candidates) and is normally 30 to 45 minutes in length. It is seen as technically based and content driven. The primary focus is to test the candidate for the threshold competencies that we have been discussing; namely, that the candidate has the intelligence, knowledge, skills, abilities, and experience to perform successfully. However, the interview team is limited to selecting only a few of the candidates for an at-the-company interview. In order to make those tough decisions, the screening interviewers have to examine personal characteristics to determine the candidates' passion for the work, including their energy and drive, and their ability to fit the culture and style of the company.

The problem facing the screening interviewers is obvious but complex. Although the focus of the screening interview is more technical and content-oriented, it is critical to begin the process of building a partnership. This involves showing the candidate respect, helping her to feel valued, and building a bond. How is this done? By being aware and by looking for every opportunity to connect. It starts right at the beginning by helping the candidate to relax and feel comfortable. This is necessary even if it is your eighth and last interview of the day. Let's look at some additional ways that screening interviewers can make the interview feel like a partnership.

Once the rapport building ends, explain the process to the candidate. By helping the candidate to understand your agenda, you can get buy-in and the interview will seem more personal. You might say, "Today, my primary purpose is to learn about your academic training, skills and abilities, and experience and your interest in joining our company and industry. That will mean spending most of our time discussing your academic background and job experience. I'll save a few minutes at the end of the meeting to answer any immediate questions you may have. Then if you interview at our company, there will be plenty of time to answer all your questions. Do you have any questions or concerns before we start?"

It is also helpful to remember that this may be the most important interview the candidate has ever had. She may have wanted to work for your company for her entire life. If a mutual interest, friend, or activity surfaces at any time in the interview, take the time to discuss it, if only for only a few moments. These are opportunities for bonding to occur and for the candidate to leave the interview with the feeling that a connection occurred.

Another opportunity develops when you ask a question that surprises the candidate or when the candidate doesn't understand what the question has to do with the position. In this instance, taking a moment to explain why you are asking the question both helps the candidate and builds rapport. You might say, "I know it seems a little strange for me to ask about your interest in music, but you know about the strong connection between music and mathematics. That is what I'm trying to pursue." You can also give the candidate time to formulate her answer. In this way, silence can help both of you to achieve your goals.

The close is a great opportunity to bond, even though the time is short. Taking the time to answer questions is a sign of respect. By this time in the interview, you will have a sense of whether this individual is likely to be invited back to the company or will be in the "might be asked back" group. If this is the case, it may be possible to extend the interview 5 to 10 minutes to answer a few more of the candidate's questions. Finally, although it seems obvious, tell the candidate that you have really enjoyed meeting her. If you can specifically refer to one of her accomplishments as being distinctive, it will go a long way toward rapport building. And remember to wish her well.

HIRING INTERVIEWS

The hiring interview is an extension of the screening process, and those candidates who are deemed to be the closest match to the Ideal Success Profile are invited to the company site. Thus the talent pool has been reduced and the best of the best remain. This is no longer about the candidate proving herself, but is about finding the best fit for the company and the candidate. The hiring interviewers usually include the hiring manager, potential colleagues, recruiters, and senior managers in the division.

The Head of Recruiting arranges the recruiting schedule in order to accommodate the executives and the candidates in the most efficient manner. For new graduates, this usually translates to a recruiting day at the company site when a series of candidates come in and have multiple interviews. The number of interviews varies but four to six or even eight is not unusual. Lunch might be scheduled with a younger member of the staff, possibly from the same school as the candidate. This provides an effective break from the interviewing routine and an opportunity for the candidate to ask questions of someone who recently made the transition. Often the day ends with a get-together and an opportunity for everyone to mix socially.

This interview is usually longer than the screening interview, 45 to 60 minutes, so there is time for the hiring interviewers to allow for bonding. Instead of a very short rapport-building period, the interviewer will have more time to concentrate on the personal contacts, interests, and activities of the candidate. At the conclusion of the rapport building, the interviewer will want to let the candidate know that the change to the business portion of the meeting is coming. A comment such as, "I've really enjoyed getting to know a little about you. Now I'd like to discuss your business (or academic) career," accomplishes the goal. The interviewer will normally test some of the same content that was accomplished at the screening interview, to justify that the candidate has the intellect, skills, and abilities to perform successfully. Then the interviewer will move smoothly and effortlessly to the way in which the candidate prefers to use personal characteristics in the work setting (style). Throughout the conversation, the interviewer will be making value judgments concerning the candidate's ability to fit in the culture of the company. As in the screening interview, the manner in which you handle candidate questions and the close will go a long way toward determining whether the candidate will want to be your partner.

When interviewers meet candidates with experience, an interesting thing happens. There is usually very little of the due diligence to test whether the individual has the necessary intellect, skills, and abilities. Presumably, this is because the candidate has a number of years of business experience and it might be embarrassing to the candidate, or the interviewer, if time were spent on skills and abilities. After all, if she was successful for a number of years at Ford Motor Company, then surely she has the skills to be successful. This is the wrong thought process. The question should be, "Are we better off hiring this experienced person or a newly graduated individual with great potential?" Once again, it is the role of the head of the interview team to be sure that the team is balanced and that there is concern for technical skills and abilities as well as personal skills and fit. One easy and efficient way to balance the team is to have each interviewer concentrate on one of the success characteristics, in addition to conducting an overall evaluation of the candidate.

It is critical that by the time the candidate leaves the hiring interview, she is convinced that she wants to be your business partner. She will need to feel equally good about each interviewer she has met, hence the need for great consistency. Each person must have treated her with respect and conveyed a feeling that they would love to have her join the team. The same behavior will need to be in evidence for the duration of the decision-making process, whether that takes a few weeks or a few months.

Earlier we mentioned that one of your responsibilities is to help the candidate achieve peak performance in the interview. In both screening and hiring interviews, rapport building, the job content phase, and the close are wonderful opportunities for the interviewer. Let's look at each of these in more detail.

> **INTERVIEW TIP**
>
> **SCREENING AND HIRING INTERVIEWS**
>
> Screening interviewers test for threshold competencies. Hiring interviewers select the candidate who is the best fit within the culture of the company and who has great long-term potential.

CONDUCTING THE INTERVIEW

What are the critical behaviors that the great interviewer needs to demonstrate when interviewing the outstanding candidate? At the beginning of the interview, let us repeat again, it is critical to establish a partnership environment where candidate and interviewer participate in a stimulating, exciting business conversation to determine whether there is an excellent match between the company's needs and the candidate's skills and interests.

It should be evident to the candidate that the interviewer has a clear agenda and he is confident and comfortable in the interviewing role. This confidence is a signal to the candidate that she doesn't have to be concerned with assisting the interviewer in keeping a conversational flow to the interview. The interviewer will handle it. The candidate only has the responsibility to uphold her end of the partnership. The confidence that this builds in the candidate helps to strengthen rapport between candidate and interviewer and conveys a tone of professionalism to the interview.

The interviewer's self-confidence and comfort level may seem like a small point but it is, in fact, huge. First impressions are as important in the candidate's evaluation of the interviewer as in the interviewer's evaluation of the candidate. When the interviewer demonstrates professionalism, the bonding that occurs is stronger and the psychological impact lasts as the candidate wrestles days or weeks later with accepting your offer versus an offer from one of your competitors.

Part of the interviewer's self-confidence is due to having a clear and concise agenda for the meeting. An outline looks like this:

Interview Format

Rapport Building

Establish/Confirm Objectives

    Transition to Business Discussion

Interviewer's Agenda

Candidate's Agenda

    Transition to Evaluation and Sell

Test Candidacy/Overcome Objections

Candidate Questions/Sell

    Transition to Close

Next Steps

Close

Rapport building will be addressed further in the pages ahead. Establish and confirm objectives is the first of a number of opportunities for you to communicate what you hope to accomplish. This should include information such as:

- The position you are discussing.
- The approximate length of the interview.
- The fact that you might take some notes.
- The approximate timelines for filling the job.

As you finish outlining your objectives, you ask the candidate if there is anything in addition that she would like to accomplish since the success of the meeting depends on each of you accomplishing your objectives.

This conversation leads right into the first of your transitions to the business conversation. Transitions are important reminders to you that you are changing direction in the interview. Since the candidate doesn't know what you are doing until you communicate the change, it is a wonderful opportunity for you to demonstrate your professionalism and to show respect for the candidate. The transition, in this case, can be as simple as, "I've really enjoyed learning a little about your personal interests and background. Now I'd like to learn something about your professional experience." The candidate has been given a clear signal that the conversation has transitioned from rapport building to the business portion of the interview. When interviewers have had a number of interviews in a compact time period, there is a real tendency to forget the courtesy of clear transitions. Don't fall into this trap.

The interviewer's agenda is constructed to find the best candidate for the position to be filled. He uses questions as a means to generate communication about the candidate's past performance and accomplishments which are the best predictors of future behavior. We will discuss questioning as a separate topic in the pages ahead. The interviewer's areas of concern are:

- The intelligence, knowledge, skills, abilities and necessary experience (professional characteristics) to do the work successfully;
- The interest, motivation, energy and drive to do it; and
- The "fit" (personal characteristics) necessary to be successful within the culture of the company.

The candidate's agenda is to demonstrate, through her competencies and accomplishments, that she is the best person to fill your open position. She could attempt to do this by being reactive to your questions and responding in the best way possible. The best candidate, however, knows that your organization is lean and that every person must be a self-starter who is expected to carry her weight immediately. In addition, if the position isn't challenging with great opportunity to break ground and learn new skills, then she won't be interested in it anyway. Consequently, within the context of your interview the great candidate will complete her own agenda which is to:

- Ascertain and understand your primary business needs and goals;
- Determine the style in which your organization carries out its business; and
- Demonstrate that she has the skills, abilities, and personality to perform successfully and to "fit" with your team.

The transition to the evaluation and sell should have the same goals of communication and showing respect that we discussed in the transition to the business discussion. You might ask the candidate, "Before we leave your business background, is there anything else you'd like to add?" This gives the candidate one last opportunity to provide additional information or discuss a skill set that hasn't been mentioned so she doesn't leave and have any regrets. Then you might transition by saying, "Now I'd like to give you an opportunity to ask me some questions."

The wise candidate will test her candidacy by asking you how you think her skills and abilities match your needs. We will look at how you might handle the candidate who is able to draw out any concerns you might have as well as the candidate who isn't as comfortable with the concept in the pages ahead. We will also look at candidate questions in more depth.

The last transition is to the close. As with the other transitions, this is an opportunity to communicate and show the candidate that you value her as a partner. The great candidate needs to understand the next steps in your hiring process and the expected time until you make your decision because she is trying to balance the opportunity she might have with your company and other opportunities she is considering. Top candidates will often tell interviewers who else they are talking to and expected time frames in those companies. This can be a frustration for interviewers who are trying to close on a candidate but, as we all know, it is a seller's market and there is no way around it. Your job is to be caring about the decision the candidate is struggling with and to demonstrate your great partnering skills so she wants to come to your company.

Your last responsibility in the interview is a strong close. This underscores your professionalism and continues to show the candidate respect. As you walk the candidate out, it is a great opportunity to tell her you are impressed with her background (if that is true) and how you particularly enjoyed hearing about one of her greatest accomplishments (speak directly to that success). In addition, tell her that you believe she would be a great fit for your team and company. So many people are reluctant to do this; if you want her on your team, tell her. You'd be amazed at how many great candidates tell us how powerful it is to be told that someone really wants her. A comment like that is often the one that seals the deal. Finally, you'll want to find the best means of staying in touch with her as she considers her options and to let her know that you, and members of your team, will remain in touch about once per week (or whatever time frame makes sense). The more often you remain in touch, within reason, the more it shows her that you really want her. Finally, say good-bye and wish her well.

Now let's go back and take a look at some aspects of the interview in more detail.

RAPPORT BUILDING

Rapport building sets the stage for everything that will follow. Interviewers come to the meeting with many other items on their "to do" list, but it is imperative to remember the many things that impact the candidate as well. It is your role to help the candidate adjust to the new surroundings. Earlier, we read about a candidate who did poorly because she spent most of the night taking her mother to the hospital and receiving some bad news about her health. Ed also had a difficult time as he tried to accommodate the interviewers.

Career Profile _____

The Raw Deal

Ed completed the three-hour drive, under highly stressful conditions, just in time for his interview. He was extremely unhappy with the executive search associate who had cajoled him into appearing for this interview on virtually no notice. The division president of the software company took no time for rapport building, but jumped right into the fact-finding section of the interview. Try as he might, Ed could not get into the flow of the interview. When he left the interview, he was very disappointed with his performance. When he returned home, he received a call from the executive search partner, who was extremely apologetic, saying that she had no idea that her assistant had forced the interview on such short notice. Unfortunately, Ed had to live with the associate's mistake and the executive's lack of sensitivity in giving him no transition time.

A successful transition is not difficult to attain, but it requires your willingness to recognize that this time is needed.

Spend a few minutes getting the candidate to talk. The idea is to engage the candidate in a dialogue in which each person talks about 50 percent of the time. The topic can be anything in which you have a mutual interest. In Ed's case, merely having an opportunity to talk about his drive might have given him a chance to make the transition to the interview. The most common ground, if the candidate has some experience in the industry, is the "who do you know" conversation. There is a high probability that you will have mutual colleagues, friends, or acquaintances. From that conversation there will probably be a war story or two. If the candidate is not from the industry or is a recent graduate, then an interesting topic can be how the person became interested in the industry. Interests outside of work also provide an excellent way to generate conversation that leads to relaxation for both of you. Rapport building is an excellent opportunity for you to conduct the "normalcy test," which is your opportunity to determine whether the candidate's interest and responses fit within the norm.

As an interviewer, how do you keep these simple thoughts in mind when you might only interview a few times a year? We recommend making the Two-Minute Drill part of your normal interviewing routine.

The Two-Minute Drill

Under the best of circumstances, none of us has more than a few minutes to clear our heads to prepare for the interview. Hence, the two-minute drill. It is in two parts: clear your head and prepare for the interview. Clearing your head refers to your need to put on your recruiting hat and to be sensitive to the needs of the candidate. This will prevent any situation such as the one Ed encountered and is an opportunity to review the Success Characteristics so you are clear about areas of concentration. If other interviewers need to be contacted, a quick call will get you on the same page. This is an opportunity to be sure that the interview site remains available for your meeting. Finally, if there are other management issues, they can be quickly completed.

Preparation for the interview begins with a review of the candidate's resume to pick up potential rapport builders. They are typically found in the Personal section. As you review the resume, remind yourself to ask the reason the candidate accepted and left each job. This is also an opportunity to spot outstanding accomplishments, experiences, and achievements that will be easy for the candidate to discuss and will be revealing for you. Finally, gaps in the resume, long tenures or short tenures at companies, or widely varying positions can identify potential problem areas.

The Two-Minute Drill
Purpose

- To Clear Your Head and Prepare for the Interview.

Clear Your Head

- Chance to put on interviewer hat: This may be *the* critical interview for the candidate.
- Remember to put the candidate at ease by engaging in 50–50 dialogue.
- Review Ideal Success Characteristics.
- Clarify roles with other interviewers.
- Address other management issues.

Prepare for the Interview

- Review resume and other candidate information.
- Select potential rapport builders.
- Ask reasons for accepting and leaving each job.
- Spot outstanding accomplishments, experiences, and achievements.
- Identify potential problems: gaps, long tenures, short tenures.

> **INTERVIEW TIP**
>
> **THE TWO-MINUTE DRILL**
>
> This is an opportunity to clear your head, think about how you will put the candidate at ease, review the Ideal Success Profile, and prepare for the interview.

JOB CONTENT

Communication is the engine that drives the stimulating business conversation in an interview, and questioning is the means of attaining the data you need. Your knowledge of the importance of communication can be used to help the candidate and you to achieve a successful meeting. When you decide that it is time to transition from rapport building to job content, it is important for you to assist the candidate by making your intentions clear. A simple statement such as, "I've really enjoyed learning a little about your personal interests and background. Now I'd like to discuss your work experience," shows respect and lets the candidate know that you will be moving to a new area of discussion.

Once the transition is made, question the candidate in a way that obtains the data you need while continuing to build the partnership. Traditional interview training teaches the interviewer to maintain control by having the candidate speak about 85 percent of the time, answering questions. Asking short, open-ended questions that require the candidate to give detailed responses will accomplish that goal. The technique does exactly what it was designed to do: maintain control.

A great candidate, however, is looking for the right opportunity to further her career. She knows that one of the most critical variables in her due diligence is to determine whether she is able to form a partnership with the people in the new setting. Her objective is not to go into an interview and present an interesting monologue. She wants an exciting, interactive business conversation that focuses on your business goals; she is expecting each participant to speak about 50 percent of the time. She wants you to judge her on how her brain works and how she would go about attacking business problems, not to judge her on how she would answer a really unusual (gotcha) interview question, such as, "If you could be any animal in the jungle, which one would you choose? Why?"

In addition, she is absolutely aware of the research that past experience is the best predictor of future behavior. Consequently, she expects you to ask her not only how she might attack a business problem, but also for examples of actual situations she has faced, what actions she has taken, and what results she has achieved. This is often referred to as PAR (problem, action, results) in interviewing jargon. She expects you to follow up the initial questions with questions that probe the how and why of her actions and decisions.

Executive Search Interview

Can you recall a great interview that you had with a highly regarded executive search professional, like the one Peter had at the beginning of the chapter? We're talking about someone who spends much of his time interviewing "A" level candidates. What do you recall about that interview? It's probable that you felt the meeting began cordially, the conversation was interesting and easy to maintain, and there was time spent on rapport building. Although the informal discussion may not have been long, it was clearly defined and gave you an opportunity to adjust to the new surroundings.

There was a smooth transition to the content portion of the interview and although you knew that the search professional would be comparing your intellect, skills and abilities, and personality to an ideal success profile, there was no evidence of it; there was no list of questions and no encumbering paperwork. He might or might not have taken notes. Your recollection is that you were asked some broad, open-ended questions designed to spark conversation. One that you remember is, "Could you tell me about one of your truly outstanding accomplishments in the last few years?" That question really got the ball rolling. You were proud as you told the interviewer a great success story. The interviewer became involved in the conversation and it felt much more interactive than a question-and-answer session. There was no attempt to trick you or catch you up. It was amazing the number of follow-up questions that were asked on the same topic. This is called probing in interviewing jargon. Now that you think about the patience the interviewer displayed, it seemed as if he would have been content to spend the whole hour on that one question. His follow-up questions addressed how and why you did things and he spent a great deal of time on your management and decision-making styles. As you recall, he was very interested in your preferences, dislikes as well as likes. Yet it never seemed that he lost the flow of the conversation. When he finished exploring one area, he would ask another open-ended question that changed the direction of the discussion, and then he probed with follow-up questions.

Another attribute is that the interviewer was truly a great listener. He was involved in the conversation and able to concentrate on what you had to say for the entire interview. When you said something unclear to him, he would ask for clarification or confirm his understanding of the situation. He seemed to have an open mind as you were discussing the way you handled difficult situations. You remember him as sincere, warm, and interested.

When it was time to conclude the meeting, he did so in a respectful manner. He did not make promises but indicated that your background was strong and on target with the search. He said that he hoped to be back to you in a few weeks but he had to be somewhat unclear because the company would decide on the timing of the interviews. The meeting ended cordially.

Questioning Style

We recommend interviewing in the style of the best executive search professional; the interview is more like a business conversation than a question/answer interview or an inquisition. Frankly, interviewing in this style doesn't come automatically and the skill has to be developed over time even by the most experienced interviewer. It takes a combination of attitude and questioning skills.

The interviewer must be willing and able to block out other pressures and come to the interview prepared to share control. Since most of us have busy schedules with great time pressures, there often isn't much time to prepare. That is why we suggested the two-minute drill as a transition from other duties to outstanding interview behavior which enables you to focus totally on the candidate and her needs in addition to your own. It is a time to replace your own agenda with a mutual agenda.

Do you remember the great interaction in the soccer dad case study we discussed earlier? Why was that interaction so positive? The dads quickly discovered that they had something in common and that offered them a place to begin a conversation. They found that it was easy and fluid. If we were to project the flow of that conversation, it might have gone like this:

MIKE: [Question] "Did you attend MIT as well?"
DAVE: [Response] "I sure did. I loved the experience."
MIKE: [Comment] "So did I. Boston is such a great town."
DAVE: [Comment] "I agree. I had never been there prior to being accepted."
DAVE: [Question] "Did you have trouble finding an apartment?"
MIKE: [Response] "I was single at the time and I was in with two other guys just off Newberry Street."
DAVE: [Comment] "I wasn't far from there. I was near Patriot Square."
MIKE: [Comment] "That's a great location. I had friends there."

An interview is different from a social conversation in that the interviewer has specific information he needs to attain. You will need parts of the interview to be question/answer and short question/longer answer/follow-up question formats and this is fine. What happens to many interviewers, however, is that they don't have the skills to use one of these styles when appropriate and then change to a conversational style in order to accommodate both agendas. Rather, the interviewer remains in control with a question/answer format with the candidate answering questions to the best of her ability. The candidate may leave the meeting with a satisfaction that she answered the questions well, but with no sense that she connected with the interviewer.

The interview research supports the idea that once the interviewer asks a question and the candidate answers it, a pattern begins that tends to repeat itself. When the candidate completes her response to a question, the interviewer immediately takes control and asks another question an overwhelming percentage of the time. This draws a response from the candidate followed by another question from the interviewer. Soon you are deep into the conversation and, unless a strong candidate does something to change the pattern, the meeting continues in that pattern. Most interviewers provide some time to answer candidate questions but this time tends to be late in the meeting and often just prior to closing the interview. Changing back to a conversational style this late in the interview often seems stilted and the interviewer is often not given credit by the candidate for building a partnership.

A different pattern happens, however, when the candidate is encouraged to participate and involves herself actively. When the candidate asks a question and the interviewer answers it, then there is a much less predictable communication pattern. The interviewer may take control back by making another comment or asking a question. There is also a reasonable probability that the candidate will make a comment or ask another question. In this less predictable communication pattern, there is a sharing of control so that an open, interactive dialogue is established. The sharing causes the candidate to feel like she is valued and her comments are respected. Simply put, there is a much greater chance that the candidate feels a partnership developing.

If you do not consciously vary the communication patterns in interviews you conduct, you may want to work on further developing the skill. The easiest way is to team with another interviewer and, prior to the interview, establish a set of goals for yourself. Ask the other interviewer to give you feedback as to how you conduct the interview. You may, for example, want to conduct rapport building for about ten minutes in a completely interactive conversation. Then you may want to take control for another ten to fifteen minutes using a question/answer/probing style, while you have the candidate conduct a life and career review. This could be followed by you probing to be sure that she has the skill set needed to perform successfully. Once this is complete, you may want to move to thirty minutes where you define a platform question (e.g., "Tell me about one of your greatest accomplishments in the last few years that involved building consensus among people or groups with differing points of view and implementing the solution.") and then, within those parameters, have an open discussion with give and take about the candidate's accomplishments. This pattern would be repeated as time allowed. Finally, you may want to conduct the trial close and then complete the interview in an open, interactive style. As you each review your performances after the interview, you'll be surprised at what you learn.

Behavior- and Competency-Based Questions

Behavior- and competency-based questions have become popular in some sectors. Each type of question is designed to uncover the traits and skills that are important to the job. After the initial question, the interviewer usually asks probing questions to get to a deeper level of understanding. Behavior-based questions often begin with a phrase such as, "Tell me about a time when you . . ." and then follow with a target area, such as:

- Persuaded team members to follow your solution.
- Handled an irate customer.
- Were forced to make an unpopular decision.
- Hired (or fired) the wrong person.
- Lost (or won) an important contract.

Competency-based questions focus on a skill or skills that will be important to job success. An example is the ability to negotiate. A series of questions is devised around the topic and discussed with the candidate. An example might be:

Competency-Negotiation

- Please describe a negotiation of which you are particularly proud.
  - What went well? Poorly?
  - What types of negotiating techniques did you use?
  - How did you create a win/win solution?
- What lessons about negotiations have you learned? Give examples. How did you learn them?
- Tell me about a legal settlement in which you were involved. What was the situation? How did you negotiate your position?
- Describe a situation in which you negotiated with others in the organization for the use of limited resources.
- Describe a situation in which you negotiated price, terms, or delivery with a difficult customer. What happened?

The important thing to remember about these questions is that they're a variation of the executive search professional's questions. They differ in that they focus more specifically on a given trait or skill. We have no problem with the use of this type of questioning to examine a specific trait or skill.

Another technique used with either new graduates or experienced candidates is case interviewing. A candidate is given a business problem that is general or that she might actually encounter on the job. She is expected to ask questions, discuss the issue, and present a solution or solutions. The objective of the exercise is to understand how the candidate would attack the problem, how she thinks.

Care must be used, however, to keep the techniques in perspective. When the questioning methodology becomes the focus of the interview, the candidate can easily get lost in the shuffle. Now we have the question-and-answer "gotcha" mentality and not the partnership model, in which you discover all the data you need and are simultaneously showing respect. When an interviewer was using competency-based questions, a highly regarded friend was asked to tell about a situation in which she was involved in a serious conflict. She answered by saying that she sought to avoid conflict and had developed a number of effective techniques to solve issues before they became conflicts. The interviewer, who felt that he needed to give her points based on her answer, became noticeably upset because the specific form of the question wasn't being answered. They almost had a conflict and our friend quickly decided that she did not want to be his partner. Over the course of the entire interview, he never asked her what techniques she employed to prevent conflict.

If you have individuals on your recruiting team who are technically oriented; who are interested in things like SAT scores, grade point averages, and specific courses taken; and who enjoy asking behavior- or competency-based questions; then we would suggest inviting them to be part of the screening team. The caution, once again, is that competency-based questions, if asked by an intense interviewer, can feel like an inquisition. An interviewer intent on "finding out" whether this person has the intelligence and skills to work in "our company" can forget the subtlety of the line between content and process in a short interview. It is the role of the head of the interview team to be sure that the team is balanced and that every member of the team has received training in developing respect, bonding, and helping the candidate feel that she wants to be your partner.

When senior-level interviewers conduct the hiring interviews of "A" candidates, we strongly suggest that you interview in the manner of Hank, the executive search professional mentioned earlier in the chapter. In this interview, showing respect and demonstrating your skills in partnering, in addition to conducting a strong content interview, are critical to the candidate. The broad-based question followed by probing inquiries to focus on the critical data achieves both objectives. In an inquisition style interview, you

---

INTERVIEW TIP

QUESTIONING TECHNIQUE

Whether broad-based and probing, competency- or behavior-based, or case interviewing, questions are used to generate communication. The type of questioning must be appropriate to the candidate.

may decide that she is a great candidate and she may decide that she has no interest in becoming your partner.

THE CLOSE

The transition to the close is another opportunity to build rapport, show respect, and inform the candidate that a change is coming. You might say, "This has been a really stimulating conversation. It has helped me to become more knowledgeable about your background. I wonder if you have any questions for me?" What happens at this point will be interesting and instructive.

In Step 5 we saw that the sophisticated candidate will test the strength of her candidacy. She might do this by saying, "I'm equally excited by our conversation; you're doing some fascinating things. Can you tell me how my skills and abilities fit with your needs?" She knows that in an hour's dialogue, thousands of words are exchanged and, since the average human being can only stay tuned in for a short time, there is a probability that she may have been off base on at least a few of her responses. It isn't because she doesn't know the answer, but because she momentarily tuned out of the conversation and lost the train of thought. Once the interviewer tells her of his concerns, it gives her a wonderful opportunity to overcome any issues in the interviewer's mind, to extend the interview (which is a very good sign), and to bring forward new skills if they haven't been mentioned previously. Not only is this candidate sophisticated, but she has a strong degree of self-confidence to carry this discussion confidently. If she does it well, it can drive her candidacy.

Your immediate reaction, like ours, may be "Isn't that the kind of step-forward behavior that we want from someone who will have the potential to make a major impact on our business?" Our answer is a resounding "Yes." However, that is a little too simplistic. That type of behavior may be absolutely necessary in a senior executive who will be conversing with Wall Street analysts and other outside constituencies, or in a sales executive who will have to convince clients who have been lost due to poor service to begin buying from your company again. That type of behavior may not be quite as expected from a scientist who is a great independent contributor and who prefers to be in the lab rather than in a meeting.

An entire new set of issues has been created with the globalization of human talent. In the United States, and in certain metropolitan areas in particular, we have come to value a straightforward, candid approach. In other areas of the country, and in some company cultures, this style is not the norm. In addition, when you begin to interview people from different nationalities, ethnicities, and religious preferences, a straightforward, blunt, in-your-face style may be regarded as disrespectful or improper.

Suppose that you were interviewing for an engineering position and, after a series of interviews, had screened the pool down to two candidates. In your final interview, the first of the two candidates did a wonderful job of testing her candidacy. She asked you if there were any concerns about her candidacy; you raised a few issues that were generated in the conversation and she gave great answers to those concerns. You did not expect the same type of behavior from the second candidate, who was from a different culture, was clearly more reserved, and seemed somewhat introverted. Let's say that you are hopeful that any engineer you hire would have the potential for sales or management, but that is not important to you at the beginning of their tenure. Initially, you are looking for an engineer with great technical skills. Just as you expect, the second candidate does an excellent job in the interview but when it comes to the end of the interview, she makes no attempt to test her candidacy.

What can you do to help to level the playing field? How about helping out? You can help her to test her candidacy by discussing any concerns that you have. Suppose that you have been working hard to develop top-notch engineers who relate well

INTERVIEW TIP

THE CLOSE

Dealing with potential weaknesses and closing the interview present excellent opportunities for the interviewer to learn about the candidate's preparation, personal style, and sophistication level.

with one another. This candidate is better prepared academically than the first candidate, but you question her ability to relate to her peers. You could say, "In our company, we feel that it is very important for every person to be a part of our team. Would you tell me about the best team that you have ever been a part of, what your goals were, what part you played, and what the team accomplished?" From this opening question, you can follow with probing questions that lead you to the information you seek. One of the real values of having a candidate answer your concerns is that you have an opportunity to evaluate how she thinks and the quality of her communication.

Questions for Your Interview Team

Another means of evaluating the candidate is considering the quality of the questions she asks. This, however, is a double-edged sword. On the one hand, it gives you an excellent opportunity to observe the quality of the candidate's thought process. On the other hand, it means that your interview team will need great answers that are well thought out and consistent from interviewer to interviewer. This highlights the need for preparation before the hiring process begins and during the process if new information surfaces.

A key question that you will be asked by an outstanding candidate is, "What makes your company special or exciting?" If your company has a slogan or motto such as General Electric's, "We bring good things to life," that is fine. For the great candidate, however, the answer will need to be much more than that. Your remarks and those of your interview team will either generate excitement or they will not. One thing is for sure! You will be asked the question in one form or another.

Additional questions will be a combination of broad-based questions that could apply in any situation and questions specific to the industry or company. A few of the questions that you might be asked are:

- What are the major issues facing you in the next few years?
- How would I know that what is said and what is practiced regarding company values are in alignment?
- Could you describe a realistic career path for me?
- Please explain the relationships among your hiring criteria, my performance evaluation, and promotional considerations.
- How do people at your company have fun?
- If you make me an offer, how specific will it be in terms of location, boss, and assignment?
- I have offers at a top-tier investment bank, an outstanding consulting firm, and a highly regarded corporation. Why should I accept your offer?
- What do you think the major challenges will be for me in the first six months to a year?
- Can you describe your mentor program for new hires and your training programs?

Answering the candidate's questions provides you with a great opportunity to sell your company and yourself. This is one of the many times when the buyer and the seller change roles. We deal more fully with the type of due diligence the great candidate conducts in the next section.

As the interview winds down, the close offers another opportunity for partnership building. Once again, the more assertive, self-assured person asks for information concerning the next steps in the process. This has to do with the candidate managing her job campaign. Every candidate has a need to know how long your process will take, but not all candidates ask. If the candidate doesn't ask, then help her out by giving her the information. You might say, "I'm sure you would like to know our timing for filling the position.

We will have one more round of three or four interviews in about three weeks. After those interviews, we will make the decision in approximately one week. I enjoyed our meeting today, and you will be receiving an invitation to return. Is there any other information I can provide you at this time?" When the candidate leaves your office, she will be appreciative of the information you have provided and the respect you have shown her.

Tactical Considerations

We are often asked a few specific tactical questions. Here are our answers.

- How many interviews (different interviewers) does it take until an offer is extended?

    In larger companies, holding 8 to 12 interviews is not unusual. In smaller companies, the scheduled interviews may be fewer, depending on the number of people in the company.

- How many interviews will a company hold in a day?

    The typical number is two or three, although four is not unusual. There are some circumstances in which the number will be higher.

- What day of the week is the best interview day?

    There is no research that indicates a given day is better or worse, although most interviewers and candidates prefer to stay away from Monday morning and Friday afternoon.

- What time of the day is best to interview?

    Early in the day is when most people are at their best.

- How important are the logistics?

    Very important. Great candidates will be evaluating everything you do and observing the administration and organization of the process every step of the way.

- Is there an ideal interview sequence, for example, human resources first, direct boss next, etc.?

    There is no ideal sequence and it wouldn't matter if there was one. Executives are too busy, and emergencies occur too often, to stick with a given sequence.

- What is the role of interviewers who are outside the division?

    Interviewers outside the division typically evaluate fit, while those inside the division evaluate technical skills, the key success characteristics, and fit.

SUMMARY

The role of both screening and hiring interviewers is to help each candidate achieve peak performance. This gives the candidate a feeling that she is valued and respected. The interviewing team benefits by being able to select the best candidate. The screening process provides a pool of the most highly qualified candidates for the hiring interviewers. Interviewers have wonderful opportunities to create a level playing field during rapport building, the job content phase, and the close. The great candidate will ask penetrating questions of the interviewers, who must give answers that are consistent and that present the company in the best possible way.

Select the Best Candidate

This is the shortest chapter in the book. If it weren't you can bet that the members of your recruiting team would not complete the paperwork to evaluate each candidate they have interviewed. Let's face it, interviewing is viewed as an important, even critical part of the job; but it is also viewed as an additional responsibility to one's normal duties.

Each part of the evaluation process must be conducted as professionally and efficiently as possible. Rating candidates is no exception. The evaluation form must be short, to the point, and extremely user-friendly. We recommend that you follow a very simple progression:

- Threshold competencies: college attended, major, grades, test scores, etc.;
- Technical skills and abilities, including specialized skills;
- Experience (if applicable), including perceived quality of the companies;
- Personal characteristics;
- Success characteristics; and
- Overall score.

Threshold Competencies

Companies often have an approved list of schools they recruit from, typically because the graduates of those schools have done well at the company. Approved schools change over time as new managers are hired and have allegiance to their schools, or recruits from the original list of approved schools don't do as well as previously, or the company's recruiters find they can attract better candidates. A candidate's grade point average and national scores, such as the SAT, are often important benchmarks. Furthermore, in some situations a company may want recruits to have taken a certain set of courses to be considered for employment.

Technical Skills and Abilities

Technical skills are important to consider because the lack of an important skill set could be a game breaker before the process even begins. The same could be true in the case of a specialized skill or skill set. It is important to test for these skills very early, before valuable time is wasted on an ineligible candidate.

Experience

Experience may or may not be a requirement for a position. A huge portion of a candidate population may be eliminated if experience is required, so that issue needs to be addressed directly. While it is true that there may be a little more risk associated with hiring an inexperienced candidate, there is also the possibility of hiring someone with more potential than you would get with an experienced hire. We never cease to be impressed by a CEO friend who is willing to take risks on inexperienced candidates. He says, "The winning candidate for the number one job in our country, the presidency, is always inexperienced upon entering the job. So why not hire a young person with great potential?"

Personal Characteristics

Personal characteristics include the candidate's attributes that will make him or her a good fit with the culture of your company.

While each company's culture may be somewhat distinct, it is probable that you'll look for warmth of personality, ability to listen, interest and eagerness to learn, and commitment to others, for example.

Success Characteristics

In Part 2 we recommended defining success characteristics for the position as a means of focusing the interview team on those abilities that have the highest correlation with success on the job. Once your team has developed the success characteristics, all you have to do is list each of them on the evaluation form and allow your interviewers to rank the candidate on each one.

Overall Score

This should be the interviewer's view of the composite picture of each candidate.

Scoring System

Use whatever system you like. Once again, we believe in using a very simple system, perhaps five (high) to one (low). There should also be a short space for specific comments by the interviewer. Comments should be as specific as possible, rather than general, and defend the score that was given. See Appen-

> **INTERVIEW TIP**
>
> **EVALUATION FORM**
>
> The evaluation form must be short, to the point, and extremely user-friendly.

dix C for a sample evaluation form. You will note that the success characteristics are the ones that were developed in Step 2: "Define the Ideal Success Profile."

PART

JUDGMENT DAY

Part 4 deals with the balance needed between the buy and the sell. As an interviewer, it is extremely important to understand the criteria that the candidate is using to evaluate you and your firm. It is the interviewer's role to select the outstanding candidate who most closely fits the Ideal Success Profile. However, it is important to remember that the candidate must want to accept the offer to become your business partner. The negotiation stage presents an opportunity to demonstrate fairness and a sense of caring.

STEP 9

Understand How Candidates Are Taught to "Buy"

"A laundry room on the first floor and plenty of closets, definitely plenty of closets." Jan was adamant about her highest priorities as she and Rob began their "must-have" list for house-hunting. Their first house had been a great starter home, but seven years and two children later, they were ready to take the plunge into the real estate pool again. This time, however, they agreed to approach the task in the same highly prepared and well-researched manner that they had conducted their job searches. For four months, Bob scoured the Internet for information about towns with reasonable commutes to New York that had well-established town centers and superior public school systems.

Jan subscribed to local newspapers in several key areas of New Jersey, Westchester, and Connecticut and traded E-mail and phone calls with friends who had moved to various towns in the metropolitan area. Together, Rob and Jan compiled their data and honed their lists until three locations, two in Connecticut and one in New Jersey, seemed to fit their criteria. Finally, they had a key meeting with their financial advisor to make sure they were united on what they could afford.

At first Rob and Jan thought they could make househunting a leisurely weekend activity, but real estate agents quickly set them straight. They learned that there was some prime real estate available, but it was a seller's market with houses selling quickly, often for the asking price or even higher. Rob took time off to spend with some New Jersey agents and Jan spent weeks with Connecticut agents. In time, each of them had several houses they wanted the other to see, fitting the requisite criteria of price, location, and "must-haves." After an exhausting weekend of open houses and consultations with the agents, they felt ready to make bids on at least two houses in New Jersey and one in Connecticut. But Jan, usually effervescent about every new step in her life, was strangely quiet. "Okay, I give up," said Rob. "There's something bothering you; are you ready to tell me?"

"Am I that transparent?" Jan smiled. "I'm not exactly sure what's bothering me. The house in Connecticut has everything we want, and the laundry room is even on the second floor, right next to the bedrooms. The one house in New Jersey is lovely, and amazingly it's $12,000 lower than our price ceiling, so we'd have some latitude to update the master bathroom right away, which is really exciting. And the other New Jersey house couldn't be in a better location; you and I could walk to the station, the kids will be able to ride their bikes to school, and any downtown that includes both a Williams-Sonoma and a Starbucks sounds like heaven to me. But . . ." Jan trailed off and gazed into the distance for a moment while Rob waited patiently.

"I can't get one house out of my head that I didn't even tell you about, because it's $85,000 above our outside limit, the commute is probably 20 minutes longer than any of the others, and the closet space is a joke." "There must be a huge *however*," Rob interjected. "You're right," Jan sighed. "I wish you could see this house; it's so clear the owners have loved their home. The perennial gardens are beautiful and you would love the vegetable garden. This is a proud Victorian on a corner piece of property with an old-fashioned wraparound porch; the wicker furniture is part of the asking price. I keep picturing us having late summer dinners on the porch, watching the kids on the swing that's attached to a huge Dutch elm. You wouldn't believe the woodwork throughout the house, and the staircase, Rob; well, I can just picture Jenny in her prom dress coming down those stairs." She stopped and there was silence between them for a long moment. "I don't know how we'll manage it," Rob finally responded, "but your instincts both in business and in our personal life have always been right on target. It sounds like your instincts are shouting to you about this house. You'd better call the agent."

Two days later, Rob and Jan signed the preliminary papers on the Connecticut Victorian for $81,000 more than they had planned to spend. Each of them had fallen in love with the house, envisioning it as the perfect place to raise their family and entertain their friends. Their carefully planned preparation had been based on logic and research, preparation that both Rob and Jan had enthusiastically endorsed. Yet their ultimate decision rested strongly on emotion. That Rob and Jan bought based on emotion is not unusual at all; it is human nature to respond subjectively, whether buying a home or car, choosing a college, or taking a new position. Although Rob and Jan allowed emotion to finalize the decision about their new home, their purchase rested on some of the "must-haves" from their original list: excellent schools and an appealing location with a well-established town center. They were comfortable buying on emotion because they were satisfied that the truly nonnegotiable aspects of their original list were included.

The Analysis Phase

The intelligent and caring candidate begins the job evaluation process in the same logical and analytical manner that Jan and Rob began the search for their ideal home. The candidate may be interested in numerous companies in more than one industry. Initially, the process is both research-based and network-based. If the candidate is in undergraduate or graduate school, then the career placement office, Internet research, classroom case studies, contacts with professors and students, on-campus presentations, and summer internships are some of the ways that students gain valuable information about companies. If the candidate is an experienced hire, there is normally a heavy dependency on networking with friends in the company and the industry as well as

Internet or library research. In addition to normal data sources, Internet chat rooms allow data gathering about the company. Often this information comes from people with a connection to the company. The objective of this initial analysis is to learn enough about the desirable industries and companies to define the companies that are highest on the target list.

The selection of the targeted company or companies within an industry requires the candidate to focus on the company, a possible position, and the people. This is a broad-brush analysis and will have to be refined once job interviewing begins. Let's examine some of the variables that a candidate might analyze in determining whether a company should be placed on her target list. (*Note:* It may not be possible to gain information about all of these variables; the objective is to get as much as possible.)

THE COMPANY

The main question is, "Will this company be functioning one year, three years, and five years from now?" The candidate will want to examine the company's financial information to see whether the company is growing, remaining static, or declining. The balance sheet indicates the funding levels (debt and equity). The cash flow statement shows the cash generation capability of the company. In addition, the candidate will want to examine the company's strengths and weaknesses versus those of the competition to ascertain a relative position within the industry. The strength of the management team and the issue of management succession also need to be examined. Understanding the ownership team and any potential changes in ownership is also important in today's business climate. Finally, the candidate will want to examine any regulatory threats to the company and how it views its social responsibility.

Some possible questions are listed here.

Adapted from *Killer Interviews* by Frederick W. Ball and Barbara B. Ball (McGraw-Hill, 1988). Reproduced with permission of The McGraw-Hill Companies.

A. Performance of the Overall Industry

- Has the industry been growing over the last five years?
- Nationally?
- Internationally (if relevant)?
- Is the outlook positive?
- What are the reasons for the trend?

B. Performance Versus the Competition

- How would you rate the company's market share?
- Has the market share been growing?
- Who are the winners among the competition?
- Is the company considered one of the best?
- What positives and negatives can occur to change the future of the company?

C. Financial Performance of the Company

- How would you rate the most recent five years of sales?
- Operating profits?
- After-tax profits?
- Cash generation?
- Are the trends positive?
- What are the reasons for the trends?
- What are the company's future projections for sales and profits?
- Are they credible?
- How does actual performance in the most recent year compare with budget or forecast?
- How does the company's return on investment compare with others in the industry?
- How about return on sales (net income as a percentage of sales)?

- How does the price to earnings ratio of the company's stock compare with that of competitors?

D. Balance Sheet Issues

- Is the debt level reasonable?
- How does it compare in percentage to other companies in the industry?
- How do the interest and principal payments required compare to the company's operating profit?
- Is the company in violation of any bank covenants?
- What are the company's plans to fund cash requirements dictated by future growth plans (i.e., capital spending, new product development, and acquisitions)?
- Has the company generated equity through public offerings in the past?
- How strong are its banking relationships?

E. Ownership and Potential Changes in Ownership

- Is the company public or private?
- If public, what is Wall Street's current view?
- If private, what are the objectives of the owners?
- If public, is the company widely or narrowly held?
- If the stock price has fallen recently, is the company a takeover target?
- How will an ownership change affect the company and the position in question?

F. Management Succession

- Is the management team experienced in the problems facing the company?
- Are the ages of key members of the management team balanced?
- Are backups in place?

- Does the company have an active management development program?

G. Social Responsibility

- Are the company's policies regarding the community sound and responsible?
- Environmental responsibilities?
- Health and safety practices?
- Are there regulatory threats facing the company?

H. Legal Issues

- Are there any major claims against the company that could impact its growth plans?
- Does the company hire outstanding legal counsel?

THE POSITION

Having interesting and enjoyable work to do is often listed as number one on job satisfaction indices. The importance of meaningful work has been well documented. The lists contain such aspects as association and friendship, purposeful activity, a feeling of personal worth, recognition, intrinsic enjoyment of the work, achievement, and accomplishment and economic reward, among others. All these relate to having interesting work.

If the candidate can secure a position that affords the correct level and degree of challenge, and if she is successful, then her sense of self-confidence rises as she achieves. While she is successful, her self-confidence remains high and the chances are good that she is regarded as successful in the organization. As that happens, a series of positive things occurs. Not only does she feel good about herself and her peers feel good about her, but her boss and senior management feel good too. She is perceived as someone who has a positive influence on the organization, someone the organization wants to keep. When she is promoted, she is given another challenging job and the positive cycle continues.

However, that's not all that goes on. Because she is deemed important, management is sure to keep her informed. She receives current communication on the state of the company (good and bad), the industry, and the competition. She knows about the efforts to improve and impediments to those efforts, and her advice is sought as to how to overcome those barriers. She is also made aware of environmental and personal factors within the company that could be roadblocks to her success.

Some possible questions are listed here.

A. General

- Does the position afford interesting and enjoyable work?
- Is the work challenging (will I have to stretch)?
- Will the position make full use of my abilities?
- Will there be freedom to perform?
- Is the position visible enough that my work will be noticed?
- Will the contribution of this position make a difference to the overall effectiveness of the company?

B. Specific

- Are the responsibilities clear?
- Will I have freedom to perform?
- Are the short- and long-term goals of the position clear?
- Are the goals reasonable?
- Will the necessary authority and resources by available?
- Who will evaluate me?
- What is the basis for my evaluation?
- Will I receive interim feedback (positive and negative)?
- Do I understand the compensation structure?
- Will I be eligible for bonuses and stock options?
- Are additional incentive compensation programs offered?

- Are benefit programs competitive (e.g., health, major medical, dental, life insurance, and retirement)?
- Are there other programs attractive to new employees?

C. Unit or Department

- Does my department have influence on critical decisions?
- Is this subdivision looked at with pride by the rest of the organization?
- Are management and employees proud to work in this organization?
- Is there a sense of direction in my functional area and in the company as a whole?

D. Communication

- Are the short- and long-term goals of the company easily obtained and understood by all?
- Is the information I generate communicated and used by the larger organization?
- Will I be kept informed regarding company progress (our position versus the competition)?
- Will my advice be sought on critical issues?
- Will I be made aware of environmental and personal factors within the company that could be roadblocks to my success?

THE PEOPLE

The relationship with the boss has long been seen as one of the critical determinants to success or failure in the job. (Relationships with senior management and others in the organization are also extremely important.) Initially, a sense of security is critical to allow the new hire to learn the things she needs to know to ensure success. This can be accomplished if the boss conveys a positive and supportive attitude.

With an initial sense of security, the new hire can approach the things she needs to learn about the organization. Knowing the short- and long-term goals of the organization and why they are the goals is important. She needs to know what is expected in her job, and she needs both freedom and guidance to move forward. She also needs feedback concerning her personal successes and failures, including suggestions for improvement if necessary.

As she gains experience in the environment, she needs an opportunity for greater independence. She wants to accept authority and responsibility for her work as well as accountability for what she does. Independence allows stretching and the development of new capabilities and skills. Achieving success through these efforts produces a larger degree of satisfaction from work.

Bosses who can support these transitions are special individuals. They need to be mature, fair, and self-confident. They must understand the need for assistance early in one's tenure with a company and the need to allow independence as soon as possible. They must believe in training and development as a means to growth. It is a great benefit to have a boss who is proud of the number of his subordinates who have been promoted within the organization. Finally, if a new hire can find a boss who will be her mentor, then she will have hit the jackpot.

Some possible questions are listed here. (*Note*—It may not be possible to ascertain much information about the people until the interviewing begins.)

A. Boss

- Does the boss have self-confidence?
- Do I sense integrity?
- Does the boss look me in the eye?
- Does the boss enjoy working for the company?
- Does the boss love his work?
- How long does he plan to be in this job?
- What is his next potential step?
- Is the boss regarded as a star within the organization?

- Does the boss speak in terms of the successes of subordinates?
- Does the boss talk about the ever-growing independence in the position?
- Do performance expectations seem high but reasonable?
- Are evaluation criteria fair and clear?
- What methods of performance feedback does the boss use?
- Does the boss recognize and reward outstanding work?
- Are training and development important to the boss?
- How many of the boss's subordinates have been promoted?
- Is the boss proud of the number of promotions received by his subordinates?
- Did the boss help to prepare those individuals for promotion?
- Is the boss receptive to new ideas?
- Do I sense the boss might be my mentor?

B. Senior Management

- Does senior management speak with pride about my potential boss's accomplishments?
- Is my potential boss regarded as a key player?
- Do I sense integrity on the part of senior management?
- Does senior management seem to care about employees?
- Do I like the senior managers I have met?
- Does the organization promote from within?
- Is there an appropriate career path?
- What promotional opportunities will there be?
- Does the organization value succession planning?

C. Others in the Organization

- Are there good working relationships horizontally and vertically in the organization?

- Do people like one another?
- Is it considered a good place to work?
- Is management held in high regard?
- Does communication flow in both directions?
- Are decisions made at appropriate levels?

The Target List

At the conclusion of the research- and networked-based analysis, the bright candidate will have an excellent idea of her target list of companies. The next step in the process will occur when contact is made with those companies and the interviewing process begins.

SUMMARY

In performing her analysis, the candidate should consider this statement: "As a prospective employee, I have as much responsibility to judge and evaluate my prospective employer as he does to judge and evaluate me. If both the employer and I do our jobs well, we enhance the likelihood of achieving a great match." The areas of focus in the evaluation are:

- Company: Will the company be a viable functioning entity in one year, three years, five years?
- Position: Will I experience interesting, challenging, and enjoyable work with an opportunity for promotion when it is appropriate?
- People: Will my boss and senior management support me and keep me informed, set challenging but attainable goals, give me independence to function, and evaluate me fairly and consistently?

Great candidates conduct this analysis in an analytical manner, identifying the best companies in an industry.

10
STEP

Conduct the "Sell" Persuasively

In Step 9 we saw how Rob and Jan approached the purchase of a new home. They agreed to approach the task analytically and they defined three "must-have" variables: a reasonable commute to New York, a well-established town center, and superior public schools. They then were able to identify a list of towns that met the criteria. Within the boundaries of those "must-have" criteria, they listened to their hearts and selected their home based on their emotions.

We saw the value of setting the parameters analytically so that any decision would be a good one, if not a great one. In the same way, the intelligent candidate defines the target list of companies through an analytical approach to the marketplace. Once the companies have been identified and the interview phase begins, a new variable is added to the mix.

That variable is people. People add a new dimension that is unpredictable and emotional. Interpersonal dynamics become an important ingredient in the ultimate decision. The top candidates are being interviewed at great companies with highly professional interview teams who are outstanding at selling candidates on the merits of their companies. It is an extraordinarily difficult process to make the buy decision for a particular career path, especially if the candidate is just graduating from college and has no experience. Interpersonal dynamics emerge when the candidate is more closely drawn to one interviewer or interview team than to another.

239

People and interpersonal dynamics, then, cause a change from logical and scientific to emotional in the buy decision. In the same manner that Rob and Jan intended to buy their home based solely on logic until emotion intervened, so too job seekers intend to make their decision based on logic until they meet an interviewer whom they really enjoy and can see as a business partner. There are other considerations, for sure, such as challenging and enjoyable work, a great company culture, a wonderful product mix, or a growing, cutting-edge industry. For many, though, it is "falling in love" with a boss, colleagues, or a particular interviewer that becomes the strongest single variable in the candidate's selection process. This fact, however, is a double-edged sword for the recruiting team. You can win the best candidate even if you aren't the best company. Conversely, you can lose the best candidate even if you are the best company if the candidate "falls in love" with someone who works for your competitor.

As the great candidate whittles his list to several companies and the final decision approaches, the thought process is no longer which company has a better starting salary, benefits, or retirement program. He will have offers from a number of the companies on his targeted list. The salary and benefits will be appropriate and the companies will be fighting ferociously for his services. He has a luxury that few candidates have; he can evaluate his interaction with all of the recruiters he has met to evaluate their potential as business partners. This involves subtle signals such as a client service approach, treating the candidate with respect, and showing the candidate that you want him on your team. When the candidate feels positively about the interviewers, you will hear statements such as:

- "These people are great. We seem to have a lot in common."
- "They make me feel like they really need me."
- "The company culture reflects what I believe."

Let's examine these concepts in more detail.

Career Profile _____

"These people are great. We seem to have a lot in common."

Kristina came to the interview solely to please Liz, her best friend. She had conducted her job search professionally and efficiently and had arrived at her decision about a job within three months. She attributed some of her short job campaign to luck, but she knew that it was also due in part to an excellent educational background, strong experience, and an extremely positive attitude. She had done everything except give her final acceptance to her new employer, and the company wanted her to start as soon as possible. She was prepared to cut off this interview when Liz told her that it would be personally embarrassing to her if Kristina did not go through with the interview, since she had gone to great lengths to arrange the meeting. Liz was clear that all she wanted was for Kristina to go through the motions.

Kristina met the chairman first, who was known to be a positive, high-energy person who could see the bright side of any situation. Winston was well-dressed and fit and emitted self-confidence. He told Kristina that he had heard great things about her and he was very pleased to meet her. The conversation initially focused on the history of Winston's company and then moved to cutting-edge issues facing the consulting industry. Although she came with few expectations, in a short time Kristina felt herself drawn into the conversation and even felt a little excited. The excitement was tempered, however, by the reality that she was committed to another company. Eventually, she felt compelled to tell Winston about her commitment. For a moment, Winston looked surprised, but he quickly continued on with the conversation.

When they finished a two-hour conversation, Winston asked Kristina to meet the head of the Chicago office, who was right down the hall. Kristina was pleased that she had been honest with Winston about her situation, but she was clearly excited by their conversation and since she had ample time that day, she said, "I'd be happy to meet him." Within a few minutes George appeared and took Kristina to his office. Kristina was struck by how well-dressed and fit George was. She knew that this level of fitness would be important to clients in Los Angeles, San Francisco, Dallas, Chicago, and New York. Within minutes she was impressed by George's intelligence and insight into the issues facing the company. Clearly, Winston's firm was at a crossroads; it would have to grow by hiring the right people or through acquisition or it would be swallowed up by a larger firm. Winston and the professionals in the firm had decided that they wanted to control their own fate. They were well on their way to becoming larger and more viable.

By the time Kristina returned to Winston's office an hour later, he had lined up three more people for her to meet. Kristina was too intrigued to say no at this point. She met Pamela next, and it was an instant replay of the meeting with George. They hit it off immediately and had a great meeting, comparing notes and sharing ideas about the state of the industry. Pamela was smart, fit, professional, outgoing, positive, and energetic. Kristina was struck by how that package, together with great dress, made her highly charismatic. Pamela had some wonderful clients and the assignments she was working on sounded particularly challenging.

Kristina completed the last two interviews that afternoon, and they were more of the same. Instead of feeling tired, as had happened in past interviews with other companies, Kristina found herself completely energized. Winston saw her on the way out and told her that his people were very enthusiastic about her. He asked if she could come back the next day to meet some more people. He never mentioned Kristina's job offer. As it turned out, Kristina had plans for the next day, but they agreed to continue the dialogue the day after. Within that three-day period, Kristina had a dozen interviews. She was fortunate to meet at least one person from the New York, San Francisco, and Atlanta offices who happened to be traveling through Chicago. By the end of the interviews, she had a second job offer.

When Kristina went home at the end of the interviews, she was shocked at what had happened. A required appearance had turned into a dozen interviews and a job offer. The more she thought about what had happened, the more she realized that she was much more like these people than those in the company that made her the first offer. Her immediate reaction was dismay. She felt as though she had sold out the first company by continuing the interview process. She came to the conclusion that she owed it to the first company to go to work for them, but her heart was with Winston's group.

Then Liz called to ask what had happened. When Kristina told her, Liz laughed. "I've heard that reaction before," Liz said. "There is something magnetic about Winston and his colleagues." When Kristina told Liz about her dilemma, Liz asked her a question. "Have you started work for them?" she asked. Kristina responded, "No, I haven't even officially accepted. But I certainly gave every indication that I would." Liz suggested that Kristina go and see the person who would have been her direct boss, explain to her that she was only completing the interviews she had scheduled prior to closing her campaign, and relate that a position was offered to her that more closely fit her career goals. Kristina knew that it would be a difficult conversation, but she knew that she couldn't pass on the opportunity to work with Winston's group. She did it the next day. The meeting went reasonably well and her potential boss was professional, although she was clearly disappointed.

That afternoon Kristina called Winston and excitedly accepted his position. When they got together, Winston asked why she accepted his offer. Kristina told Winston that she had spent a lot of time thinking about that in the last 72 hours. She responded, "I was struck by the intelligence, skills, and experience of the staff. I believe that I can learn from them and perhaps share something that I have learned. There is an amazing sense of energy and everyone is so positive and can-do. I think that is a must in a consulting environment. Perhaps most important for me, however, is that I think you and your people are great. I absolutely want to work with you."

Career Profile _____

"They make me feel like they really need me."

From the moment Jon made contact with the finance division of the top-ranked technology company, he had a great feeling about the place. It was December and he was three months into his first year of study toward his MBA. He remembered that, due to his difficulty in scheduling more than one day to visit the company, the head of the recruiting team was accommodating in scheduling seven interviews on the same day. As Jon was driving home he recalled the warm feelings he had toward those who had given their time so generously. The fact that he was offered a summer internship the next day only magnified those feelings.

The lines of communication remained open during the next six months and Jon reported to work in June. He was impressed that the division head took the time to meet him, in addition to the person who would be his boss for the summer. Jon was also impressed that he was assigned a mentor who was a graduate of the college he was attending and was closer to his own age. The mentor was available for companionship, assistance, or discussion about what it was like to work for the company. It clearly gave him an alternative to asking the boss a sensitive question.

After a short orientation period of a few days, Jon was assigned to a project for the summer. The organization was studying new models of investing retirement funds and he was asked to assume one discrete piece of the project. His boss told him that the organization maintained a tight control on head count, and the firm employed summer interns in meaningful roles that were important to various projects. This really impressed Jon, who never thought that he would be given such valuable work. Soon he was working as hard and long as any of the full-time employees and feeling highly productive and part of the team.

In addition to normal work activities, the head of summer interns sponsored a series of luncheons designed to provide socializing and networking opportunities among the interns and an opportunity to hear a guest speaker who headed one of the major business units. The interns learned about the various opportunities at the company. The highlights of the luncheon series were presentations by the CEO and CFO, both of whom were highly recognized in the industry. Jon remembered how the CFO came over and spoke with him personally at the end of the luncheon.

Another added bonus to the summer was the opportunity to see how research and manufacturing operated. This was especially valuable for those interns who had been assigned to a corporate function. It gave them an opportunity to meet with all the finance interns and to see how various parts of the company interrelated. Jon knew that at this company, there was a policy of rotation of the finance people to gain skills and understanding of all the areas within the finance division.

Jon knew from the beginning of his internship that the culminating experience of the summer would be a presentation of his project to the CFO and a number of her senior managers. The presentation would count for about 40 percent of his summer evaluation. Jon's boss and mentor were each extremely helpful in his preparation. His boss helped by giving him assistance in the manner in which data was collected and presented at the company. His mentor was helpful in giving him personal and professional background information about the senior managers as well as what they liked and disliked. With the help he received, and the great project he had been assigned, Jon received high marks for his presentation and the summer's work.

> ### INTERVIEW TIP
>
> **VALIDATION**
>
> **If the candidate feels that you genuinely need and want him or her, that will help you to recruit him or her.**

As Jon evaluated his summer, he realized he loved everything about the experience. The Director of Recruiting had planned and implemented an outstanding program. The other interns were bright, challenging, and fun people and would prove able colleagues. Everyone at the company was bright and had the experience to teach Jon new skills and to offer him exciting challenges. But at the top of Jon's list, he remained incredibly impressed with how fast the organization had brought him in, given him meaningful work, and made him feel really needed.

Career Profile _____

"The company culture reflects what I believe."

Chad resigned from his corporate finance position with a large auto manufacturer. As a fourth-year financial analyst, he felt that he had learned all that he could, in part because the huge acquisition that his company had recently completed meant that the company's appetite for deals would diminish until the most recent acquisition was assimilated. During that time, he learned that he really enjoyed analyzing companies and assessing their value.

In a short time Chad was having serious conversations with three companies, one consulting firm and two investment banks. The large consulting firm described itself as a meritocracy where Chad would come in as a senior associate and then progress at his own pace. He was told that his degree of success would determine his compensation. This sounded good to Chad. He knew that his initial position would be one of servicing clients and his compensation would be about the same as others in his grade. His real agenda, however, was to determine when, and under what conditions he could develop his own business. Although there was some reluctance to deal with this issue, he was told that he would be expected to sell add-on business immediately as a result of great service, and that within three to five years he would be in a position to move to new business development. When Chad asked how much of his business initially would be add-on business, the answer was a very small percentage. One part of the compensation that seemed intriguing was that the company would sometimes take equity positions in client companies as part of their fees. Over the course of his interviews, Chad discovered that senior managers were the only ones who received equity.

The first investment bank was a large, well-established organization with a practice in the auto industry. Chad was told that the firm was interested in him due to his experience on the client side. This was seen as a real asset. He would become a member of the auto industry team as a senior associate and would service the business. He was told that the team functioned as a tightly knit unit where everyone in the group did his or her part to help the group achieve its goals. When Chad asked about the compensation, he was told that he would be paid approximately the same as other members of his class, but there could be differentiation for outstanding service. It became clear to Chad that if he joined this company, it would be for the long term. His advancement to vice president and principal would be within defined time limits and his compensation would correspond with his title. The meritocracy would depend upon his business successes and the bonus would recognize a certain degree of that success. There were no guarantees that he would reach the managing director level. When he asked how one became more involved in new business development, he was told that it was a developmental process and that principal and managing directors handled most of the new business activities.

The second investment bank had quite a different feel from the other two firms. It was a relatively new firm that had been created about five years ago, when three former partners left an established firm. The entire company consisted of six people and an administrative assistant, and their total focus was the automotive industry. Chad was savvy enough to focus on the state of the company to attempt to discover its long-term viability before discussing a possible position. What he heard pleased him. It appeared that enough of the partners' business relationships remained loyal to them to give them an excellent chance to survive and prosper. The partners were honest with Chad in telling him their strengths and weaknesses. They could definitely provide advisory services and some finance-related services, but there were also things that they could not do. When Chad asked how the firm operated, one of the partners laughed and said, "With only six of us, we work together." Chad asked how he could be helpful. He was told that the firm had just received two major new pieces of business and they needed a financial analyst to help with the projects. The fact that Chad had client-side experience was viewed as a large plus.

When Chad asked about the progression to new business development, he was given a different answer than in the larger firms. He was told, "As soon as we have confidence that you will be able to represent the firm professionally." Chad was asked about the possibility of bringing business from his former company. He told the partners that his work was well-respected and he had asked the firm for their business when he landed. He had been told that it would depend on where he landed but that the door was open. Chad also asked about how the compensation system operated. He was told that on each deal, the majority of the fees went to the firm but there was a bonus pool to be divided up among everyone who worked on the deal. This was in addition to the base salary and end-of-the-year bonus.

Chad spent time evaluating the companies and their cultures. He enjoyed all of the people that he met and felt that they were fun and intelligent and would make excellent business partners. He eliminated the consulting firm based solely on his greater interest in investment banking. His decision basically came down to culture. He had to choose between the larger bank, which would clearly be there for the long haul but where his progression would be slower and more measured, or the boutique where the jury was still out regarding the viability of the business. The boutique, however, was closer to a meritocracy in terms of productivity and would provide an opportunity for new business development. Chad's life circumstances and risk profile were such that he felt the culture of the boutique offered him the best risk/reward quotient at this stage of his career. He joined the team with much excitement and enthusiasm.

WHAT IS THE GREAT CANDIDATE EVALUATING?

These case studies illustrate what the outstanding candidate who is bright, intuitive, and mature is thinking as he gets to know the interviewers personally. As the interview process winds toward its conclusion, it is not hard to image the questions he might be asking himself regarding the respect he has been shown, the mission, vision, and values of the company, and the excitement factors that will make it challenging and exciting to work at the company.

Respect

The primary question is, "Am I treated with respect and is it clear that I will be treated as a business partner?" Part of being a partner includes the offer of meaningful work where I can learn new skills and contribute to a winning team. The evaluative questions the candidate asks himself are:

- Did each person I meet treat me with respect and as a partner?

- Did each interviewer greet me in a warm, friendly manner?

- Are noninterviewers equally friendly?

- Do company staff treat each other with respect?

- Is "treating employees well" equal in the company's value formula with "producing outstanding products" and "profit for the shareholders"?

- Do my potential boss and others on the team really want me to be their partner?

- Do I believe my boss will provide me with security until I become fully oriented, then give me freedom and accountability to stand on my own?

- Is there a challenging position for me where I will be able to learn new skills and contribute to the organization?

- Has the position been identified with me in mind as opposed to merely filling a position on the organization chart?

- Has a possible career path been clearly explained to me?

> **INTERVIEW TIP**
>
> **PEOPLE**
>
> You win the outstanding candidate by showing respect and offering him or her a chance to work on a winning team with great people.

Mission, Vision, and Values

The issue here is, "What is the relationship between the mission, vision, and values statements and the way the place runs?" The blessing and curse in getting to know the candidate better is that he gets to know you better and he gets to see your warts as well as your strengths. Smart, intuitive people can see and understand how the place is really run. The evaluative questions the candidate will ask are:

- Do the people I meet articulate the mission, vision, and values well?

- Do they believe the mission, vision, and values?
- Is there consistency among the interviewers?
- Do outsiders verify that the company and its people represent their mission, vision, and values?
- Are others whom the company is trying to recruit representative of those values?
    - Are values discussed as a distinct topic?
    - Are the company's products and services consistent with my values?
    - Does the company culture seem consistent with my expectations?
    - What are the five values I would use to describe my impressions of the company?
    - How closely does that list compare to the stated company values?

> **INTERVIEW TIP**
>
> **VALUES**
>
> The outstanding candidate will evaluate whether the mission, vision, and values statements are consistent with the way the company is run.

The Excitement Factors

The relevant question is, "What factors make this a special and exciting place to work?" There is no question that new graduates want that excitement factor. They're asking, "Impress me. Show me what you can do. How will you help me?" The evaluative questions the candidate will ask are:

- Are people having fun at this company?
- Is the industry growth-oriented?
- Does the company reputation establish it as one of the top in the industry?
- Is the division highly respected within the company?
- Does it enjoy a cutting-edge reputation?
- Will I learn state-of-the-art skills that will add to my marketability?
- Am I proud of the company's products and services?

- Are senior management of the company and my division highly regarded in the workplace?

- Are the people high-energy, creative, and exciting to be around?

- Is it possible for me to make a contribution relatively quickly and be recognized for it?

- Will I be comfortable here?

- Will I be paid an excellent salary?

> **INTERVIEW TIP**
>
> **EXCITEMENT**
>
> The question, "What makes your company a special and exciting place?" must be answered impressively if you are to win the superior candidate.

HOW THE GREAT CANDIDATE BUYS A COMPANY

As the candidate reduces the list of target companies, he becomes like the college coach who has a list of recruits or the company executive who has a list of potential candidates. The dramatic change from 10 or 15 years ago is that the outstanding candidate is evaluating target companies in the same way that the company is managing its list of potential candidates.

Typically, the company manages the list of candidates against the number of openings and attempts to keep as many of the top candidates as possible interested until the offers are made and the positions filled. In that way the offers can be made to the "A+" players and, if the openings are not all filled, then the company can go back to the "A" candidates and so on, until all the openings are filled. Today the top candidates are managing their top choices in the same manner. The complexity of the recruiting process increases significantly when both the recruiting team and the candidate are managing lists.

CHALLENGES FACING THE RECRUITING TEAM

By now it is clear that the challenges facing the recruiting team, even in the great company with the outstanding reputation, are much greater today than ever before. We have also seen that the outstanding candidate will have offers from more than one great company. This gives him leverage to whittle his opportunities to a short list from which he can make his final decision. He will then be in a position to go beyond his "must-have" list to seek the greater subtlety of his "would like to have" list.

From the short list of great opportunities, the decision is more emotional and is based upon building relationships with an interviewer, boss, or the interview team. It is during this phase of recruiting that the team faces its greatest challenge. The great candidate is ultrasensitive to personal interaction, both good and bad, and is able to discriminate intuitively between the sincere and the rote gesture. The recruiting team must include people who are totally committed to a client-centered approach, as distinguished from the notion that they are doing candidates a favor by interviewing them. The notion of the importance of the client is the critical notion of the sell, so let's repeat it.

Every member of the recruiting team must be totally committed to a client-centered approach. No exceptions. No slip-ups. No excuses. The responsibility is even greater than this. Earlier, we spoke of the importance of making it an honor to be on the recruiting team for the department, division, or organization. The honor is not a lifetime appointment; rather, it is earned in every recruiting season. Each member of the recruiting team will work for many hours trying to recruit the "A" player. Even if you do everything right, you are only going to win some of the time.

That's life and that's okay. What you can't afford is to lose any of the share you would normally win due to human error or, worse, a lack of caring by a single person. If any member of the recruiting team is not 100 percent attuned to the need for client service, then he or she should be replaced. Furthermore, if any individual in the company who is not on the recruiting team but comes in contact with candidates acts inappropriately, then he or

> **INTERVIEW TIP**
>
> **COMMIT TO BEING CLIENT-CENTERED**
>
> Every member of the interview team must be committed to a client-centered approach. No exceptions. No slip-ups. No excuses.

she should be removed from any contact with candidates. It is the role of the head of the division and the recruiting team to protect the company's franchise.

What, then, are the specific challenges facing the recruiting team? Let's look briefly at some of the research findings and then see how they can be applied in conducting the sell. The challenges fall into two major categories: building relationships and conducting and managing the sell.

BUILDING RELATIONSHIPS

It is critical that each member of the recruiting team review what behavioral research teaches us regarding human drives and motivators. With this knowledge, it is possible to focus on the process of being client-centered. Some of the major findings that affect the recruiting process and the way it makes us feel are:

- We are self-centered and seek praise. (If someone wants to praise something that I have done, I am usually going to react well to the comment and the person.)

- We think of ourselves as winners. (I am likely to rate myself higher in self-evaluation surveys than might truly be the case.)

- We are strongly driven from within and self-motivated. (I am capable of being a self-starter who seeks to be highly productive.)

- We act as if express beliefs are important, yet actions speak louder than words. (I will not miss any of your actions and they will tell me, more than all your words, whether you respect and value me.)

- We profoundly need meaning in our lives and will sacrifice a great deal to institutions that will provide it. (I want to work for a company that makes products I am proud of and for which I will go the extra distance.)

- We want to be part of a winning team. (I want to work for a boss and team who are highly regarded and who make me feel proud to be associated with them.)
- We buy based on emotion. (I want to associate with people whom I like and respect.)

CONDUCTING AND MANAGING THE SELL

It is equally critical to do a great job of conducting and managing the sell. It is extremely hard to have a team of people work for weeks and months to land a highly recruited candidate, only to have him tell you that he found a position that "more closely fit his career plans." This is often a nice way of saying, "I found a group that I love more than you." Too often the hiring teams in great companies lose "A" players because they don't remain in contact often enough or because they manage the sell poorly. Managing the sell requires attention to a number of items. They are:

- A remarkable people orientation;
- An intimate understanding of recruiting;
- A sense of timing;
- An ability to resolve issues;
- Advance notice;
- A great network;
- Involvement of senior management; and
- Measurement and feedback.

As you read each principle and its case study, ask yourself, "Do I have the right people on my interview team?"

A Remarkable People Orientation

One the most important decisions the head of the recruiting team faces is deciding the composition of the recruiting team. The key is to select people who truly enjoy and care about people. These people seem to have an intuitive sense about doing the right thing when it comes to human relationships. Maturity and a sense of self-worth are key ingredients in a person before he or she can reach out to someone else.

Career Profile

It's Nice to Have a Friend

Yoko was tight on time for her final presentation as an intern. She had proven her skills over the summer and she knew that she had done well. Today, however, was different. Her boss had told her that she had an emergency meeting and that set a number of wheels in motion. Not only did it mean one less friendly face in the audience, but it meant that Yoko had to rent a car, which was time she didn't have to spend. When one or two other glitches came up, Yoko began to sense that this would be one of those days when what could go wrong would go wrong. This was not the way she had hoped her final presentation would go.

For the first few minutes of her presentation, Yoko was clearly nervous. Then she noticed that Russell, a vice president who was sitting right in front of her, seemed to be very interested in her presentation. He nodded affirmatively when she made a salient point and, since the meeting was informal, asked appropriate questions and made supportive comments. Soon she began to relax and her presentation improved dramatically. The presentation was well-received by those in attendance. When she was debriefing later with the Director of Recruiting, she told him how much Russell's support meant to her. The Director told Yoko that Russell was one of the most intuitive people in the department; he had the ability to understand when someone needed help and to do the right thing in providing that support.

An Intimate Understanding of Recruiting

Building a partnership with the candidate begins with the first contact and is a fluid give and take between the buy and the sell.

Knowledge of the rules of the game is critical in today's highly competitive marketplace.

Career Profile _____

Know Thy Strengths

Joseph knew every strength of his large conglomerate as well as each perceived weakness that would be thrown back at him as he prepared for his presentation to MBA students at a highly acclaimed graduate school. He knew the students would be direct and that challenging work, a chance to learn cutting-edge skills, and an opportunity to make an impact quickly would be important to them.

The presentation went extremely well, and after it Joseph welcomed questions from the students. It didn't take long before the discussion focused on a comparison of working for a large company, a consulting firm, or an investment bank. A student asked, "Granted your firm has a great reputation; but many of my classmates are focused on consulting, due to the variety of assignments across a range of industries, or investment banking, to learn cutting-edge finance. Aren't they compelling reasons?" The boldness of the remark caused a momentary hush in the room as the students waited for Joseph's response.

Almost instantly, a huge smile crossed Joseph's face and he said, "They certainly are. If you were to join our company you'd have a chance to do both. As you may know, we rotate executives through a series of positions in an effort to expose them to a broad range of opportunities so they can get close to the business. We are proud of the reputation we have earned as being at the cutting-edge of finance. As you grow with us, you would be in an excellent position to become a line manager and run your own business." Joseph knew how well he had responded when there was spontaneous applause from the students.

A Sense of Timing

Timing means more than returning calls quickly. Have you ever noticed how some people just seem to have a knack for calling at the right moment or saying or doing the right thing? It's not just luck; they have trained themselves to be attuned to the needs of others.

Career Profile
The Big Decision

Michael was really struggling with his decision, and it was a momentous one. Harvard Medical School or Johns Hopkins Medical School? Johns Hopkins or Harvard? Michael approached the decision in the same technical, analytical manner in which he had approached his engineering studies at Purdue University. It obviously worked well, since he had been awarded one of the highly prestigious Whitaker Fellowships for complete tuition reimbursement at the school of his choice. Michael had selected a career in medical research and, through his own research and discussions with friends, had defined a list of questions upon which to rate the schools. The list read, in part:

- How much research is done and what kind is it?
- Is the emphasis more academic or on clinical medicine?
- How many endorsements are there for research?
- How much autonomy does the research function have?
- What is the financial stability of the institution?
- How strong is the faculty?
- How closely tied are the hospital and the research facility?
- How international is the medical education and the hospital?

It was a disciplined way to approach his task. It helped Michael to screen his list down to his two finalists. However, it no longer helped him to discriminate between those last two enviable choices.

As the decision time drew to the final hours, Michael decided to have one final round of conversations with his proposed professor-mentor in each institution. He called and both professors were out. Michael could do nothing but leave voice mail messages, which he did. That evening at midnight Michael received a call from the professor at Johns Hopkins. He apologized for the late hour but said that he was in the airport in Chicago, awaiting a continuing flight to a conference where he would be the keynote speaker the next day. The professor and Michael had a productive conversation that lasted for almost an hour and covered a wide range of topics, including the difficulty of Michael's choice. The professor acted primarily as a mentor, helping Michael sift through his thoughts. When the conversation ended, the professor told Michael that he hoped he would come to Johns Hopkins and wished him good luck in making his decision.

Michael heard from the Harvard professor the next afternoon. The conversation was shorter than the one the night before, but very congenial. Michael was surprised at his own reaction. He had clearly made the decision to attend Hopkins the night before and now was merely seeking confirmation to justify the decision. The attention that the Hopkins professor gave to Michael at just the right time was deeply appreciated. It also won Hopkins a prime recruit.

An Ability to Resolve Issues

You will only know about a candidate's issues if you remain in close contact. When you do, personal or professional concerns can be understood and addressed immediately and in a way that will be meaningful to the candidate.

Career Profile _____

How Did You Know?

Paige was up to her eyeballs in work, with her MBA semester exams staring her in the face and her sister's wedding scheduled in less than a week. She was needed at home by Thursday night at dinnertime and she wasn't at all sure she'd be able to pull it off. The final straw was when the airline told her that she had called too late and there were no available seats for Thursday. When she hung up, she was in tears.

Five minutes later, the phone rang. It was Adam, the Director of Recruiting at the firm where she had done her internship last summer. He was calling to wish her well at her sister's wedding. Paige was dumbstruck; "I can't believe that you remembered my sister's wedding." "When we discussed it last summer you seemed so excited. How are you managing everything on your plate?" Paige responded, "Not very well." She then told Adam about her dilemma with the airline and the flight home.

Adam offered, "Let me see if there is anything I can do; sometimes our internal travel agents have pull with the airlines. You understand that you'd have to pay for the trip." "Of course," Paige answered. "If you could help, I'd be really grateful." Adam was on the problem the first thing the next morning and within two days, he was able to produce a ticket. Paige was extremely appreciative when Adam called her back. She made it home and had a spectacular time at the wedding. Several months later, when Paige accepted a position at Adam's company and rejected three other outstanding offers, she told her new boss that a major factor in helping her to decide on accepting the offer was the kindness that Adam had shown her.

Advance Notice

One important way of addressing your career progress is to ask yourself, "Am I being kept in the communications loop in every direction?" Individuals can understand and adjust to change if they are kept informed. This is also true for new hires. It is often a number of months from the time an offer is made until the candidate accepts, and then even more time until work begins, so it is possible that changes may need to be made regarding the position. Direct, clear communication is critical in these cases.

Career Profile _____

Changing Direction

Maria couldn't have been happier with her decision. She decided just before Christmas to join the human resources department of the conglomerate in her home state of Michigan. She was to join one of the divisions as an associate in employee relations in June, after graduation.

From the time Maria agreed to join the firm, her new boss put Maria on the mailing list for the company newsletters, the annual report, and other special publications. As Maria read the newsletter in the early spring, she began to get an uneasy feeling. It seemed that the division's profitability had declined and a management study had been undertaken to evaluate the problem.

Maria wasn't sure what to do. As a new employee, she didn't think she should be calling her boss, but the future of the division was of critical importance to her. Shortly thereafter, the telephone rang. It was Ralph, the vice president of human resources. After some initial pleasantries, Ralph confirmed that the division wasn't doing well. It seemed that new technology was changing the way the industry operated and the division was behind the technology curve. He told Maria that the company still very much wanted her but, in an effort to be honest, he thought he should tell her that there was a possibility the division could be sold or merged with another division and moved to a new location. Maria asked Ralph what he thought she should do. They had an open discussion; Ralph asked her how important it was for her to move back to that part of Michigan. She indicated that it was very important because her fiance lived there. Ralph advised her to conduct a job search for other opportunities in the city and to remain in close contact with him so he could inform her of developments within his company.

Within three months, Maria had two other offers, although they were not as appealing as Ralph's. She felt a little apprehensive about calling Ralph, but she did and she told him about the other offers. He was very understanding. He then said that there were better business signs at his division. The technology that they lacked had been developed much more quickly than expected, and there was an 85 percent probability that the division would not be sold or moved. He was careful to indicate, however, that it was 85 percent and not 100 percent. He indicated that he thought her job was safe and that he still wanted her to join the company. Maria was excited as she thanked Ralph for communicating openly and honestly with her. She accepted the offer to work on his team.

A Great Network

Taking the time to get to know key people on the faculty and administration of the schools you recruit from can pay huge dividends at recruiting time. The same is true of influential colleagues from the candidate's former companies, staff members from your firm who attended the same school, and those who might have similar interests to the candidate.

Career Profile _____

The Basketball Coach

Ted had hit a wall in his efforts to recruit Erik. He had done everything he could think of and he wasn't sure that he had made any significant headway. Ted knew that Erik was in real demand and had three offers beside the one from his company. One day, he decided to have lunch with an old friend from production whom he hadn't seen for a number of months. Once they caught up on personal issues, they began to discuss business issues. Eventually, Ted mentioned the problem he was having recruiting a highly desirable candidate. His friend asked about the college the student was attending. Ted responded, "The University of Texas." His friend thought for a moment and then said, "We don't get too many from that part of the country, but we did recruit one young man from Texas a few years ago. I think he was a football player." Ted told his friend that Erik was a basketball player.

That afternoon Ted's friend called him and said that he had spoken to the former football player from Texas. His friend asked Ted if he'd like to speak with him. "Sure," Ted responded, "I'm not sure what good it will do, but I'd love to talk with him." They did speak. Ted learned that the former football player had friends at Texas who were very close to the basketball coach. Ted asked if they could make a connection for him. Within a short time, Ted had been introduced to the basketball coach via telephone, and they agreed to meet on Ted's next trip to Texas.

They met three weeks later and Ted felt they had a cordial, productive meeting. He learned that Erik was from a single-parent family and had a very close relationship with the basketball coach, who had become a father figure for Erik. As the end of his college years loomed, Erik leaned heavily on his coach for mentoring. Ted didn't try to oversell or strong-arm the coach on the merits of his company, but he did have an opportunity to present his organization in the best possible light. Ted felt that a real connection was established.

When Erik decided to accept a position with his company, Ted was ecstatic. It wasn't until a few months later, however, that Ted found out what really happened. Erik had joined the company and he and Ted were having lunch for the first time. Ted asked how the first few months had gone. Erik told Ted that he was having a great time and he owed it to his basketball coach. He explained that he had made the decision to stick close to home and accept a position with a small company that would be very comfortable for him. When he was reviewing his thought process, the coach asked some questions that led Erik to reconsider his decision. It was these conversations that eventually convinced Erik to reach out and take the riskier, but much higher potential, position with Ted's company. Ted recognized that some of the content of those discussions came from his meeting with the coach.

Involvement of Senior Management

Engaging the assistance of visible and highly regarded senior people to contact the candidate is a tangible sign of the degree to which he is valued. Time is precious at the senior ranks, so care must be given to the priority of winning the candidate and the timing of the contact.

Career Profile

The Spur-of-the-Moment Barbecue

Brett knew that he only had 72 hours, because Lori was committed to making her decision before noon on Monday. Part of his frustration was that he hadn't been able to get Lori together with four of the most senior managers in the department. Brett took the time to speak with Randy, the division head, one last time. Randy was candid in say-ing, "Look, you aren't going to get us together today because we have all been on the road. Why don't you invite Lori and the others to my house on Sunday and we'll grill some chicken?" For the first time, Brett had some hope.

He quickly contacted the other managing directors and all but one could make it. He then contacted Lori and asked if she was available. Initially she said that she couldn't make it but, once she realized that it included the senior managers in the division, she asked Brett for some time to try to reschedule her appointments. A few hours later she called Brett back and told him that she would be able to attend the barbecue.

On Sunday, Brett asked Lori to come a little early so she could spend a little quality time with Randy. They had a relaxed 30 minutes together before the other guests arrived. Randy had a chance to learn about Lori and her skills, interests, and long-term goals. By the time the others arrived, Randy had given Brett the indication that he thought she was terrific.

The barbecue could not have been more successful. The manag-ing directors made Lori feel at ease from the start. There was a lot of conversation about where everyone had been that week. Lori had re-cently traveled to China and she was more than happy to join in the storytelling. Every once in a while there was a discussion of business for a short period of time, and then the conversation moved back to personal interaction. It was clear that Lori was very comfortable with herself and the group interaction.

On Monday, when Lori accepted the job offer from Brett, she told him that she had been "blown away" by the barbecue. She said she couldn't believe that four senior officers of the company would take their precious personal time on a Sunday afternoon to meet with her. Furthermore, she thought they were great and she had decided then and there that this was the right situation for her.

Measurement and Feedback

Data is critical to any recruiting effort. Are we winning our share of recruits from our target and stretch colleges and of experienced executives we recruit? Should we be upgrading the colleges we re-cruit from? What is the feedback from the students and experi-enced candidates we are trying to recruit? Do we need to change the composition of our team during the next recruiting season? As a result of the changes, is our recruiting effort more successful?

Career Profile _____

Increasing Diversity

The recruiting team was faced with a real challenge from the head of the division: Increase the diversity among recruits receiving offers. The newly appointed Director of Recruiting gathered, studied, and analyzed the data from the past five years. Indeed, the statistics were not good. The number of women and minorities receiving offers was clearly lower than the targeted levels. A number of initiatives were un-dertaken to identify the cause of the problem. One initiative was to identify and meet with firms that were acclaimed for their efforts in this area. The basic strategies generated from the initiatives centered around expanding the eight target and stretch colleges, attending se-lected conferences focused specifically on diversity, and using the in-ternal network better within the company.

Short-term (one-year) and long-term (two- to-three-year) goals were put into place. The short-term goal was to increase by two (out of a class of 20) the number of minority hires. This represented an in-crease of 10 percent. The long-term goal was to put a recruiting structure in place that would address the problem. It is not an easy task to establish a presence on a new college campus, so the decision was made to select only two new colleges for the immediate recruit-ing campaign. After a careful analysis, the two colleges were selected because they seemed to be particularly fertile for recruiting, seemed to be at the correct academic level, and perhaps most important, the company had a minority alumna who was willing to be the school contact.

In addition, teams were sent to two conferences specifically geared toward recruiting minorities. The teams were trained to look for experi-enced hires as well as new graduates. The conferences were selected in part because they addressed the minority issue and they drew people who lived in the Southeast, where the company was located.

The third component of the plan required senior management endorsement, internal communication, and networking. The division head was cooperative in scheduling time on all upcoming agendas to endorse the diversity issue as one of her major objectives. This spurred the internal newsletter editorial staff to grant the Director of Recruiting a column to inform staff of activities and accomplishments. Soon members of the staff began to generate the names of potential candidates they knew or who were brought to their attention.

The results for the first year were encouraging. For a while it looked as if there was a possibility of landing four minority candidates. The organization learned that increasing the company's diversity wasn't going to be as easy as it looked when they received two rejections. In the end, however, they landed two candidates, met the initial short-term goal, and were encouraged to continue the progress.

SUMMARY

Once the outstanding candidate has completed an analysis of the industry and companies and established top choices, the interviewing process begins. The candidate will have more than one company interested in him and will be in the fortunate position of being able to go beyond his "must-have" list to the greater subtlety of his "would like to have" list. This includes the evaluation of emotional considerations, such as:

- *Respect:* Am I treated with respect and is it clear that I will be treated as a partner?
- *Mission, vision, and values:* What is the relationship between the mission, vision, and values statements and the way the place is run?
- *Excitement factors:* What factors make this a special and exciting place to work?

A highly regarded interview team who can convince an outstanding candidate that he wants to be their partner must be totally committed to a client-centered approach. This involves understanding the human drives and motivators that would make someone want to be your partner. They include:

- We are self-centered and seek praise.
- We think of ourselves as winners.
- We are strongly driven from within and self-motivated.
- We act as if express beliefs are important, yet actions speak louder than words.
- We profoundly need meaning in our lives and will sacrifice a great deal to institutions that will provide it.
- We want to be part of a winning team.
- We buy based on emotion.

The interview team must also do a great job of conducting and managing the sell. This requires attention to a number of items, including:

- A remarkable people orientation;
- An intimate understanding of recruiting;
- A sense of timing;
- An ability to resolve issues;
- Advance notice (of any changes);
- A great network;
- Involvement of senior management; and
- Measurement and feedback.

11
STEP

Negotiate a
Win/Win Package

As the interviewing process draws to a successful end, two things should be occurring simultaneously:

1. You are coming to the conclusion that you have identified the best candidate for the organization.
2. The candidate has decided that your company has all the ingredients to challenge and excite her, and you have sold her on becoming your business partner.

THE PSYCHOLOGY

The key to negotiations, as in other parts of the methodology, is to continue to build the partnership with the candidate, because you will become business partners when the process is completed. Consequently, your goal and the candidate's goal are the same: to reach a fair and equitable compensation structure in exchange for becoming an impact player in a challenging job with specific targets that are critical to the company's success. It would seem that building and maintaining a solid relationship should be an easy task, since by this time the candidate and you are "in love" with one another.

Assuming that the strong relationship built to this point will automatically carry you through negotiations can be a fatal mistake, however. There is serious business yet to be transacted. The interview process is a series of ebbs and flows between the buy and the sell. Business concepts are discussed in greater or lesser detail and conversational flows are often interrupted as one or the other presents an idea, discusses a point, or makes a suggestion. Multiple interviewers add the strength of a more in-depth examination of the candidate and a better employment decision for the company, but tend not to bring clarity and finality to job expectations or set specific performance goals. The negotiation, then, is often about setting clear and measurable performance expectations with you (the potential supervisor), in addition to finalizing a fair and equitable compensation structure.

Being able to negotiate substantive issues while maintaining a solid relationship needs to be a key competency of the senior executive. In fact, the impact or "A" player is more than willing to participate in these discussions, will not accept a position without resolving them, and wants to be involved as an active participant. The expectation is that a partnership model will be utilized whereby each participant will:

- Show the utmost respect and approach the negotiation from a win/win point of view.
- Remain engaged by listening carefully and attentively.
- Understand the issues fully before attempting to resolve them.
- Demonstrate openness in discussing critical and difficult issues.
- Generate alternatives by using a creative problem-solving approach.
- Request clarification when there is ambiguity.
- Reach agreement and end the negotiation when fairness and equity have been attained.
- Let the candidate know how much she is valued and that you are looking forward to having her on your team.

INTERVIEW TIP

PSYCHOLOGY

Negotiating substantive issues while showing respect and maintaining a solid relationship is key to reaching an agreement.

Following these principles gives the candidate assurance that her thought process is sound and that she is making the right decision in joining your company and your team.

THE PREPARATION

A number of factors determine the compensation that an organization is willing to pay an outstanding candidate. They are:

- the job's relative position in the organization's corporate structure;
- the market value for the position;
- the current compensation of the candidate; and
- the budget of the department.

The job's relative position is important because it sets the salary parameters within the organization. It is a time-honored principle that the boss makes more than the subordinate, while making less than his boss, and so on. There are, of course, exceptions such as a highly paid salesperson making more than a sales manager, but they are still unusual. Setting salary parameters is helpful to the organization and still leaves a good deal of room for flexibility. In larger companies, for example, there are often two or three salary levels for a given position.

The market value for the position is a critical determinant when trying to attract an "A" player. It takes constant work to remain in touch with the moving target called the marketplace. By definition, the "A" player is the best candidate who will attract the best offer from a number of highly competitive organizations who know that human capital is what will set them apart. Consequently, this is an area where a company must do its homework. There are a number of ways for research analysts to remain current. The Internet has numerous company sources and compensation surveys to provide data. There are numerous research companies that provide up-to-the-minute comparisons of positions in given industries. Your organization may be able to gain competitive compensation information from an executive search firm that is conducting a search for you. Personal networking for information within an industry can also be extremely beneficial. Finally, the process of interviewing itself is the process of giving and receiving information and can lead to valuable data.

The critical message is that without current market information, you cannot even compete. Having the data doesn't yet mean that you will be able to compete, but it is a prerequisite. With that information, your organization has to make a decision about the level at which you want to compete. A large conglomerate, for example, can make a decision to compete against other large corporations for the best young MBA talent at one compensation level. If, however, the decision is made that the competition should include consulting firms and investment banks as well, then the compensation parameters will be different.

It is important for senior executives to deal with the issue of a less than adequate compensation structure. The decision to raise the starting salary for the next recruiting class causes internal consistency issues, including salary compression at certain levels. Yet this is the type of tough decision that often needs to be made if a company is to remain competitive.

The current compensation of the candidate will also be a factor in the overall decision. Under normal circumstances, when a candidate has been paid at market rates, a company is willing to pay a premium of 10 or 15 percent to attract talent. For the best talent, however, this yardstick may not be applicable. The decision will ultimately rest on a combination of the organization's ability to pay and the candidate's value to the organization. The candidate's value is a major piece of the total puzzle; that is why a great candidate is taught not to bring up salary until the organization has fallen in love with her. It is at this time, when the organization truly wants her, that her negotiating leverage is at its greatest.

The departmental budget is surely an issue. There may be certain times when a highly desirable candidate is lost because the company just can't afford her. No company should allow itself to be placed in this uncomfortable position. The interview team needs to understand the parameters within which it will operate. If it needs to end a relationship with a candidate, that should be done in the early stages of the relationship and not during the negotiating period.

> **INTERVIEW TIP**
>
> **ASSESSMENT**
>
> From the beginning of the first meeting, assess what type of offer it will take to hire the candidate.

EARLY DISCOVERY

As we have seen, it would be unusual and unwise for an interview team to reach the negotiating stage with a candidate whom it just couldn't afford. Consequently, some compensation probing needs to be done early in the process to make sure that valuable time will not be wasted. This is usually done by a screening interviewer, who determines that the candidate is within the salary parameters (or close enough to continue the discussions). There is little if any negotiating room at the lowest level (entry-level BA graduates), but negotiating room increases with each step up the corporate ladder. Fortunately, at the entry level, candidates normally have a reasonable idea of the salary level through contacts with older students, professors, the career placement office, and other sources. Interviewers, have to be sure their starting salary is competitive, but they don't have discovery issues because the candidate is just graduating and doesn't have a current salary.

A recent MBA candidate presents a more complicated picture, because she will often have three to six years of experience at a great company or companies. Consequently, right up front it is important to begin to assess the type of offer it will take to land her. It is important to understand the competition and to understand the motivations of the candidate. The more intuitive the interviewer, the better the read on the probability of the candidate having a high interest level in your company. A small segment of a typical dialogue might sound like this:

INTERVIEWER: What was your salary prior to going back to school?

CANDIDATE: I was at $65,000 plus a bonus.

INTERVIEWER: In addition to our company, what other kinds of companies interest you?

CANDIDATE: I'm looking at the consulting industry and investment banking in addition to two competitors of yours in pharmaceuticals.

INTERVIEWER: What are the most important criteria in making your selection?

CANDIDATE: Criteria?

INTERVIEWER: Yes, I mean things like learning cutting-edge skills, high compensation, balance between work and family life, travel, and so on.

The answer to this question and the discussion that follows will give you the intuitive data that will help you begin to assess the candidate's potential fit in your company and the chances of having her accept your offer.

The experienced candidate presents a more complicated challenge, for a number of reasons. She may be in a job title that is not easy to quantify; she may be overpaid or underpaid; or her salary may have been depressed due to the inordinate value of her stock options. At this early stage in the process, you need to have some data to determine whether it makes sense to continue talking. A small segment of dialogue might sound like this:

INTERVIEWER: What kind of compensation package are you looking for?

CANDIDATE: I'd really have to find out more about the job challenge and responsibilities before I could attach a price tag.

Let's say that is not enough information for you to reach a comfort level.

INTERVIEWER: I need a little more information. Can you tell me how much you were making in your last job?

CANDIDATE: My base was $125,000 and my bonus ranged between $25,000 and $50,000.

At this point, as long as that salary level is within the parameters or close enough, you should stop the probing. However, if that salary is not within the parameters, then you need to let the candidate know immediately. You might say:

INTERVIEWER: You have a terrific background and we are interested in you. Unfortunately, your salary is outside of our range, and I don't think that it makes sense to get too far into our discussions.

CANDIDATE: Can you tell me the range you have in mind for the position?

INTERVIEWER: The maximum base we would pay is $100,000 with a 30 percent bonus.

CANDIDATE: Is that firm?

INTERVIEWER: I'm afraid that it is.

CANDIDATE: You're right. I'm looking for a little more than that. I'm disappointed because I'm excited about your approach to the business and I can see that you really have a great organization. I hope that you'll keep me in mind if a position opens at a higher salary grade.

INTERVIEWER: I certainly will. I hope that we can stay in touch.

It is certainly better to find out now than to waste the time of 8 to 12 interviewers and then determine there is no way that a match can be made.

REFERENCES

Once you have made the decision that this is the outstanding candidate who can help to impact your business, and just prior to the actual offer, you should complete your reference checks. The purpose is to verify, with individuals who have worked with the candidate or who have knowledge of her, that the professional and personal characteristics she has represented are real.

The best organizations will typically be interested in reference checks related to the past ten years of the candidate's career. They will want to speak with a subordinate, a peer, and a boss among the references. For an experienced candidate, it is not unusual for a company to want to speak to five or six references. Since this is a time-intensive activity for the hiring manager or the head of recruiting and because candidates are becoming more sophisticated in preparing their references for the telephone call, it is easy to rationalize that the reference check is not productive or necessary. That is a major mistake. The best organizations check references, because they are helpful in adding the final pieces to the composite you are forming regarding the candidate's fit within your organization.

In conducting the reference check, you will know a great deal more about the ideal success profile for your company than the reference does. Typically, the best approach is to build rapport with the reference first, to the degree possible. You might be able to find out about the reference's background and give some of your own. You can include some of the complimentary things the candidate has said about the reference. Giving the reference a short background on your organization and the position you are trying to fill will help him to understand the context of your need. Then it becomes possible for you to ask him to put himself in your shoes. You might say, "Our company has been stalled at $25 million in sales and we need a dynamic COO to partner with the CEO to drive the business to the next level." This comment may be enough to generate active conversation about the candidate.

If that comment doesn't generate conversation, the reference may say, "How can I help you?" You might respond with, "I understand that you were Sally's boss at company X and I'm interested in hearing about the value that she added." As the reference begins to provide information, a dialogue will often be easy to foster. In this scenario, the conversation is fluid, with excellent give and take about the information you seek.

In some cases, however, the reference will not be so forthcoming and will only respond to your questions. You will then want to ask specific questions about the issues that face your company. You might say, "One of Sally's responsibilities would be to oversee information systems, which is an area in need of immediate help. Can you tell me how Sally helped you in this area?" Once a discussion topic is open, your follow-up questions can focus on the ideal success profile. If the company's culture is highly team-oriented, you might ask how Sally might go about solving problems in the information systems area. When that topic has been exhausted, you might ask about Sally's abilities in other areas that are necessary to the growth of the company.

It is important for you to ask for information in a priority ranking, because time may be limited. It is time consuming to reach references; some will be more forthcoming and give you more time than others. You need to be flexible. The close should be cordial and brief.

In addition to verifying the candidate's professional and personal characteristics, the reference check can provide you with critical information regarding those skills and abilities that the candidate most enjoys using in the workplace. You should enter the reference check conversation assuming that it will not be easy to attain the information you seek. That will heighten your ability to listen for sound bytes of information that may prove important to you later when you present the offer. If the reference is forthcoming, then your work will prove more fruitful.

Suppose, for example, you mention that negotiating with your suppliers has been an area of real concern (Sally continues to be the candidate in question). Let's assume that the reference responds immediately saying, "Sally loves negotiating and she's great at it. She is extremely thorough in her preparation and is always better prepared than her counterpart. One of her strongest traits is her ability to understand not only what she is trying to achieve but also what will create a win for the other side. This puts her in the enviable position of working toward a win-win solution. I've been amazed to watch Sally complete the most difficult negotiation while winning the respect and admiration of the other person." In this case, you were fortunate to receive much more than a sound byte and it certainly sounds like negotiating is a skill that Sally enjoys using.

As you listen to the various references you will begin to build a composite of Sally's strongest and weakest skill sets. Let's assume that you have gathered evidence that Sally is absolutely great with people in every phase of business. The references support her ability to forge a partnership with the CEO to drive the business forward. Her ability to seek ways to find win-win solutions gives you confidence that she will work well with the management team and workforce in managing the day-to-day operations of the company. You are also comfortable with her abilities to manage relationships outside the company, ranging from public relations efforts to difficult negotiations. You also determine that her most challenging assignment will be the management of the information systems area because it is where her own skills are the least strong. This is a minor red flag for you; if she is hired, she will need technical help in this area. You are comfortable that other members of the management team have strong skills in information technology.

> **INTERVIEW TIP**
>
> **REFERENCES**
>
> The best organizations check references that relate to the past 10 years of a candidate's career and speak with bosses, peers, and subordinates.

Suppose that the CEO, upon hearing the data gathered from the reference checks, is really excited that he has found a great partner. Now the ball is in your court to present the offer to Sally. You are now in a much better position to structure and present the offer because you have learned from the personal interviews with her and from the references who have actually worked with her.

THE OFFER

Throughout the interviewing process, the members of your team will be evaluating the motivations that drive the candidate and assessing how best to construct the offer. This information will be valuable to you as you ready yourself to make the offer.

When presenting the offer, you need to be a compelling salesperson on behalf of your organization, yet promise only what can be delivered. The point to remember is that a great candidate buys based on emotion. Let's repeat that: The great candidate buys based on emotion. She buys because you really want her to join your team and be your business partner. She buys because others in your group also want her and believe she can make a significant contribution. The candidate buys because you work for a successful company that can teach her new and marketable skills and because she can learn from smart, caring colleagues. She buys because she feels that you will mentor her and protect her while she is learning, and then give her freedom to produce and to accept accountability for that production. The candidate buys because she senses that you really care about your people, help them receive promotions, and allow them to grow even if it means moving outside your area. She buys because you will pay her well.

At the beginning of the meeting, tell her that you are making her an offer and how excited you and your group are about the possibility of her joining your team. Be enthusiastic. You need to reiterate the exciting things that your group is doing and how she can make an impact. This is where your preparation is critical. What were the motivating factors driving her? If learning new skills is critical, then reiterate that she will have an opportunity to learn new skills from highly respected people in the field. If travel is important, then remind her that she will have the opportunity to travel to South America, Europe, and Asia.

When selling the offer, make it come alive. It is far more appealing if it is specific. Tell her who she will report to, which job she is to fill at which location, where she will have an office or cubicle, and how she will make a bottom-line contribution to the organization. Help her to understand the skills she will learn in the first six months to a year and how she will grow.

After reiterating how much you want her to join the company, make her the salary offer and remind her that your company pays competitively within the industry. Let her know about the outstanding benefit package your company offers that represents 25 to 40 percent of salary in monetary terms. If she has questions about any aspect of coming to work with you, take the time to answer them. An example might be a concern about the anticipated time to advancement. You can help her to understand how a typical career might develop, being careful to indicate that progress is dependent on outstanding accomplishment.

If the candidate indicates her excitement with the offer and asks for time to consider the offer, give it to her while indicating your interest in understanding her considerations and time frames. In addition, let her know that the offer letter spelling out the terms of the agreement will arrive shortly. Care must be used in this regard, because colleges often establish time frames for degree candidates, to provide them time to consider multiple offers. Once the college's policy has been met, then you have the right to establish a reasonable time frame within which to expect a decision. When dealing with an experienced candidate, time frames are much tougher to predict, due to work schedules, negotiations, and unforseen factors.

> **INTERVIEW TIP**
>
> **THE OFFER**
>
> When presenting the offer, be a compelling salesperson on behalf of your organization, yet promise only what can be delivered.

NEGOTIATION

After your offer is made, the candidate has the option of accepting it, rejecting it, or attempting to improve it through negotiation prior to making a final decision. If the outstanding candidate has more than one offer, her leverage in negotiation increases dramatically. In addition, she knows that the greatest negotiating leverage she has ends when she accepts the job. The complexity of the negotiation process increases from new graduates through middle-level experienced candidates to senior experienced candidates.

Your organization will have done its research and arrived at an entry-level position title, salary grade, and starting salary for the incoming class, including your firmwide benefit package. Some firms establish small equity participation right from the beginning of a candidate's tenure. Often there is a sign-on bonus. When dealing with new graduates, the flexibility to negotiate will be within fairly tight limits. When moving to candidates with advanced degrees, such as an MBA or an advanced science or engineering degree, the degree of flexibility increases. Your highest-ranked candidates might receive $5,000, $10,000, or even $15,000 more in their base salary than others in the class, and their sign-on bonuses may be significantly larger than those offered to others. There are often incentives offered in a given industry, such as a plum assignment with a higher bonus potential for someone in the financial services industry. Individual considerations can be made, such as an interest-free loan to a candidate with large college loans or help in relocation. Once again the negotiation is conducted within fairly predictable parameters.

FOCUS ON THE ISSUES

Focusing on the issues is critical to keep personalities and emotion out of the equation. It is not always easy, however, to identify the driving motivators, so the interviewer must receive help from the candidate. The amount and quality of the information you receive depends upon the strength of the relationship you have built with the candidate. In addition to building the relationship, it is critical to listen for signals throughout the interview process so that when negotiation is appropriate, you will know what drives the candidate. There are certainly broad generalities that give general guidance, such as the fact that new graduates are probably going to be more concerned about the here and now and less interested in retirement perks; someone with children ready to go to college will need as much base salary as possible; and a candidate with a successful career and grown children might welcome an opportunity to take a bet on a start-up situation with low salary and a great deal of stock. However, there are lots of exceptions. It is the interviewer's job to understand the candidate's motivations.

Suppose that you are negotiating with a candidate in the $100,000 to $150,000 range and that you have determined and confirmed with the candidate that the number of dollars of take-home pay is the most important need. She moved to the metropolitan area a few years ago, and the increase in expenses coupled with having a young child in private school have been a greater drain on her resources than she had imagined. Let's follow the negotiation.

INTERVIEWER: I'm really excited to offer you the director level position. The base salary will be $105,000 (the candidate's salary was $100,000 previously) with a maximum 35 percent bonus. You will also receive our very strong health benefit package, disability insurance, life insurance, 401K, and pension program. The level also entitles you to two weeks' vacation.

CANDIDATE: I'm really excited and flattered that you are interested in me. I'd like the weekend to think it over. If I have any questions, could I get back to you?

INTERVIEWER: Absolutely. Please do.

CANDIDATE: Oh, there is one more thing. Would you mind if I contacted your vice president of human resources to learn more about the benefit package?

INTERVIEWER: I think that makes a lot of sense. I'll tell him that you will be calling him.

You have your vice president call the candidate the next day, and they meet to discuss the benefit package. While they are together, the vice president indicates how excited he is that she is considering joining the organization and floats a trial balloon by asking, "How are you doing with your decision?" The response is that she is really excited but that she is wrestling with a few outstanding issues. When he asks which ones, the candidate indicates that the base salary is only five percent higher than her previous salary, the bonus is the same percentage, and the vacation is less than in her last position.

When you meet, again you are prepared—you know the important issues. After a cordial greeting, you have another great opportunity to build rapport and continue bonding. You then review the position as you have discussed it, including the goals and objectives for the first 6 to 18 months, job responsibilities, resources, and evaluation procedures. Once that conversation is over, you ask the candidate how she is doing with her decision.

CANDIDATE: As I indicated the last time we met, I'm very flattered that you are interested in having me join your team. I'm just wrestling with a few issues.

INTERVIEWER: Can you tell me about them?

CANDIDATE: Sure; they're base salary, bonus, and vacation. I also have a question about eligibility for stock options.

INTERVIEWER: Shall we take them one at a time? Let's talk about the base salary first.

(*Note*—Get to her number one concern.)

CANDIDATE: I know that you have advocated for me and I appreciate it. My concern is that my research indicated I was underpaid previously, plus I had not had an increase in over a year.

INTERVIEWER: What were you hoping to receive?

CANDIDATE: My research indicated that approximately $115,000 was the market value for a position with this responsibility.

INTERVIEWER: What are your concerns about the bonus?

CANDIDATE: My bonus potential was 35 percent in my last position. There is more responsibility in this job.

INTERVIEWER: Did you receive the maximum each year?

CANDIDATE: No, but I received close to it.

INTERVIEWER: Can you tell me about your concern with the vacation?

CANDIDATE: Once again, my research indicated that a position at this level carried three weeks of vacation.

INTERVIEWER: What was your question about eligibility for stock options?

CANDIDATE: I wondered whether this position was eligible for stock options.

INTERVIEWER: You've raised some challenging issues. Rather than respond on an individual basis, I'd like to take some time to evaluate these issues and come back to you with our best offer. As you know, we want you to join us, and we'll do the best we can.

You have now given the candidate the opportunity to raise the most important concerns that she has, and they are out on the table. You now have an opportunity to evaluate the total compensation package and make a judgment concerning your final offer. Suppose you decide that the candidate you have is an impact player and you want her to join your team. You invite her to return, continue the rapport building, and then get to the issue at hand.

INTERVIEWER: I'm sure that you're anxious to hear our thoughts about your compensation package. I understand from our previous conversations, that the base salary is particularly important to you. Consequently, we are prepared to offer you $120,000 in base salary. At that increase in base, and our company salary grade restrictions, we will have to keep the bonus at a maximum of 35 percent. Since I was able to raise your salary grade to a 14, you will be eligible for three weeks of vacation time. In regard to your question about stock, you will be able to purchase stock. Our stock options begin at salary grade 15 and I am sure that you will be at that level soon. How does that sound?

CANDIDATE: That's great news. That is a very fair package and I accept. I want you to know that I am very excited about joining your team. When would you like me to start?

INTERVIEWER: The sooner the better. How much notice do you have to give your employer?

CANDIDATE: I wouldn't want to leave without giving at least two weeks' notice, but in the interest of being fair I'd like to give three weeks' notice. Do you have a problem with that?

INTERVIEWER: No, not in general. In the third week, however, on Thursday we have a series of very important meetings. Do you think that you could come?

CANDIDATE: I'm sure that I can work it out. What time would you like me here?

INTERVIEWER: That's Thursday, the 25th, at 8 A.M.
CANDIDATE: I'm looking forward to it.

CREATIVE SOLUTIONS

Negotiation with senior-level experienced candidates often requires creative problem-solving abilities. You have most likely
gone to the outside because you have a particularly challenging
assignment that needs a fresh look, or an assignment that requires
skills or experience that your people inside the organization don't
have. The outstanding candidate is going to look very closely at
the business model that you intend to employ, and will often negotiate over the job to be done as well as her compensation. If a
deal is to be struck, it often takes creative solutions and thinking
"outside the box."

Suppose that you are a public consumer products company
with $1 billion plus in revenue. You have a $150 million dollar,
high-profile division that is not in the same core business and is in
need of new leadership because it has been languishing with no
clear direction. You are interviewing a new potential president for
the division. You have had a series of meetings with the candidate
and 10 members of your organization have also met the candidate.
Your team has come to the conclusion that this candidate is the
best person for the job. At the end of the last meeting, the candidate told you that she had some concerns regarding the financial
commitment the organization needed to make in order to jump-
start the division. You suggested that since she had been given the
financial data regarding the division, she come back with a realistic plan detailing what she would do and what it would cost. Let's
pick up the conversation when she comes back and after the rapport building.

INTERVIEWER: Did you have a chance to think some more about
    the business?
CANDIDATE: Yes, I did. We have talked about a number of the
    ideas, but two areas continue to concern me.

INTERVIEWER: What are they?

CANDIDATE: First, if you really want the business to grow to $225 million as we discussed, I believe that it will take an investment of $10 million over the next two years.

INTERVIEWER: How would you use the money?

CANDIDATE: In various forms of advertising and buying shelf space. I've documented how I would use the money in the report I've prepared for you.

INTERVIEWER: I'd like to take some time to digest the report. Thanks for doing the analysis. What is your other concern?

CANDIDATE: The division is not the largest division in the company. I've read some reports that X (the largest division) hasn't been doing well. I've been in a "drowning man" syndrome once before and I don't want to go through that again.

INTERVIEWER: The "drowning man" syndrome?

CANDIDATE: Yes. The "drowning man" sucks any and all resources to try to save himself. I'm sure that you understand that I'm not saying X is drowning, rather that the division might suck the resources as it gets back on a strong footing.

INTERVIEWER: I understand what you mean. There is no question that X needs to move in a new direction, and we are addressing those needs. What you need to understand is that the division you and I are talking about is extremely important to us. We are committed to making it a much larger part of our organization.

CANDIDATE: That's great to hear, but do you understand my concern? I know that you are committed to do what we have talked about. I also know that when large amounts of money are involved, more than one person is involved in the decision making.

INTERVIEWER: I do understand your concerns, and they are valid. Are there other concerns with the business?

CANDIDATE: If we can work out those two, then I'm sure that you and I will be able to partner to work out the other issues.

Now you've identified the key issues of concern to the candidate in achieving the goals of the business. It is equally important to discover how you're doing in reaching agreement on how the candidate will be compensated.

INTERVIEWER: Can we switch gears and talk a little about the offer that we have made you?

CANDIDATE: Certainly. Could you review the offer as it stands at this point?

INTERVIEWER: We were prepared to offer 100,000 in stock options; a $400,000 base salary; a target bonus to 60 percent of salary; a great benefit package including pension, a 401K, and life insurance to three times salary; and a car allowance that would include enough to pay for a garage in the city. Does that sound like what we have discussed?

CANDIDATE: Yes, it does.

INTERVIEWER: Have you had a chance to digest it?

CANDIDATE: I think I have. Would you like my reaction?

INTERVIEWER: Certainly.

CANDIDATE: I think it is a very generous offer. As you know, the $400,000 base is a solid increase over my present base, and I appreciate that. The stock options are a combination of covering the options that I will lose if I leave my present company and options for your organization. The benefits and car allowance sound fine. The 60 percent target bonus is less than what I have now, and I'd like to talk about that. The biggest issue, however, is that I have been forthcoming from the beginning in saying that if I'm going to leave the great situation that I have now, there will have to be a way for me to feel that I have an ownership piece in the venture.

INTERVIEWER: Doesn't the stock accomplish that?

CANDIDATE: Not really. The stock is in the corporation of which my division would be a part. But the vast percentage of growth (or decline) will be due to forces that are outside my control. In addition, the stock grant is what is traditionally given to employees these days, and I want to be more than an employee.

INTERVIEWER: What are you looking for?

CANDIDATE: I will need your help with the answer to that question. I understand that as a public company you can't give me a five percent stake in the company. The thought that has occurred to me is a second bonus, predicated on the company hitting certain targets.

INTERVIEWER: You've obviously been thinking about this. What are you thinking?

CANDIDATE: Well, I was thinking about a second bonus of two percent of the revenue above $175 million.

INTERVIEWER: We are obviously into territory now that I can't give you an answer to today. I'm going to need to look at your business plan and talk to my colleagues. Then I'll be able to tell you how much compensation we are prepared to offer.

CANDIDATE: That's more than fair. I just want to reiterate what a great team I think we could make together.

INTERVIEWER: Thanks. I think so, too.

Now it's back to the drawing board. The remaining issues have been defined, and you have to make the decision as to whether the candidate's requests are reasonable and possible, or whether one of the issues represents a game breaker and no agreement is possible. Let's assume that this is a really important area for development and, after analyzing the situation, you decide to proceed with the candidate. You call the candidate back in, once again use the time for rapport building and bonding, and then get to the business conversation.

INTERVIEWER: I've been thinking about our last conversation. We agree with your point that there needs to be a commitment to the finances for this division, independent of the organization as a whole. Consequently, we are in the process of having our finance division undertake to set up the division as a completely freestanding operation with its own set of financial statements. I was able to get a commitment for $7.5 million dollars, with a promise to look at the progress at the end of the first year. If objectives are being met, then the additional money will be forthcoming. How does that sound?

CANDIDATE: Great, regarding the freestanding operation of the division. I have some concerns about the infusion of cash, because it is going to take some time to turn around the division. We talked about my belief that it would take between two and three years to complete the turnaround.

INTERVIEWER: I understand that, but that is the maximum amount of money I could get coming out of the gate. You are going to have to make a decision as to whether you trust me. I'm telling you that if we hit our targets, and I'm willing to set them realistically, I will be able to get additional funds.

CANDIDATE: The feedback I have received about you in the marketplace is really outstanding. People say that you are true to your word and can be trusted. I trust you.

INTERVIEWER: In terms of your compensation, we are willing to give you the equivalent of ownership. We are prepared to offer you two percent of the revenue above $200 million dollars, as a pool for you and your management team. This was a very unusual arrangement for the corporation and the first time that anything like this has been done, so I can't move on the maximum percentage of standard bonus. That would have to remain at 60 percent.

CANDIDATE: Thank you very much for your efforts on my behalf. I'm going to need a few days to get together with my financial advisor. I should be back to you before the end of the week.

INTERVIEWER: Good. I think that you know we really want you and we see a great opportunity for you here. More than that, I am personally looking forward to working with you. I think that we will make a strong team. When do you think you could start?

CANDIDATE: Thank you. I feel the same about working with you. It will take a month for me to wrap up my current work and give my company some time to find a

> **INTERVIEW TIP**
>
> **CREATIVE SOLUTIONS**
>
> Generate creative alternatives by using a problem-solving approach to resolve difficult negotiations.

replacement. It is really important to me to leave in the most professional manner possible.

INTERVIEWER: We want you to do that as well. I'll wait to hear from you.

This negotiation might end in a few days, when the candidate comes back to you and indicates that she is prepared to accept the offer except that she feels badly about having to take a cut in the bonus potential. You agree to match the 75 percent that she had at her former company, and she excitedly accepts your offer.

INTERVIEW TIP
AGREEMENT
End the negotiation and reach agreement when fairness and equity have been attained.

We have seen that the degree of complexity increases from negotiating with a new graduate to the senior-level experienced candidate who might become the president of the company or division. In each instance, however, the principles of showing respect, solving problems, and seeking a win/win solution are critical.

SUMMARY

Negotiating substantive issues while maintaining and furthering a solid relationship is a key skill set for the head of the interview team. The expectation is that a partnership model will be utilized whereby each participant will:

- Show the utmost respect and approach the negotiation from a win/win point of view.
- Remain engaged by listening carefully and attentively.
- Understand the issues fully before attempting to resolve them.
- Demonstrate openness in discussing critical and difficult issues.
- Generate alternatives creatively, using a problem solving-approach.

- Request clarification when there is ambiguity.
- Reach agreement and end the negotiation when fairness and equity have been attained.
- Let the candidate know how much she is valued and that you are looking forward to having her on your team.

12
STEP

Seal the Deal

Creating an outstanding interview team in today's environment requires a senior management that is passionate about the vision to hire truly outstanding talent and communicates it clearly. You have internalized that mandate, including establishing a sense of urgency with specific goals and timelines. Your recruiting model is established and fits your industry and company. You have developed the Ideal Success Profile and have set in motion the implementation of the process, which rests with your highly energized and motivated team.

Your interview team understands and is committed to building a partnership with the candidate. Each interviewer will show the candidate utmost respect as he or she conducts a fluid buy/sell interview in a seamless fashion. The buy entails testing for professional characteristics: the intelligence, skills, and abilities, and any necessary experience to demonstrate the threshold competencies. It also includes searching for personal characteristics: the candidate who is the best fit with the culture of your company and who has great long-range potential. An important component of fit is finding the candidate with the interest, motivation, energy, and drive to want to be on your team.

Throughout the process, each of your interviewers will be mindful of the fact that it is fruitless to determine that you have found the perfect candidate and then discover that he or she doesn't want to be your partner. Consequently, your interviewers will be constantly searching to discover the candidate's needs to be addressed at the time of the offer. The salary negotiation stage is one last opportunity for you to reach a win/win settlement and reinforce the candidate's desire to become your partner.

Now the training is complete. Your team has the interviewing skills to seal the deal. It takes more, however, than preparation and interviewing skills alone to hire the superstar. It takes sincerity, honesty, and a commitment to do the right thing for the candidate as well as for your organization.

As we have stressed throughout the book, people want to feel valued and respected in every aspect of their lives; the interview process is no exception. Recently, a friend was involved in a series of interviews which underscore the importance of the interviewer making a personal connection and building a partnership with the candidate.

A highly regarded financial services firm put on a full court press to recruit Rick, their number one candidate. After a morning of final interviews with Kate and Marshall, the two most senior members of the firm, Rick accepted their invitation to join them for lunch at a venerable private club nearby. Since he had spent several hours with Kate and Marshall in a number of interviews throughout the process, Rick felt comfortable and relaxed with both of them although he was aware that the lunch was still part of their interview process.

After scanning the menu, all three ordered the summer fruit plate. When the beautifully presented lunch was placed in front of Rick, he quickly decided he could easily negotiate all of it while paying attention and contributing to the conversation except for a formidable wedge of cantaloupe. As lunch progressed, however, both Kate and Marshall commented on how spectacular the melon was and Rick felt compelled to try it. A few minutes later he scooped his spoon into the crescent of cantaloupe and then watched in horror as the piece he was trying to manuever onto his spoon spiralled several feet into the air and then fell, ricocheting from the shoulder of a nearby patron to a serving tray where it divebombed a soup plate, landing with a commanding "thunk." Rick froze, mortified by his gaffe until the obvious absurdity of the situation made an irrepressible grin spread across his face. He glanced at Marshall and Kate and was immediately relieved to see their shoulders shaking with silent laughter.

"I certainly hope you can chip out of the rough better than that," Marshall said smiling. "Frankly, that's the way many of my tee shots have landed," Kate added. All three dissolved into laughter; when they resumed the conversation, Rick thanked them for easing the tension of an awkward moment. "I really didn't know how you'd respond to my mistake," he confided. "You know," mentioned Kate, "my dad always believed that it was important to walk in someone's moccasins before judging them. I remember very well what it felt like to be on the candidate's side of the interview table and it's hard to be on display like that nonstop." "Besides," Marshall interjected, "we have to be able to see the humor in things. Our work is high powered and stressful; nothing is more effective than our ability to be able to laugh together."

It probably doesn't surprise you that although Rick received four outstanding offers, he accepted the one from Kate and Marshall's firm. He felt valued and respected throughout the interview process and believed his outlook on life matched well with all the people he met there.

We're positive that you will win top talent like Rick through your finely honed interview process and the caliber of your well-trained, personable interview team. It's an exciting and rewarding adventure to make the impact hire; enjoy the journey!

APPENDIX A

Key Interview Tips

RECRUITING PROCESS

1. The Vision—The role of the CEO or division head is to create the vision and the sense of urgency to hire impact players. (Step 1, p. 53.)

2. Head of Recruiting—The Head of Recruiting must be held in high regard and must understand the psychology of recruiting "A" players from a technical and intuitive point of view. (Step 1, p. 53.)

3. Alignment of Staff—A core group of line executives and recruiters who are "A" players themselves should be selected to implement the program. (Step 1, p. 53.)

4. Ownership—Ownership of the process is in the hands of the hiring manager, who holds ultimate authority and accountability for the hiring process. (Step 1, p. 53.)

5. Credibility—Think carefully about the answer to this question: "When I have to make a critical hire, one that will have a major impact on my career, who do I want on my interview team?" (Step 6, p. 161.)

6. Commit to Being Client-Centered—Every member of the interview team must be committed to a client-centered approach. No exceptions. No slip-ups. No excuses. (Step 10, p. 239.)

7. The Stakeholders—The interview team may include stakeholders who represent corporate or client interests, as well as divisional representatives. (Step 1, p. 53.)

8. The Policy—Clear, concise recruiting policies and procedures must be in place. (Step 1, p. 53.)

9. Questions About an Open Position—All questions regarding the position, the duties, the type of position, and the potential career path need to be answered before the interviewing process begins. (Step 1, p. 53.)

10. Communication—There simply cannot be too much communication about the organization's commitment to hire the best. Use every means possible. (Step 1, p. 53.)

PREPARATION

11. Success Characteristics—The interview team defines the four to seven critical characteristics that determine success within the culture of the organization. (Step 2, p. 75.)

12. Evaluation—To make the best hiring decision, rate each of the final candidates on every success characteristic. (Step 2, p. 75.)

13. Intelligence, Skills and Abilities, and Experience—The candidate must have the intellectual background, skills and abilities, and experience necessary to perform successfully. (Step 4, p. 109.)

14. Interest—The candidate must have the interest, motivation, energy and drive to join the team. (Step 4, p. 109.)

15. Fit—The candidate must demonstrate the interpersonal skills that result in an outstanding fit within the culture of the company. (Step 4, p. 109.)

16. Fitness—Exercise on the day of an interview enables you to relax and gives you a chance to focus. Exercise at a level of 75 to 100 percent of a normal workout. (Step 3, p. 95.)

17. Listening Ability—The ability to listen carefully is critical for evaluating the candidate and learning what it will take to land him or her. (Step 3, p. 95.)

18. Screening and Hiring Interviews—Screening interviewers test for threshold competencies. Hiring interviewers select the candidate who is the best fit within the culture of the company and who has great long term potential. (Step 6, p. 161.)

19. Professional and Personal Characteristics—Professional characteristics (intelligence, skills and abilities, and experience) are the threshold competencies. Personal characteristics (strong people skills) represent long term potential. Both are extremely important in an outstanding candidate. (Step 6, p. 161.)

20. The Two-Minute Drill—This is an opportunity to clear your head, think about how you will put the candidate at ease, review the Ideal Success Profile, and prepare for the interview. (Step 7, p. 189.)

BUILDING THE PARTNERSHIP (BEHAVIOR IN THE INTERVIEW)

21. Interviewer Dress—Interview dress should be professional and on the conservative side for the industry and company. (Step 4, p. 109.)

22. Initial Greeting—A warm smile and a firm handshake make a strong first impression. (Step 5, p. 135.)

23. Presence—Each person's presence is observed early in an interview. It includes warmth, confidence, fitness, grooming, and choice of dress in addition to enthusiasm, interest, energy, and mental alertness. (Step 3, p. 95.)

24. Energy—An energetic and enthusiastic interviewer emits a positive, can-do attitude. (Step 3, p. 95.)

25. Rapport Building—Rapport building is the first step in forming a bond with the candidate. (Step 5, p. 135.)

26. The "Normalcy" Test—This test determines whether there are differences between a candidate's actual and

expected behavior that go past "normal" or "reasonable" and into a red-flag zone. (Step 4, p. 109.)

27. Form a Partnership—The partnership (buy/sell) model allows you to gain the information you need while building a strong relationship. (Step 6, p. 161.)

28. Business Conversation—The goal is to create an exciting, stimulating, 50–50 business conversation throughout the interview. (Step 6, p. 161.)

29. Questioning Technique—Whether broad-based or probing, competency- or behavior-based, or case interviewing, questions are used to generate communication. The type of questioning must be appropriate to the candidate. (Step 7, p. 189.)

30. Respect—Engaging in interactive conversation shows the candidate you care about his or her thoughts and ideas and demonstrates the utmost respect. (Step 6, p. 161.)

31. Needs Development—Allow the candidate to develop and confirm your business needs and to sell his or her ability to accomplish the goals. (Step 5, p. 135.)

32. Raising Concerns—Observe whether the candidate draws out concerns you have about his or her candidacy and attempts to overcome them. (Step 5, p. 135.)

33. Candidate Questions—The interview team must have great answers for candidate questions. The quality of the questions provides additional information about the candidate. (Step 7, p. 189.)

34. Eye Contact—Make eye contact throughout the interview, particularly when the candidate asks about perceived weaknesses of your company. (Step 5, p. 135.)

35. Timetable—Let the candidate know about the interview and decision-making timetable, to allow for adequate planning on his or her part. (Step 5, p. 135.)

36. The Close—Dealing with potential weaknesses and closing the interview present excellent opportunities for the

interviewer to learn about the candidate's preparation, personal style, and sophistication level. (Step 7, p. 189.)

EVALUATION OF THE CANDIDATE

37. Evaluation Form—The evaluation form must be short, to the point, and extremely user-friendly. (Step 8, p. 221.)

THE SELL

38. Partnership Potential—Demonstrate character, integrity, and fairness through your interview behavior. The outstanding candidate will evaluate whether you have the potential to be an excellent business partner. (Step 6, p. 161.)

39. The Candidate Buy—The candidate buys based on emotion. (Step 10, p. 239.)

40. Validation—If the candidate feels that you genuinely need and want him or her, that will help you to recruit him or her. (Step 10, p. 239.)

41. Challenging Work—A great candidate must be offered work that is challenging and visible and that will increase his or her skills, abilities, and marketability. (Step 6, p. 161.)

42. People—You win the outstanding candidate by showing respect and offering him or her a chance to work on a winning team with great people. (Step 10, p. 239.)

43. Values—The outstanding candidate will evaluate whether the mission, vision, and values statements are consistent with the way the company is run. (Step 10, p. 239.)

44. Excitement—The question, "What makes your company a special and exciting place?" must be answered impressively if you are to win the superior candidate. (Step 10, p. 239.)

NEGOTIATION

45. Psychology—Negotiating substantive issues while showing respect and maintaining a solid relationship is key to reaching an agreement. (Step 11, p. 267.)

46. Assessment—From the beginning of the first meeting, assess what type of offer it will take to hire the candidate. (Step 11, p. 267.)

47. References—The best organizations check references that relate to the past 10 years of a candidate's career and speak with bosses, peers and subordinates. (Step 11, p. 267.)

48. The Offer—When presenting the offer, be a compelling salesperson on behalf of your organization, yet promise only what can be delivered. (Step 11, p. 267.)

49. Creative Solutions—Generate creative alternatives by using a problem-solving approach to resolve difficult negotiations. (Step 11, p. 267.)

50. Agreement—End the negotiation and reach agreement when fairness and equity have been attained. (Step 11, p. 267.)

APPENDIX B

The Two-Minute Drill

PURPOSE—TO CLEAR YOUR HEAD AND PREPARE FOR THE INTERVIEW

Clear Your Head

- Chance to put on interviewer hat: This may be *the* critical interview for the candidate.
- Remember to put the candidate at ease by engaging in 50–50 dialogue.
- Review Ideal Success Profile.
- Clarify roles with other interviewers.
- Address other management issues.

Prepare for the Interview

- Review resume and other candidate information.
- Select potential rapport builders.
- Ask reasons for accepting and leaving each job.
- Spot outstanding accomplishments, experiences, and achievements.
- Identify potential problems: gaps, long tenures and short tenures.

APPENDIX C

A Sample Evaluation Form

CANDIDATE:

INTERVIEWER:

POSITION:

We appreciate your willingness to assist in the interview process. As you know, we want to create the most professional recruiting process with the least administration possible. Please circle your score for each area and your composite score. Any comments should be as specific as possible, e.g., "in the top 10% of all candidates I have seen," or "is lacking the following courses . . ."

3 4 4+ 5 5+   Threshold competencies: college attended, major, grade point average, standard test scores, etc. (Must have 4 or above.)
Comments:

3 4 4+ 5 5+   Technical skills and abilities, including specialized skills. (Must have 4 or above.)
Comments:

3 4 4+ 5 5+   Personal characteristics, including warmth of personality, commitment to others, listening skills. (Must have 4 or above.)
Comments:

1 2 3 4 5   Experience (if applicable), including perceived quality.
Comments:

SUCCESS CHARACTERISTICS FOR POSITION

1 2 3 4 5   Demonstrates the presence to command respect and confidence from senior management through every level of the organization.
Comments:

1 2 3 4 5   Sets and meets aggressive targets while building partnerships in fast-paced, multitask environments.
Comments:

1 2 3 4 5   Solves complex problems through evaluation, analysis, creative solutions, and marshalling resources to implement the plan.
Comments:

1 2 3 4 5   Builds powerful global teams with sensitivity to diversity and cultural differences.
Comments:

1 2 3 4 5   Overall Score—Comments:

Index